JAN '93 $X10.95

The Domestication of the Human Species

D1157784

The Domestication
of the Human Species

Peter J. Wilson

YALE UNIVERSITY PRESS

NEW HAVEN AND LONDON

Copyright © 1988 by Yale University.
All rights reserved.
This book may not be reproduced, in whole
or in part, including illustrations, in
any form (beyond that copying permitted by
Sections 107 and 108 of the U.S. Copyright
Law and except by reviewers for the public
press), without written permission from the publishers.

Designed by Sally Harris
and set in Meridien type by
Graphic Composition, Inc., Athens, Georgia
Printed in the United States of America by
Braun-Brumfield, Inc., Ann Arbor, Michigan.

Library of Congress Cataloging-in-Publication Data

Wilson, Peter J.
The domestication of the human species / Peter J. Wilson.
p.   cm.
Bibliography: p.
Includes index.
ISBN 0-300-04243-4 (cloth)
0-300-05032-1 (pbk.)
1. Social evolution.   2. Architecture and Society.   3. Dwellings,
Prehistoric.   4. Land settlement patterns, Prehistoric.
5. Neolithic period.   I. Title.
GN360.W55 1988
306—dc19   88-5516
CIP

The paper in this book meets the guidelines for
permanence and durability of the Committee on
Production Guidelines for Book Longevity
of the Council on Library Resources.

2   4   6   8   10   9   7   5   3

*To the households of Norbury, Sunapee, Taunton, and Portobello—
the four quarters of my world.*

What I resent is that the range of your vision should pretend to be the limit of my action.

—Henry James, *Roderick Hudson*

We see but one aspect of our neighbour, as we see but one side of the moon; in either case there is also a dark half which is unknown to us. We all come down to dinner, but each has a room to himself.

—Walter Bagehot, "Shakespeare," *Literary Studies*

Contents

Preface

Anyone who writes today about tribal, peasant, rural, village, Neolithic, or domesticated societies invariably does so from the perspective of membership in an urban industrial society. This includes anthropologists as much as sociologists and historians. We write as heirs to the ambivalence felt by the sophisticated city dweller toward the bumpkins of the romantic countryside; it is as inheritors of civilized barbarism that we look upon the noble savage. These ambivalences have been subtly documented by Raymond Williams (1975) and more recently by Keith Thomas (1984); and both Brian Street (1975) and Ronald Meek (1976) have pointed out the intricacies in our perceptions of those who live beyond the sphere of our own civilization.

From this point of view "they," the other world of tribespeople, "natives," and peasants, live in societies that are "kinship based," and we have proposed that the purpose or function of this kinship organization is to secure social solidarity and coherence. These societies—the basis of the ethnographic discourse—not only depend on kinship where we have developed democracy, they espouse one way of thinking while we embrace another: they are "pre-logical" or "bricoleurs" while we are scientifically rational; they are pre-literate but we are literate; they are pre-capitalist, we are capitalist; they are pre-modern, we are modern. They tend to lack privacy whereas the right to privacy and freedom is central to our view of life; they are close to nature and we are buffered from nature by our technology; they are collectivist and we are individualist; they tend to emphasize the social costs and benefits of undertakings whereas we accentuate the rational, economic aspects in a search for efficiency.

The position we take is one that looks back and across from the urban society of which we are members. This has nothing to do with whether our viewpoint is judgmental, whether we look down on the rest of the world. That possibility does not concern me, for there are plenty of discussions about cultural relativism, pro and con. What does concern me, and what I try to exemplify in this book, is that the vantage point conditions what is perceived, and so if one could try to take another vantage point one would see different things. Social scientists see other societies through an implicit, comparative lens, their own society. When, for example, we speak quite neutrally about "pre-capitalist" society we isolate out economic practice as it is found in our own society and study the other society in those terms, comparatively. Because capitalism depends on relations of production, materials of production, capital, and so forth we look for the precursors or analogues of these in what we have been pleased to acknowledge as precapitalist. But this cannot be an accurate reflection of how the society in question theorized or practiced, because for them capitalism was a future and an unknown. Their way of making a living had to be framed in terms of the past and the present. Here I am not talking about the "emic" interpretation of a culture, the method that purports to show how people see things from within their culture. My analysis is far too broad and general to make such a claim. No, what I want to do is to look at ethnography's societies (or what I shall call *domesticated society*) from a "Paleolithic" viewpoint, from the basis of hunter/gatherer society, instead of from the observation post of urban industrial society. Instead of looking back and down, I shall try to look up and around. The reason for this is simple: what domesticated societies could do, and were doing, they could only gauge and compare with their contemporaries and with what had gone before. Only in recent times could village societies compare themselves with a possible life quite different from any they had experienced, with a future development already visible in their present. Until recently there was no "developed" world to serve as the future present for an "undeveloped" world.

The point of view I shall try to take, then, is a more realistic one toward the actual course of the evolution of human society. Certainly I am on dangerous ground, for I too am an ambivalent member of an urban industrial society who can, presumably, only look back, down, and across. I have to admit this is true, but, being aware of the situation, I have tried to step outside my context and look at things from the point of view of Paleolithic hunter/gatherer society. I may not have achieved all the consistency necessary, but I have tried.

My time scale is large—somewhere between the time scales of human evolution and prehistory. This is because in trying to see beyond the ethnographic trees to the evolutionary wood I think I discern that a major modification of the human organism, namely its ability to pay attention, occurred when a major cultural innovation, domestication, was adopted. This has not hitherto been considered as even a possibility in the body of social theory, while it has been considerably downplayed by archaeologists in favor of agriculture and pastoralism. If nothing else, adopting the Paleolithic point of view allows me to "see" and put forward alternatives to present-day wisdom, and this, I hope, will be considered a viable argument that can be adopted, adapted, and disputed on its own terms.

I mentioned evolution. This book evolved from an attempt to write a sequel to my earlier *Man, The Promising Primate* (1980). In a way it *is* a sequel, even though its terms of argument are quite different, for it reflects the radical influence of culture on biological adaptation. Although there is an evolutionary theme, and hence a reductionist argument running quietly through the book, I have not tried to speculate how one thing, form, or trait evolved into another. I have not been at all concerned with origins, either of things or of institutions. I have nothing to say, for example, about the *origins* of domestication or sedentism; I make no effort whatsoever to track the "rise" of kingship in the different civilizations that I mention—Egypt, Mesoamerica, or Southeast Asia, for example. Such indeed is the breadth and imprecision of the concept of domestication with which I operate that many scholars may well accuse me of conflating village life and the rise of urbanism. If I had the patience and scholarship of a Paul Wheatley, for example, I might have taken the more historical line. But to have done so would have confounded my theoretical purpose. This I can, perhaps, best expound by an example.

I just mentioned Paul Wheatley, whom I have never met but whose work I hold in high regard. His inquiry into the origins of the ancient Chinese city is, in fact, an inquiry into the origins of urban life in all parts of the world; or, at least, it is a synthesis of what we know so far about the subject. Stated too simplistically, but for the sake of brevity, Wheatley pulls away "theories" that account for urbanism and central political authority by "realistic" and "materialist" arguments, such as propounded by Witt-fogel arguing in favor of hydraulic bureaucracies. Instead Wheatley pro-poses, very cautiously, that the "ideal type [of] ceremonial center . . . has strong claims to be considered as a functional and developmental stage in the evolution of city life" (1971:328). He has scrupulously traced this in-fluence in China and has surveyed the literature for comparative evidence from other parts of the world. But he gives us no idea as to *why* this might be so. Why should building be such an all-consuming undertaking? Why should people not rest content with building effective shelters but rather spend most of their time, effort, and resources on elaborate and monu-mental ceremonial centers, palaces, temples, shrines, mausoleums, and so on? What sort of motive could there have been? What sort of conditions would make such enterprises possible? If human beings had been content for several hundred thousand years to roam shelterless and with only a minimal technology, why, all of a sudden (historically speaking), should they become seemingly obsessed with architecture, with not just settling down in one fertile place protected from the elements but erecting build-ings and cities that contested with nature itself for grandeur?

I hope that, in trying to answer such "grand" questions as these I have not engaged in speculations so broad and general that they lack value for more specific theorizing. I have tried, at various points in the book, to demonstrate the value of my argument for particular ethnographic theo-rizing by analyzing and attempting to explain specific ethnographies and specific ethnographic phenomena. But, in general, my purpose is not to examine the specific archaeological steps that led up to settlement and sedentism, or to formulate a paradigm for the evolution of political hier-archical society in different parts of the world, or to redescribe the structure of ethnographic, domesticated societies. My purpose is to point out that, from a hunter/gatherer point of view, domestication is the most radical and far-reaching innovation that happened and to try therefore to analyze its consequences. Why was it so radical? Rather than try to form a paradigm of political evolution I am concerned to reexamine our ideas of power. What does power look like from a Paleolithic point of view and how might it "take off" when domestication becomes a fact of human life? If residence and coresidence are so radical and important when looked at from the

Paleolithic point of view, then what bearing does domestication have on the nature of the everyday life of the people who live in huts, houses, and villages? There may be cultural variations of domestication, but if there are, they are variations on a theme. And what I want to do is establish the theme.

Acknowledgments

This book has had many lives, and I thank all those who have assisted in its deaths and rebirths. I thank the University of Otago for granting the year's leave of absence that allowed me to work out my ideas and a first draft, and I thank the Master and Fellows of Churchill College, Cambridge, for their hospitality and stimulation. My gratitude to my colleagues in the Department of Anthropology at Otago and to Charles Higham for taking over administrative duties. I picked the brains of James Woodburn and Nurit Bird and became all the wiser for doing so. I hope they will condone what I have said here. To James and Lisa Woodburn and Ray and Eva Abrahams I extend the thanks of the Wilson family for all the pleasures of their company in Cambridge.

The final version(s) of the book were written while I was recovering from an accident. I doddered around as Kirsten Mackay typed frantically, rushing to the library and bringing me books and notes. Lynn Marsh and Ann Trappitt at various times have also typed their fingers to the bone on my behalf, and "super-trooper" Paul Armfelt got the mess in order. Had it not been for Charles Higham's continuous efforts on my behalf, from keeping me intellectually awake to the inspiration of lending me his portable electronic typewriter, everything would still be grounded.

I am grateful to Ellen Graham of Yale University Press, who says "no" more constructively and helpfully than any author has a right to expect and whose approval is all the more gratifying. Various versions of the book were given careful and thoughtful consideration by several anonymous readers and their reactions and comments have been of considerable help to me. I hope that the end result justifies their trouble. The end result also owes much to the scrupulous editing of Laura Jones Dooley of Yale University Press. That which is correct stands, that which remains in error is no fault of hers.

I especially want to thank Islay Little and her frontline staff at the desk at Otago University's central library. For many years they have helped to make the library the happiest of hunting grounds for my forays.

And, finally, my love and thanks to those who make my house my home—Marc, Duncan, Robin, Ian. And Joan.

Introduction

> Most of the rules of conduct which govern our
> actions, and most of the institutions which arise
> out of this regularity, are adaptations to the im-
> possibility of anyone taking conscious account of
> all the particular facts which enter into the order
> of society.
>
> —F. A. Hayek, *Law, Legislation and Liberty*

Ⅰf Hayek is correct, and I am sure
he is, then there is no chance whatever of a true and successful social
theory that will account for what has happened and will predict what will
happen. Nor, for that matter, is it possible to pin down human activity to
a single basic causal factor, to come up with a clear-cut answer to the
demarcation problem of what unambiguously differentiates the human
species from all other species. Grand theories that work upward and outward from "the" basic discriminator—the capacity to truck, barter, and
exchange, the capacity to produce, the ability to reason, the necessity to
control the sexual instinct, or the instinct for aggression, to cite some well-
known examples—just do not account for everything, and they predict
little. Because of this many scholars disapprove and discourage the pursuit
of "grand" theory and its attempt to discover and articulate human universals. For them the differences between societies and their conditions of
existence offer most promise of enlightenment. And in a certain way they
are right. That certain way is local, small scale, and comparatively unin-
spiring. The functionalism of Durkheim, which proposed that what people
were really doing when they performed exotic rites, or devised strange
institutions, was striving for social solidarity, may be teleological and not
too accurate on detail, but it opened huge possibilities for study and inspired social scientists to produce outstanding detailed works. Lévi-
Strauss's analysis of kinship, alliance, and exchange may have been shown
to be inaccurate in its details, but no one can question that he has managed

to insist we look differently at the world. The fact is, I think, that to get an idea across it has to be exaggerated, lifted out of the confusion and multiplicity of real life, and placed on its intellectual pedestal. It has to pretend to autonomy and omniscience so as to goad others to challenge. There is, surely, some truth in even the most monolithic of social theories, and criticism helps to distill that truth, render it down to size, and mix it in with all the other distilled truths. The single central idea and its elaboration provides inquiry with a good wall to bowl against.

Emotion and instinct have so far provided the ammunition for basic social propositions in global social theories: Machiavelli elevated fear to the status of a first principle in the science of human motivation and saw its political implications (Smith 1985:38). Hobbes, Mandeville, and Smith seized on self-interest and Rousseau on compassion. Ever since Malthus, and Darwin's borrowing of his basic idea that reproduction outstrips production, broad social theory has adopted a tough, realistic stance, arguing that human practices and institutions were determined ultimately by the clash between population pressure and the scarcity of resources.

I am not trying to snuggle what I have to say up to these big names and thereby gain some sort of vicarious credibility. I do want to point out that all emotions and all instincts depend for their working on the senses. Emotions and instincts are usually aroused, and arousal is a sensual activity whereby the organism integrates with the environment, especially with other organisms. So, in a way, the senses are more "basic" than the instincts and emotions, and yet they have not been seriously called on to found a social theory. Only one social theory, as far as I know, presupposes the senses as its source, but it does so indirectly and unintentionally. Hayek (1960) and Popper (1972) propound a theory that stresses the importance of human ignorance on our inability to know everything that goes to make up and move events and institutions. Insofar as theories of knowledge incorporate the ideas of Locke and especially of Hume about sensory data, then such social theories as those of Hayek and Popper are based to some extent on the senses. What I want to argue in what follows is not that "society" grows out of the senses, or that all human activity and institutions may be reduced to the character of the senses, but that a critical strand in human behavior and in the evolution of human institutions has been spun out of factors relating to the senses. That the instincts rather than the senses have so far provided the starting point for much theorizing suggests that the senses have been taken for granted. It suggests especially that nothing in the human career has happened to have either furthered or threatened the functioning and efficiency of the senses since the emergence of Homo sapiens. I think this assumption is incorrect. I suspect that within the enormous span of hominid evolution there have been two major "events" wherein the relation between the senses and the environment were put under stress and rendered problematic. The first of these events revolved around the gradual shift of hominids from an arboreal environment to a plains life. I have argued elsewhere (Wilson 1983) that this made grasping redundant for locomotion and intensified the use of grasping for tactile sensing and manipulation. Such sensing requires increased cross-modal referencing between touch and sight, which in turn calls on more cognitive interpretation.

But I am concerned with the second "event" here. It is recent, having begun perhaps no more than fifteen thousand years ago. Nor, in all likelihood, was it the "result" of, or a response to, drastic and far-reaching environmental changes impinging on the human species. Rather, it may have been an activity originating in the initiative of people, possibly in response to environmental modifications. I refer to the adoption of the practice of living in permanent homes and settlements, a practice that probably began in southwest Asia about fifteen thousand years ago and either spread throughout the rest of the world or was taken up at different times or independently hit upon. Archaeologists, who tend to emphasize the beginnings of agriculture and herding rather more emphatically than the beginnings of settlement, tend to see this change (the agricultural revolution) as being a response to a food crisis occasioned by climatic changes (for example, Cohen 1977), a typically realistic, Malthusian argument. There is, however, some evidence for arguing that settling in relatively permanent dwellings came before and independently of agriculture and hence was not occasioned by a food crisis. I do not want to get embroiled in an argument about this point. I merely want to take up the implication that what I shall call *domestication* can be conceived of as an independent innovation and even that the domestication of plants and animals follows the domestication of human beings and is inspired by it. I shall leave entirely open the question as to why people at a particular time and place adopted the built environment as their context for living.

I shall also leave unattended the relation between domestication, sedentism and mobility. Pastoral nomads, for example, are in my estimation domesticated because they reside together in permanent communities and frequently carry their dwellings with them. They visualize their living group as an ongoing structured community that varies little even though it is moved from place to place (see, for example, the various essays in *Pastoral Production* [1979]). In a recent study Eder (1984) reports that the Batak foragers were even more mobile when they relied on hunting and that foraging seems to place them on the threshold of sedentism, but even their mobility seems to me domesticated, because when they move they retain their settlement pattern of "small groups of households."

A general understanding of the term *domestication* is adequate for my purposes. Domesticated people are those who live (and mostly work) in houses grouped together in hamlets, villages, and small towns as distinct from people of the past and the present who use only temporary dwellings or no dwellings at all (that is, Paleolithic and contemporary hunter/gatherers) and people who live in large cities and work in factories, offices, and so on. I want to show that domesticated society relies to a great extent on the house as both a dominant cultural symbol and a central rallying point and context for social organization and activity. By implication the extent to which domesticated society exists amid modern industrial urban society, or even alongside it, suggests that its ideas, understandings, and practices are current. Insofar as modern social ideas and practices have their origins in the past, they are closely related to the ideas of domesticated society.

The two theses, that human evolution and conduct is as much a sensory matter as a matter of the instincts and that domestication is a significant evolutionary event, come together as follows. I maintain that attention, particularly visual attention, is of primary importance to the operation of the drives, instincts, emotions, feelings, and bodily processes of human beings and thence to the survival and well-being of the individual and the species. I argue this as economically as possible in chapter 1. With the adoption of the built environment—that is, domestication—the ability of people to pay attention to each other in the governance of their interaction and in their dealings with the environment is drastically modified. Without people necessarily knowing what has happened, as long as they choose to live in houses behind walls, they are beset by, and have to cope with, problems of attention. At the same time new possibilities for thinking and acting, for creating and expanding, are opened up. Recognizing and developing such possibilities comprises a considerable slice of cultural and political development.

4

In chapter 2 I continue the theme of chapter 1 in trying to demonstrate how much modern hunter/gatherers govern, organize, and monitor their interaction and activity by an uninterrupted and unimpeded attention. This chapter is more than just scene setting. It is, I hope, a contribution to ethnographic synthesis and theory. Nurit Bird has written that hunter/gatherer ethnography lacks a theory of social organization, and I have taken the liberty as a purely armchair observer of proposing one (Bird 1986). Even if the workers in the field reject my theoretical offering, I still think that the point for my general argument remains valid. Hunter/gatherer societies are marked by an emphasis on "focus" in contrast to domesticated societies, which are distinguished by an emphasis on the boundary.

In chapter 3 I take up the domestication theme, briefly establishing it as a historical (more correctly a prehistorical) event. This may seem unnecessary to some, but since psychoanalytically oriented social scientists in particular have attributed primeval, womblike significance to the house and have implied that the human "need" for shelter is innate and natural, and since people in general take housing for granted, a reminder that domestication is a cultural event is not out of place. In the remainder of this chapter I turn from prehistory to ethnography and attempt to show that the house, especially its geometry, should be viewed as a technical and cognitive instrument, a tool for thought as well as a technology of shelter. If this is recognized and appreciated then it is possible to understand and fathom the how, and perhaps the why, of the structuring of human relations and activities so typical of tribal, traditional, and peasant societies described by anthropologists and so atypical of hunter/gatherers.

Chapter 4 begins the exploration of what I consider to be among the direct and most important consequences of domestication for life in society and for social theory. My basic contention is that settlement and domestic architecture impose conditions on living that provide a basic spatial structure. Simplistically stated, domestic walls divide space between the public and the private, a division that is most important for the development of both the avoidance and the enhancement of human attention. This has considerable implications for motivation—the motivation to exploit possibilities for concealment and to exploit the opportunities for display. I argue, further, that the basic spatial structure has to be associated with the development of a universal aspect of social structure in domesticated societies: the development of the role and status of neighbor. I believe that to recognize these factors is to question much of current social theorizing, for example, the assumptions that production is materially motivated and that such production is fundamental. Production, I suggest, may well be aesthetically motivated and treats subsistence as an incidental. Further, the proposition that traditional societies are kinship societies, that kinship is economics (religion, politics, and law), as Godelier (1977:124) put it, may be only partially accurate. They are equally, if not more so, neighbor societies in which the principal political activity is hospitality. In short, in chapter 4 I argue that conceptually isolated institutions such as economics and politics are quite differently motivated than we have hitherto understood them to be and that they are premised on the house: their anchor is the domestic condition, however far they may depart from it.

In chapter 5 I continue this argument in relation to the metaphysics of politics—that is, trying to understand the growth of human concern and preoccupation with power. I do so by arguing that the development and enlargement of architecture from the house to the palace, and from the grave to the tomb, provided both a technical and a conceptual stimulus for a preoccupation with the theory and practice of sovereign power. In the second part of this chapter I look at power as a condition of life among neighbors in the domestic setting. Whereas the monumental possibilities of architecture provide the real and the surreal conditions for the accumulation of power, the situation of neighbors sharing the same community provides conditions requiring the dispersal and distribution of power. To examine this situation I analyze witchcraft, which seems to be an institution of beliefs (and to some extent practice) common to domesticated societies but uncommon in both hunter/gatherer and urban industrial societies.

1

Attending to Assumptions

T he widest context for social science, which is also the boundary preserving the human being whole and entire before inquiry crumbles it into cells, pulses, and genes, is the probable fact of human evolution. Or, as Robert Young has put it: "The point about evolutionary theory is that it is the central conception linking humanity and social theory to natural science" (1985:238). The conceptual area covered by the theory of evolution is the world of the between: it is both the world between the individual and his or her constitution and the world between the individual and the external environment. The process of evolution, natural selection, is the process that translates interaction between individuals into exchanges of genes; at the same time, it is the process that translates individual interaction into transactions with the environment. The forces of selection are the acts of individuals that elicit reactions from the environment and the acts of the environment that elicit reactions from individuals. As far as human beings are concerned these forces of evolution have become concentrated and have developed as culture, which has grown to be a larger and deeper buffer between individuals and between individuals and the environment.

For much of hominid evolution—that is, during the time when the genus Homo was coming into being—evolutionary selection and change was internal, biological, genetic bodily change, as when four-leggedness gave way to bipedalism or the cerebral cortex enlarged. But as the abilities these developments sponsored matured as language and toolmaking, culture evolved into that which came between the organism and the environment—a mediator, a buffer, a barrier. Tools and language are still the principal means by which humanity makes active contact with the environment, but they have also become the means by which culture itself is reproduced, furthered, and developed, the means through which human productive capabilities are both expressed and realized. The species with culture, then, is confronted by both the natural environment *and* the cultural environment. Human relations of interaction, adaptation, and dialectics—human evolution, in short—must be tripartite, involving the species and the natural and cultural environments. For culture comes between individuals and the natural environment not as a passing or transparent feature but as a permanent and material world external to both the human species and nature. It is a force that impinges on its creators as well as on their natural environment.

If this is the case, then no account of human nature and human evolution can overlook the possibility that radical changes in the human career, active forms of selection, may have originated in the conditions and problems inherent in the coexistence of people in a dual environment: that which is natural and that of their own making, the cultural. Furthermore, the forms of adaptation and selection pertaining to human evolution may be cultural as well as biological—human individuals having to survive in a cultural as well as a natural environment.

The products of culture tend to accumulate and take their place in the world as well as to become obsolete and extinct. Earlier anthropologists were often tempted to see in cultural history a parallel with natural selection, identifying traits as being selected for their fitness (or efficiency). Karl Popper (1972:106–7) has argued that even human ideas and beliefs come to assume an objective existence in the domain of culture as inhabitants of a World III. In an archaeological time-scale, culture in all its varieties and complexity has only recently taken its place as a world of its own, as a mediator and buffer between the human being and the natural environment, as the partner and rival to nature. As this has happened, people have increasingly had to learn not only how to use their culture but how to live with its dangers and advantages. We adapt to culture with as much, if not more immediacy as we adapt to nature. Culture has also deeply affected the ways in which individuals live with one another in their pursuit of survival and well-being (or of "fitness"). Indeed, it might not be going too far to say that in modern human societies individuals face greater and more immediate problems in adapting to their culture than they do in coping with the natural environment. However, the increasingly active and massive presence of culture is something that has developed. It is the content or subject matter of human history. As culture has developed it has come to loom ever larger not only as a means of mediation with and control of the physical environment but also as a world in itself that appears more and more independent of both humanity and nature to become a source of problems in its own right.

Neither language nor the first tools seem to have changed the living environment of people or altered the landscape in any appreciable way (though conceivably they made a difference to human conduct). For the tens of thousands of years that form the bulk of human existence the species can be said to have lived a predominantly "natural" life out in the open, distinguishable possibly in degree, but not in kind, from the life of other animals. The living environment of early Paleolithic human beings in all likelihood remained as unaltered by their presence as did the prehuman environment. Culture was a thin buffer, a help to the hand, a diffident mediator. Selection remained natural.

I propose that the first cultural move or development that physically altered the landscape, that was a designed protective move against nature, and that, in retrospect, can be seen to have been a, if not the, growing point for the expansion of the world of culture, was the adoption of architecture for shelter and settlement as the more or less permanent living condition of the species—that is, the designed construction of permanent shelter as distinct from the temporary use of natural shelters or the erection of flimsy, impermanent shelters. I shall call this process *domestication*.

From an evolutionary point of view domestication has clear and precise beginnings. Human settlement began at some time between fifteen and five thousand years ago in some parts of the world (notably southwest Asia, and possibly Egypt). It is still not 100 percent complete throughout the world. From the historical and prehistorical point of view, these dates are hardly precise. But archaeology, ethnography, and history provide us with details of the process and its consequences. The adoption of domestication sets in motion the process of community living and creates the conditions for the political life, the public life, and the private life. Even more importantly, it sets these lives in motion to become dialectical factors in the evolutionary process. Domestication may enhance the survival and well-being of people, but it is also a barrier between people and between

9

people and the natural environment and so could be expected to create new problems or demands. In other words, it is reasonable to ask whether domestication perhaps changes "human nature," steering it in one direction rather than another, or triggers dormant possibilities. An affirmative answer would mark humanity's first move to combat nature that simultaneously sets in motion an unforeseen reaction affecting the innermost aspects of the human person. I propose that this is in fact the case, that domestication not only establishes a meaningful buffer and mediator between humanity and the natural environment but brings in its wake, perhaps as an unforeseen consequence, a series of new situations between individuals that arise from the imposition domestication places on biological features of the individual.

From the study of nonhuman primates and from the study of the ethnographies of people who live in the open like other primates—a condition which roughly matches that of Paleolithic people—I propose that a primary feature of human adaptation is a heavy emphasis on visual perception and attention. The visual sense is dominant among many primates, and hence among human beings, although this does not mean that the other senses have atrophied or have no use. Given this assumption, which I seek to establish in this chapter, I propose that a likely consequence of domestication was (and is) the effect it has on visual perception and attention and therefore on all the activities that depend on vision or involve it. The most salient of these activities, particularly for the student of human affairs, is the interaction between people, or their social life. In which case, what this book is about is the effect of domestication on human social life.

A Visual Order

Among mammals, primates are exceptional for their highly developed visual sensitivity (Fobes and King 1982:219). Where most other mammals rely on smell and hearing to guide them through the environment and to lead them to its bounty, primates depend on first seeing the world and then hearing, smelling, touching, and tasting it. Vision in primates is a specialized adaptive sense in an order noted for its morphological conservatism and propensity to remain primitive and generalized (P. J. Wilson 1983; Rosen 1982).

Vision tends to be a primate specialty because most primates are arboreal and, by and large, rather big to be living in trees. Large arboreal animals

10

"must judge distances and the strength of support with precision," and so, for them, "vision is the paramount sense" (E. O. Wilson 1980:251). Primate vision is distinguished by great acuity, or the ability to discriminate in detail; by stereoscopic sight, which allows for depth perception; and by color viewing, which not only permits a more exquisite discrimination but enriches the organism's experience of the world (Fobes and King 1982; Humphrey 1984:146). But not all primates, and certainly not the nocturnal ones, are possessed of equally acute perception or can see in color.

The specialization of primate visual capacities is particularly important for, and adaptive to, navigational demands: primates find their way about the world and locate food and mates by looking for them. Vision is thus an active modality closely linked to locomotion, so much so that any modification in one might well have consequences for the other. Among those primates—particularly certain hominoids—whose size has forced them to move around on the ground as much as in the trees or who have been "forced out" of the trees by competition with other species, the resultant modifications of the structure and function of the limbs have had far-reaching effects on the role of vision. As I have suggested elsewhere (1983), among the hominids, the readjustment of an arboreally evolved being to terrestrial conditions renders grasping obsolete for locomotion and therefore frees it entirely for such functions as holding and manipulation and for tactile exploration. This means a closer and much more intense linkup between touch and vision and between limb or digit movement and seeing. For upright human beings, vision and its integration with other sensorimotor capacities has become even more crucial and distinctive as a prime component in "intelligence"—the perception and grasping of the nature of the world.

Another aspect of the same process has meant that vision has become a more salient feature of communication and hence of expression. Primate vision has developed in general at the expense of smell, though olfactory sensitivity among primates is far from having been phased out. The forest air currents that carry smells are easily blocked, whereas sound waves, though muffled, can often carry considerable distances, and some primates like howler monkeys or gibbons have become vociferous communicators. Communication by sound (and hearing), especially over long distances, has become important to many primates in the forest, so much so that some, as part of their tactics for survival, are able to disguise their sounds and make them hard to localize (Rosen 1982).

Intimate communication at close range among primates has come to de-

11

pend on visual signals as well as the voice. The original modification of the snout area to accommodate the enlarged and forward-facing eye sockets resulted in an increased prominence of the eyes and a reduction of the snout. As is well known, among infant humans the presentation of the eyes more than any other feature enables recognition; reciprocally, the large eyes of the infant appeal to the adult, and the portrayal of large, round eyes is the principal device artists use in sympathetic anthropomorphosis of animals. Even more important, the reduction of the snout allows for the installation of extensive and mobile facial musculature in the higher primates, especially humans. Because of this, human beings and apes have a range of facial expressions and individual looks that greatly enlarges the repertoire and variety of intimate communication and identification. The freedom of the forelimbs from the requirements of locomotion enables the individual to develop a repertoire of gestures. Hominids—and especially Homo sapiens—have combined these gestures with facial expressions and bodily postures to develop an extensive nonverbal mode of communication. This emphasis on the visual may also have contributed to the development of a wide variety of visual marks of identification, such as colored coats, individualized features and bodily conformation, and the like.

A number of qualitative implications arise from the shift of emphasis to the visual sense due to the basic differences between sight and the other senses. Smell is chemical in origin, and odors are received directly by chemoreceptors. Smell is difficult to detach from its source, although chemical vapors may linger after the source has disappeared. But smell remains a direct reception. Touch is more immediate than smell, because touch relies on pressure and hence on direct contact between sensor and object. Sounds, too, originate from a source directly and are received as pressure in the ears. But the sights we see are the reflections and refractions of light, not the sources of light. Sight and sound, then, are relatively more detached from their sources than smells, tastes, and touches. Sound reception entails translation from wavelength to pressure, rather like feeling at a distance; sight reception involves translation from wavelength to retinal image, then to photochemical reaction, which involves rods and cones, then to electrical energy firing along the optic nerve and ending in the visual cortex (Gregory 1979; Frisby 1979). Seeing is thus a more complex process than the other sensory modes, and its product is far removed from its stimulus—that is, what we "see" is distant literally and qualitatively from the object. Seeing, on which human beings rely so extensively, is, in fact, perceiving.

Seeing Is Perceiving

According to John Frisby, "seeing has puzzled philosophers and scientists for centuries, and continues to do so" (1979:25). He relegates the classical theory of vision, the theory of the retinal image or inner screen, to a vague and minuscule relevance. Any theory of an inner image that replicates the object outside "leaves all the information about the scene implicit within the new image. That is hopeless" (ibid.:156). His objections are similar to those of J. J. Gibson, a pioneer of the ecological theory of seeing. Gibson points out that any theory which proposes a reality as being seen in representative images supposes a never-ending regression of homunculi, and "the little man would have to have an eye to see it with, of course, *a little eye* with a *little* retinal image connected to a *little* brain, and so we have explained nothing by this theory" (1979:60). So not only is what we see removed from the object, it is not even an image of it. What do we see? According to Gibson, we have a physiology geared to apprehending invariant features in an ambient optic array, features such as occlusion, movement, and brightness. We take these and other optical elements and with them construct objects in the world not only by means of inner physiological activities but also through a complex and ongoing synthesis of the whole organism's activities:

> Natural vision depends on the eyes in the head on a body supported by the ground, the brain being only the central organ of a complete visual system.
>
> When no constraints are put on the visual system we look around, walk up to something interesting and move around it to see it from all sides, and go from one vista to another. This is natural vision. [Ibid.:1]

These activities pick up the information that composes the environment, especially its invariances and movements as they relate to the organism: "Perceiving is a registering of certain definite dimensions of invariance in the stimulus flux together with definite parameters of disturbance" (ibid.:249).

If the classical theory of seeing via the retinal image "proposes a symbolic description as the basis of seeing" (Frisby 1979:8), then the ecological approach to perception relates it more to a theory of general signs. If symbols must have a referent to convey meaning, signs, which are by definition partial, cannot alone portray objects in their entirety. Not even the total inventory of such invariances as edges, occlusions, textures, movements, angles, and colors, which are picked up by the visual system from the ambient array, will add up to the object, the view, the picture of the person we actually see. Gibson's ecological theory does not overcome the objection that "seeing must be a symbolic process because the world itself obviously does not exist inside our heads" (ibid.:156).

The ecological theory leaves us with the problem of explaining the "gaps" between those bits of information in the stimulus flux that we pick up or select out. Gibson, aware of this problem, suggests that "to perceive is to be aware of the surfaces of the environment and of oneself in it," and knowing, therefore, is an "extension of perceiving" or an awareness of surfaces (1979:158–59). But as I understand the ordinary sense of the terms *knowing* and *perceiving*, they refer not only to surfaces but also to what lies beneath or might be contained within surfaces and to what connects surfaces together. Knowing must be more than superficial. It must shed light on what is otherwise concealed.

Perhaps the most widely accepted theory of perception, especially visual perception, argues that vision and perceiving are largely cognitive processes. Visual perception relies on inference, decision, and categorization (Bruner [1957] 1973). In this view, perception is a synthesis, collation, and interpretation of information gathered via various means and media. In making this synthesis the brain (the mind?) must not only transform the variable data into equivalences but also establish connections among the data. For Bruner all perception is generic, and this means categorization. In turn, decisions must be made about the assignment of data to categories, and this involves discrimination, or choice. The organism seeks to achieve a condition of perceptual veridicality with its environment. This Bruner equates with model building, a process in which the mind (?) represents the relations between the properties of objects and the events the organism encounters as accurately as possible. So, rather than the "inner eye" perusing an image, the brain itself constructs a model that represents, or symbolizes, the world outside. This allows for the possibility of inaccuracy and misrepresentation, which is made explicit in Richard Gregory's analysis of visual perception as a mode of hypothesizing about the world "out there."

Error is intrinsic to perception. Occasions for error occur particularly when cues from the environment and the objects in it are equivocal (Bruner 1973:29–30), or when they are more symbolic and less signlike, or when a perceiver approaches a situation with inappropriate categories with which to predict, interpret, or cope with the environment. It is im-

14

portant, and not unexpected, that Bruner singles out as the prime example of a source of perceptual unreadiness the equivocal nature of cues to identity in interpersonal relations. Here the external signs of inner states, the signs of intention and disposition, are notoriously uncertain and inconstant. In perceiving and identifying others the problems of categorization become severe, because the categories are symbolic and appearances need bear no relation to them (ibid.:32). Visual disguise and deception are relatively easy to assume.

Exactly how we see and perceive is still largely unknown in many respects. But the very complexity of seeing indicates that it is more likely a matter of interpretation than of direct access, of structuring, destructuring, and restructuring, for how else can we get the world inside our heads the way we do? Gibson's ecological approach attempts to get rid of the passive receiver and replace him with an active viewer fully integrated with the environment, not standing off from it. But even this active viewer, picker-up of visual trifles, must *interpret* selections or findings, piece them together, and propose connections between the separate parts. To see a building on one occasion, to walk around it, and then at another time and place to see a pile of bricks as a building on the basis of past experience involves inference, induction, and hypotheses, all highly subject to uncertainty. Seeing and perceiving, which to English speakers are the equivalent of believing and knowing, are intrinsically uncertain.

And so, while the visual sense is of prime importance to primates, and especially to human beings, as the means of negotiation with the physical environment and the environment of fellow beings, it is notoriously and intrinsically error prone. Such a reliance on an uncertain tool is conducive to persistent inquiry, but it induces a state of ongoing anxiety, especially with regard to fellow beings. The seeing, perception, and understanding of others occurs most immediately within a framework or context of a social arrangement by means of which individuals more effectively pursue their survival and well-being. Attention operates within this framework at the same time as it serves to support the structure.

The Primate Social Context

The senses mediate between the individual and the environment, including the other individuals surrounding any subject. Primates live in a wide variety of physical environments as well as in different forms of living

15

arrangements. Even if we consider only the higher primates there is considerable diversity, as the following summary indicates.

The orangutan is largely arboreal, though the heavy male must spend some time on the ground. The orangutan lives a solitary life, probably because it is a large eater and must be constantly on the move in search of food (Rodman 1979). Nevertheless, females are accompanied by their dependent offspring for a year or more, and adult males and females "contrive" to cross each others' path frequently. Males tend to range over a territory that excludes other males but includes females. The social contact between adult orangutans tends to be far more frequent between the sexes, and the female often initiates contact (Schurman 1981:131). The female's solicitation and the male's presentation are almost exclusively visual, consisting of looks, gestures, and then touching. Orangutans build nests in such a way that they can obtain an unobstructed view of a large segment of the forest around them (Maple 1980:26).

Gibbons, which are exclusively arboreal, live in a monogamous breeding unit of adult male and female with their immature offspring. Mature offspring are expelled. Gibbons acknowledge territorial boundaries, which are patrolled and protected by the adult male (Gittens 1980). The "family" unit is often close-knit, and both parents pay considerable attention to the infants, inspecting them visually and grooming them (E. O. Wilson 1980:258). The male gibbon patrols the perimeter of his territory and maintains contact with the female and their offspring both visually and by sound. Gibbons are, in fact, famous for their vocalizing.

Gorillas spend most of their time on the ground. They live in multi-male, age-graded groups numbering between five and thirty individuals (Rosen 1982:21). The group is dominated by a large, silver-backed male who heads a number of junior, subordinate, black-backed males, a number of females, and their young. Lone males are common, however, and small, all-male troops have been observed (E. O. Wilson 1980:265; McKenna 1982:93). Mountain gorilla groups often occupy quite small ranges of between four and eight square kilometers, and these home ranges change little in size and position over the years (Dixson 1981:108). Groups do vary by distances traveled and membership composition, however. Younger males are particularly mobile. New groups form when females leave their natal groups to join lone males or other groups (ibid.:104). Gorillas build nests to sleep in at night and sometimes for their midday siesta. They sleep on their own and hence build nests from about the age of two and a half years (ibid.:122).

16

Most writers agree that the life of the gorilla is quiet, calm, and low-key. Individuals often spend the day lying around or wander off feeding on their own without making any particular effort at contact with fellow group members. Consequently, gorillas communicate with one another rather less than other primates. The most spectacular communication is a sequence of nine actions comprising the display that includes the famous chest beating (ibid.:129). For all their inactivity, gorilla facial musculature is well developed, and gorillas are capable of a wide range of facial expressions.

From an evolutionary point of view the gorilla and the chimpanzee are genetically (and phylogenetically) close to human beings. The phenotypic similarities among them may, then, be taken to indicate a common primate nature. Unfortunately little is known quantitatively about gorilla senses. Qualitatively they are most likely on a par with other apes and humans. What has struck many observers of gorillas is the striking and expressive nature of gorilla eyes:

> All their emotions are in their eyes, which are a soft dark brown. The eyes have a language of their own, being subtle and silent mirrors of the mind. I could see hesitation and uneasiness, curiosity and boldness and annoyance. Sometimes, when I met a gorilla face to face, the expression in its eyes more than anything else told me of his feelings and helped me decide my course of action. [Schaller 1967:119]

Or "A gorilla's eyes are most expressive and during threat they change from their normal soft hue and grow hard, staring fixedly at the other animal" (Dixson 1981:131).

Perhaps most puzzling about gorillas is that while they seem to many human observers to compare most closely with humans in sensitivity and intelligence, they seem to have arrived at such a level without the apparent stimulus of intense competition from either conspecifics or other species and without having to cope with environmental disasters and pressures, at least as far as we know.

If gorillas seem to be the epitome of relaxation, if not lethargy and boredom, chimpanzees often strike human observers as hyperactive. Chimpanzees live mostly in the forest and spend a great deal of time on the ground. They live in groups of up to eighty individuals, but this larger grouping subdivides into smaller ones whose membership is always changing. This has led commentators to describe chimpanzee group structure as fluid or open (Reynolds 1966). Usually the females move between groups, though young males may roam on the periphery. The large, inclusive groups range over their territory, which varies in size from about five to twenty square kilometers. Troops generally have little to do with neighbors, but they occasionally meet, and such contact seems to arouse great excitement, followed by withdrawal. However, Jane Goodall has reported on the violent destruction of one group of chimpanzees by another (1979).

While the gorilla sometimes seems scarcely to notice its companions, the chimpanzee engages in a close, active, intimate, and lively social life of considerable variety. In their interactions chimpanzees rely considerably on visual communication, both sending and receiving, as well as on extensive vocal communication. They possess mobile faces and can perform a wide variety of easily observable facial expressions. These are correlated with a repertoire of sounds, enabling them to communicate extensively and probably in some detail about their environment, their feelings and emotions, their state of mind, their intentions, and each other (Goodall 1974). This audiovisual communication, together with tactile grooming, comprises the bulk of chimpanzee social life itself and is supplemented by periodic cooperation in such activities as hunting and meat sharing (Teleki 1973).

The primate reliance on vision and visual perception is marked among chimpanzees and is especially revealed through their development of contrived strategies of visual deceptions. For example, Fifi and Figan, two chimps observed by Jane Goodall, had figured out how to open banana boxes. They also found out, however, that when they opened the boxes, higher-ranking animals would descend on them and take away the bananas. "So they just lay around, together with Flo, waiting for the others to go. (Having opened the boxes) they just sat with one foot keeping the lever closed, casually grooming themselves and looking anywhere except at the box. Once I timed Figan sitting thus for over half an hour" (1974:144).

A second example shows chimpanzees capable of even more subtle and sophisticated visual deception. Yeroan pretended to have hurt his foot, but he did so only in the presence of his rival, so he "kept an eye on Nikki to see whether he was being watched" (de Waal 1982:48). De Waal provides another example worth citing. Two chimps pretended to be walking in the same direction. If they were not being watched by others in the group they could dodge behind a tree. One of the chimps, Dandy, made advances to a female while looking around to see if any of the other males was watching (ibid.:48–49). De Waal concludes that chimpanzees are "masters of pretence," and although this may be too sweeping, it is clear that chimpanzees make considerable use of revelation and deception and of cultivating an appearance.

Chimpanzee vision is much the same as human vision (Fobes and King 1982), and their special appreciation of the visual, as well as their eye-hand coordination, is indicated by the interest and enthusiasm that some captive chimpanzees have shown for painting (Morris 1962). The psychological and existential significance of visual perception to chimpanzees may be further illustrated by citing the experiments of Gallup (1977) and his associates (Gallup, Wallnau, and Suares 1980), which suggest that chimpanzees (and orangutans) may possess self-consciousness. Animals were first shown their reflections in a mirror; then they were anesthetized, and a red dye was applied to their eyebrows or ears. When they came to, they were shown their reflections, and on seeing their altered appearance the chimpanzees touched the colored areas.

Among chimpanzees sexual activity is particularly stimulated by visual cues. When the adult female enters estrus her genitalia swell and assume a vivid coloration. Sexual behavior also includes much posturing and gesturing. However, the other senses, particularly smell and touch, are also active in sexual life and social life in general.

Like other apes, chimpanzees build sleeping nests high in the trees. These nests, however, tend to provide comfort rather than shelter. They are unroofed and do not obscure a view of others, nor do they completely conceal an individual from others' view.

Attention

Given the emphasis on visual matters and, among chimpanzees in particular, a preference for an active social life, the higher primates, including human beings, place great weight on attention. The strong nurturing and emotional ties between mother and infant, so crucial to individual survival and learning, rely as much on the constant attention each pays to the other as on feeding and touching. It has been argued that among humans such visual attention is often sufficient to maintain attachment. When a parent figure goes out of sight the infant becomes agitated and anxious, but as long as the parent figure remains in view, the anxiety is allayed (Bowlby 1973).

But attention is important among primates in a more general and far-reaching political manner as well. Michael Chance has proposed that the various forms of hierarchy found in different primate social organizations are kept in operation by different, and appropriate, modes of attention structure (1967; 1976). *Hedonic* attention relies on rewards and approval in return for display; *agonistic* attention binds individuals with threats. These are complemented by *centric* attention, in which an individual is surrounded by others and is the focus of their attention, and *acentric* attention, in which individuals in a group continuously divide their attention between themselves and the objects of the environment (Chance 1976: 322–24). Acentric societies, exemplified by the patas, the langur, and the gibbon, tend to disperse when danger threatens; centric societies, being centripetal, coalesce around a dominant, focal male, as do gorillas, chimpanzees, macaques, and baboons.

Thus the achievement of a unitary social life in which distinct individuals form a cohesive group depends in large part on each individual paying attention to the others, on watching and being watched. It depends equally on primates giving impressions and signals that are meaningful to others who are attending.

The adaptive advantages of relying on visual attention and, almost equally, on auditory signaling over the olfactory communication typical of most nonprimates have been pointed out by John Tylor Bonner. He suggests that audiovisual structures, unlike olfactory signals, would not need to undergo any genetic change for a new repertoire of audiovisual signals to be invented. At the same time, audiovisual signals can be detached from the originating context and used elsewhere, whereas olfactory and tactile signals are bound to their context. As well as the advantages of variety and flexibility, however, such versatility and complexity may confuse and deceive (Bonner 1980:110).

The advantages of a dependence on visual perception and attention are especially strong with regard to the exploration and exploitation by primates of the natural environment. The features of the environment are relatively constant and invariant, so that apprehending the objects of the environment *at a distance,* as is possible through vision, is unlikely to be any more mistaken than apprehension through smell. But seeing a prey at a distance gives a predator a distinct advantage over one who must first smell the prey. In the case of hominids, a combination of vision with manipulative motor skills made possible the eventual manufacture of tools, utensils, and weapons, and this probably gave hominids a major and irreversible adaptive advantage over other species.

The problems of reliance on visual signs and attention refer preeminently to relations between conspecifics, to social life. All higher primates can vary their expressions at will and so alter their appearance. This allows individuals to mask their feelings and conceal their intentions if they so desire. The deceptions practiced by the chimpanzees Fifi, Figan, Flo, and Yeroan are examples of this capacity. Disguise presupposes the separateness of appearance from substance, and this ability to manipulate appearances, more than anything else, turns primate action into what Nicholas Humphrey calls transaction: calculated exchanges of actions and reactions in which each individual tries to manipulate the others the better to obtain specific ends (1984:20). Being able to separate appearance and to superimpose it on an alien substance as disguise, or to assume an appearance that belies feeling or intention, creates the primary condition for having to calculate behavior and activity, which is an outstanding characteristic of primate, and especially human, conduct. Being unsure of the relation between another's appearance and intentions or feelings demands calculation and breeds uncertainty.

The primate emphasis on visual perception and visual display contributes to the more detailed, nuanced, and direct expression of mood, intention, and feeling than seems to be the case among other species. This in turn contributes to the more intense and varied emotional and intellectual lives lived by primates, particularly humans. Primates, especially gorillas, chimpanzees, and human beings, live as much to keep each other company as to live simply in each others' company. Among humans, these characteristics are vastly furthered through the expressive use of language.

The Living Environment

Although some apes build sleeping nests, the higher primates do not alter the natural environment for their shelter or comfort. The flow of attention and perception that regulates social life is subject to interference from natural barriers only. Individuals in the same group remain more or less constantly in view of one another and can easily monitor, be sensitive to changes, and react to each other appropriately and accurately. Although observers and commentators have more or less completely anthropomorphized primate life, superimposing the notions of public and private life onto nonhuman primates seems, at first glance, to be the limit. And yet there are intimations that chimpanzees, for example, occasionally deliberately withdraw from company:

21

During the ten years since I left Gombe Stream, the importance of these consortships has been repeatedly confirmed. Males lure single females away with them. The pairs avoid the activity centres of the main community, indeed several other consorting couples have used the same quiet little valley where I found Olley and David. After an absence of a few weeks, or even months, the pair return to the main group, when the female is usually pregnant. [MacKinnon 1978:78]

Another way to avoid attention is to keep on the move and to seek different companions frequently, a tactic analyzed by Albert Hirschman as the exit option (1970). The active social life of chimpanzees is likely to produce emotional collisions from time to time. This they may counter by engaging in extensive mobility, leaving each other's company before tension erupts. Gorillas, by contrast, seem to do little, spending most of their time feeding, resting, and lying around. Their mobility is correspondingly minimal.

There is enough evidence to warrant the assumption that a reliance on visual attention and perception is an invariant aspect of primate nature. It follows, then, that visual attention and perception are central aspects of human nature. The particular character of vision differentiates it from the other senses and, among other things, renders it peculiarly vulnerable to such uncertainties as illusions, misperceptions, and mistaken identities. Although vision is often regarded as the touchstone for truth and for establishing reality, it is a composite process that relies especially on inference and generally on cognition.

This emphasis on vision developed while the various primate species continued to live in a manner that did not disturb or reorder their immediate living environment. The only obstacles to an accurate viewing were natural or came with the withdrawal of individuals out of sight. Not even the simple sleeping nests built by some primates were sufficient to interrupt or conceal the view. Since the senses, especially sight, are the prime mediators between individual and environment, a stable and sympathetic balance between sense and environment has probably been crucial in primate life.

Given these assumptions, how has this relationship worked for human beings during the course of their evolution, prehistory, and history? Have the problems of the relation between vision and environment contributed to, if not determined, forms of human practice whose origins and raison d'être have been misinterpreted or mistakenly identified—that is, inadequately explained by existing theories?

22

2

The Opening Society

There is no need to elaborate a fantasy when a
genuine analogy is at hand.

—D. D. Raphael, *Justice and Liberty*

H unter/gatherer societies are the
logical, and in their archaeological form, the chronological beginnings for
any inquiry into the evolution and nature of human society. Because it is
known that prehistoric societies subsisted by the hunting/gathering mode
it is thought that modern societies subsisting in the same way present a
modern analogue. And while the ethnographic analogy may not be entirely reliable it will display the effect of limiting factors. In any case, modern hunters are manifestly a more satisfactory analogy than modern tribal
peoples or peasants. The conditions of life contingent on hunting and gathering indicate a minimal sociology, suggesting what is absolutely necessary
and sufficient for the survival and well-being of a human society. A minimal sociology identifies the need from which the luxuriant growth of social
organization has sprouted.

Social and political philosophy does not always look for the literal origins of human society but posits them from a rendering down of modern
society. But one imagines that if someone's hypothetical original state was
found to conform to the archaeological evidence, it would claim for itself
absolute priority, correctness, and legitimacy. Theories, like statuses, rely
on genealogy for their authentication, and genealogies rest on the sanctity
of the founding ancestor, the Creator.

Although conditions in the Paleolithic era differed vastly from the present and no modern ethnography could ever claim to model reliably the
earlier condition, contemporary anthropology can and does expand and

23

qualify our ideas about possibilities and limitations of human society. For a long time the general idea of the earliest hunter/gatherer society was of an opportunistic life lived on the edge of survival. It was dominated by the male, and, while not quite the nasty, short, and brutish life immortalized by Thomas Hobbes, it was a life marked by peremptory violence. Earliest man was thought to have been a creature very much at the mercy of the environment and a merciless hunter in everything he did. On the other hand, many of the myths of our own civilization, the mythology of Plato's *Republic*, or of Genesis, for example, have depicted the earliest stages of human existence as a Golden Age, an Eden of abundance and peace, happiness and security, from which we have declined.

In recent years anthropologists have carried out detailed, intimate studies among some of the few surviving hunter/gatherer peoples of the world. They have produced an ethnographic record that is fuller, more understanding, and more detailed than any studies that might hitherto have provided a basis for theoretical and evolutionary speculation. However, modern hunter/gatherers are no more or less reliable models for the Paleolithic than earlier ones, perhaps even less so, for most exist virtually by permission of neighboring tribal agriculturalists, who despise them at the same time as they recognize them as serving a useful purpose. Modern ethnography does, however, provide a convincing, detailed analytical picture of a new range of social possibilities that have an empirical foundation. For example, it has long been stressed that early (or simple) societies were kinship based, and this presumption has been the starting point for both historical reconstruction and logical construction of human society in general. It is now apparent from modern studies that while kinship is certainly present it is by no means the central, master organizing principle of social life. From the logical and chronological point of view kinship need no longer be considered the inevitable starting point of a human sociology.

The ethnography of modern hunter/gatherers is itself conditioned by modern anthropological theory, and this in turn is largely founded in the study of sedentary agricultural societies. The idea of social structure, for example, and its subtheories of kinship, descent, and alliance, is based on the experience and contemplation of largely African tribal societies. A modern anthropologist is brought up to assume that the societies of the anthropological universe are fundamentally kinship and descent based. And so, when fieldworkers have come to contemporary hunter/gatherers they have looked at them through theoretical spectacles that posit a social structure founded in some way on kinship. They have found something of a different stamp, but they have had to analyze their observations in terms of the models they possess. As a result such societies have suffered from "negative description": they are said to lack the various features of social structure or to possess them only in some stunted and deficient form. Modern hunter/gatherer societies are viewed by implicit comparison with tribal peoples and not in their own right. Many anthropologists are well aware of this situation and are seeking to formulate the principles of hunter/gatherer life in positive form. In so doing, they are, of course, having to rethink social theory in its entirety. One example is James Woodburn's identification of basic hunter/gatherer societies as exhibiting features of what he terms *immediate return systems*. Such a system stresses that subsistence activities, and by extension social activities in general, are conducted on the premise that investment yields an immediate return. Such people will not employ an elaborate technology, construct facilities for storage or trapping, or enter into any long-term commitments. This contrasts with *delayed return systems*, which typify agricultural communities but also apply to some hunter/gatherer societies or aspects of them.

This model is obviously economically biased, and while it is most useful, I would like to try in this chapter to offer a synthesis of hunter/gatherer ethnography based on a noneconomic model. This is partly because if it is true that hunter/gatherers can gain their living relatively easily and without the pressure of scarcity and cutthroat competition, then the heart of their social lives may well consist of interests that are not overwhelmingly economic. This is also because an overall aim of this book is to pin down and describe the source and development of regulatory or moral aspects of human social life. And partly I am trying to formulate a model of behavior and activity that other models can only describe negatively, as without structure. I am seeking to extract a strand from the skein of social life and to trace out its evolution as a function of the adaptation of people to each other and their environment under changing conditions. Hence, the model of hunter/gatherer social life I put forward may be understood as continuous with a model of tribal social life but, in the passage from one form to the other, has undergone an evolutionary transformation.

The Open Life and Intimacy

Modern nomadic hunter/gatherers living in tropical, subtropical, and temperate climates lack a solid or permanent architecture. Many arctic peoples, however, do live in substantial dwellings, though not throughout

25

the year. In general, tropical people live in flimsy shelters or lean-tos that take no more than an hour or so to build and last only a few days. In some cases people live around the fire in the open, perhaps covering themselves with sand and resting their belongings in the hut. Even a trained archaeologist may discern little evidence of an occupation site a week or so after its inhabitants have departed (Yellen 1977; Gould 1980).

Socially this means that, as among the !Kung San, "daily life goes on in full view of the camp" (Lee 1979:461), and thus, as Nurit Bird describes for the Naiken of southern India, "mere physical propinquity creates intense familiarity between people. . . . a state of involuntary intimacy characterises the social setting" (1983:119). Not only are people in full view of one another, but in many instances "they like to sit close together and interpersonal contact is frequent and extensive" (Silberbauer 1981:285). Such intimacy and exposure is enhanced, particularly in tropical areas, through an absence of clothing and little ornamentation.

This intimacy, involuntary or not, means that people spend much of their time within what Edward Hall calls the range of intimate and personal distance: "At intimate distance the presence of the other person is unmistakable and may at times be overwhelming because of the greatly stepped up sensory output. Sight (often distorted), olfaction, heat from the other person's body, sound, smell and feel of the breath all combine to signal unmistakable involvement with another body" (1966:110). It would be risky to generalize about the effects of this intimacy, because it is probably interpreted differently among various peoples. But such stepped-up sensory exposure is likely to result, among all human beings, in considerable sensitivity among individuals—something that can work two ways. Individuals who are especially sensitive to the nuances of human communication may be easily upset or, because they can read the slightest signs, extremely considerate. Whether hunter/gatherers are supersensitive either way is hard to tell from the literature.

George Silberbauer writes that the sensitivity of the G/wi of the Central Kalahari to one another is so acute that we might be tempted to attribute them with extrasensory perception. He suggests (1980) that this is produced by open and intimate conditions rather than any unique physiology and gives an example:

> The G/wi customarily scan each others' behaviour so keenly as to read a clue as slight and fleeting as a momentary change in the set of a man's neck muscles, from which they know he has struck a difficulty in the work he is

doing, a work that demands the concentration of his attention to the exclusion of conversation around him. The consequent withdrawal into silence is explained, and potential frustration and annoyance thus avoided.

Other writers, without being as specific, imply that the open, intimate life of the camp provides for a high degree of interpersonal sensitivity; Patricia Draper drew attention to the crowded intimacy of the !Kung camp and noted how the constant presence of so many people monitoring each other's behavior and moods prevents conflict (Draper 1973; 1978). The Mbuti pygmy camps include huts built of leaf fronds, and these do obscure people from view, although Pygmies spend most of their time in the open. The huts are flimsy, however, and the intimacy of life is indicated by Turnbull's observation that if a man's wife nags him at night he need only raise his voice to get friends and relatives to help (1962:124). The close involvement of Inuit Eskimos with one another within the confines of the snow house or the tent and their resulting sensitivity is documented extensively by Jean Briggs (1970), an extraordinarily sensitive observer whose abilities were in a sense honed by the open and intimate living conditions into which she entered.

Living under such intense intimacy can conceivably be a strain: other people's idiosyncracies grate more easily and trivialities become magnified; as Simmel (1954) observed, the indiscrimancy of intimacy can itself produce tension and conflict, which in turn may lead to an exaggerated fear of violence. Marjorie Shostak notes that the !Kung dread the prospect of tempers flaring out of control (1981:306), and so, too, do the Inuit Eskimos (Briggs 1982). Though open and intimate, camp life is not without its tensions, and occasionally these erupt into open conflict and fighting (see Turnbull 1982:122–24; Lee 1979:382).

In some cases, among the !Kung, for example, any attempt by a person to withdraw psychologically from company is strongly resisted. If a person becomes sullen and withdrawn he or she is not allowed to remain so, and to seek solitude is regarded as bizarre behavior (Lee 1979:461). Such a reaction may be construed as a deliberate attempt to maintain an open life through the exercise of constant surveillance. Individuals may not, on their own initiative, achieve privacy within the open company.

But they are allowed privacy through civil inattention. It is "considered bad manners" for other people to look at a married couple engaged in conjugal sex, which is carried on discreetly underneath a blanket, though in full view (Lee 1979:461). Such inattention is carried to an extreme

27

among the Naiken, who, it will be remembered, live physically so much in view of one another that they are subject to involuntary intimacy. The Naiken seem to ignore one another to the extent that they appear totally disinterested—when sitting together, for example, they look in different directions, utter infrequent observational sentences, and appear to lack interest in each other (Bird 1983:163). Like many nomadic hunter/gatherer people, Naiken deportment is marked by considerable reserve. *Nachika* almost amounts to avoidance between certain persons, for example, between children and parents-in-law of the opposite sex (ibid.:118), but nachika is reserve between people in general. To outsiders, such as the Mopala laborers on the estates where Naiken gather wages, this reserve appears almost autistic. Bird suggests that nachika minimizes or counteracts the involuntary intimacy that comes from the open life led by the Naiken.

An Unbounded Life

Hunter/gatherer nomadic groups are small, face-to-face units that range over vast, relatively empty spaces. This is particularly true of modern nomadic hunters, who live in marginal areas. These coresiding groups are continually on the move: they may pitch a camp at one spot for a few days or weeks but rarely longer; once an area has been picked over for food, another zone must be exploited.

The eastern Hadza studied by James Woodburn (1968: 49) numbered about 400 people occupying about one thousand square miles. About 460 !Kung lived in the Dobe region of around nine thousand square kilometers, which they shared with 340 Bantu (Lee 1979:41–42). Generally speaking, "hunter densities rarely exceed one person per square mile; most of the accurate figures reported at the conference ranged between one and 25 persons per square hundred miles. . . . Birdsell cites a figure of 500 as the modal size of tribes in aboriginal Australia. . . . Twenty-five to fifty persons were the figures most frequently reported for the size of local groups or bands among modern hunter-gatherers" (Lee and DeVore 1968:11).

Such a small and, as we have seen, intimate group could, if it remained permanent in composition, close in on itself. But the social composition of these camp groups is universally described as fluid and flexible (Turnbull 1968; Woodburn 1968; Lee 1979; Morris 1982). Turnbull first noted that the prime way in which tension is relieved and open conflict forestalled is by exercising what Albert Hirschman has gone on to elaborate as the "exit option": individuals are free to leave one camp and join another if relations get too sour and tense (Turnbull 1968; Hirschman 1970).

The low population density, small groups, and large areas seem to go along with an absence of formal boundaries to mark exclusive territories. !Kung boundaries are "vague and not defended" (Lee 1979:350); Pandaram "territories" overlap, and individuals claim that they go where they please (Morris 1982:185); Hadza move freely from region to region (Woodburn 1968:105); boundaries and trespass are rare and of little consequence to the Mbuti Pygmies (Turnbull 1966:277); and among many, if not most, Australian aborigines exclusive territorial and social boundaries are inappropriate (Munn 1973:11; Gumpert 1981: 116; Hamilton 1982).

Yet all ethnographic accounts note a strong association between people and territory, especially landscape, among hunter/gatherers. Ingold (1983) suggests that hunter/gatherers are concerned not with the surface of the land but with objects and features of the landscape: paths, tracks, sacred sites, haunts, water holes, and the like. He argues that such markers serve, among other things, as signposts to indicate the relative disposition of people in a landscape and that this function of signposting differs from the way in which boundaries may serve as fences to keep others out (ibid.:21).

Bushman "territories" center around water holes, and the hole itself, plus the land immediately surrounding it, is said to be "owned" by the K^nausi group (Lee 1979:334). Ingold disputes this, saying that the land around is not included and that the !Kung name simply means location (ibid.:16–17). The water hole is the "place where I belong" (Wilmsen 1980:19), but this surely means more than location: it is identification, and the idea of ownership, if it must be invoked, is in the sense of the person "belonging to" (being owned by, originating from, identified with) the place. Mbuti Pygmies look on the forest as "their territory" in the sense that it is the place where they belong rather than the place that belongs to them (Turnbull 1966:176). Even the Naiken of southern India, among the least committed of people, turn to ancestors who reside in a landmark rather than within bounded territory to clarify their identity with one another (Bird 1983:221). In his comparative study of northern hunter/gatherers, David Riches (1982:119) argues that rather than association with land being synonymous with a right of exclusion, people claim to identify with, and be identified by, their customary association with an unbounded but focused area.

The association with territory, with landscape and its objects, identifies an indigene, a native of the place, one whose life begins and focuses at this spot. The individual and the world fuse at this spot or marker, and it acts as a sort of magnet that attracts (and repels) the individual and distinguishes him or her from others whose focus or center lies elsewhere. I would suggest that the objective or etic comparative position that should be adopted from this identification with land, landscape, and objects, is not "ownership" and "tenure" but "identity." Ownership seems to be an alien concept, one that has not properly come into being among hunter/gatherers (though it can easily transpire). The relation of person to materials is basically one of sharing, and this is an ethical rather than a natural or altruistic relationship. But sharing artifacts does not stop individuals from identifying with them: !Kung arrow makers impress their individuality on weapons; ornaments and designs, both secular and sacred, individual and communal, are continually employed in identifying persons to each other. And so, too, water holes are not exclusive preserves whose value is viewed as solely economic and utilitarian. Sacred sites, paths, and water holes may be shared in a physical sense, but they cannot be claimed equally by all as foci, anchors, or epicenters of existence.

Boundaries, then, do not enter into the matter. Hunter/gatherers revolve around a focus, sometimes physically, always spiritually and socially. The region around the center point fades in its attractive powers, in a manner of speaking, or it may "overlap" with the "radius" of another center of attraction. Since these foci and zones are unbounded they can hardly exclude others. But people moving in and out come within and move out of a "zone of influence" or of another's belonging, and it is in this respect that "permission" is asked (and granted) to enter. This is a way of life that emphasizes openness, and I suggest that any notion of closure such as might be imposed by the concept of boundary is foreign. On the other hand, any tendency for formlessness or anarchy is counteracted by emphasizing focus, attraction, identification with, and belonging to.

The hazy, ill-defined sense of boundary is suggested by the findings of some ethnographers reporting what might perhaps be considered the extreme cases where people do not, apparently, organize their taxonomic thinking in culturally or socially uniform or consistent categories. These are the hunter/gatherer peoples of southern India: the Paliyan, the Hill Pandaram, and the Naiken. These people operate with what Gardner (1966) has called "memorate knowledge," knowledge derived from individual experience unmodified by any such socially shared or transmitted

process as education. Nurit Bird (1983:54) found that her Naiken informants could agree on names for a small core of familiar plants, but their
information did not coincide. Brian Morris has argued that since the notions used to identify plants and animals and other natural phenomena are
independent of each other and of other cultural domains, they can have
little symbolic power. Hence the anthropologist is unlikely to discover a
unified conceptual system constituted by symbols and their transforma-
tions—a savage mind such as Lévi-Strauss (1966) and Rodney Needham
(1979) have claimed to identify (Morris 1976).

Memorate knowledge is not, perhaps, typical of all hunter/gatherers.
The G/wi are said to have systematic knowledge of many aspects of the
world, such as the weather, the composition of plant communities, and
animals, particularly mammals, and their knowledge is consistent among
individuals (Silberbauer 1981:chap. 3). Some anthropologists find memorate knowledge hard to accept, and Morris's claims have been challenged. But ethnographers of other hunter/gatherer peoples offer hints that
confirm a relative inconsistency in classification, which in turn points to a
lack of development of the boundary concept. Jean Briggs suggests that
the contradictory behaviors identified among the Inuit Eskimo, especially
in the games played by children and by adults with children, "help to
destroy any compartmentalisation." Moral and behavioral values in this
case are not promulgated and absorbed as clear-cut, unambiguous imperatives, and therefore life is not an undeviating invariant bounded by experience: "The sense of danger is created by making children aware that
contradictory and imperfectly compartmentalised and rationalised values
exist, but, even more, by pointing up, or even creating, contradictory feelings about each of the opposed values" (1982:119).

In their attitude toward the natural resources of the landscape, and perhaps in other aspects of life, the !Kung do not divide according to categor-
ical boundaries. Lee feels sure that classificatory ambiguities do not represent lapses or omissions and believes that "the !Kung consciously strive to
maintain a boundaryless universe because this is the best way to operate
in a world where group size and resources vary from year to year"
(1979:335).

I am, however, suggesting rather more than that. I suggest that the very
structure of nomadic hunter/gatherer life cannot be conceptualized by the
observer through any technique that uses such boundary concepts as fron-
tiers, categories or compartments. These societies are better conceived and

described as they seem to conceive and describe themselves—that is, as being held together by mutual attraction and common focus. Socially, hunter/gatherers assort themselves and their thoughts far more as the occasion demands. Ideals and ideas grow far more openly and obviously out of interaction than even the anthropologist may be ready to acknowledge (cf. Holy and Stuchlik 1983).

Beholden to None

Hadza men and women often go off for weeks at a time to roam, hunt, gather, and live on their own (Woodburn 1980). Among the Pandaram, "individual men and women are often self-sufficient," and even elderly persons are expected to look after themselves (B. Morris 1982:130). Dependent behavior, except in small children, is looked down on by the Inuit Eskimo (Briggs 1982:129), while among the Naiken an old man would prefer to go cold through the night rather than ask his brother, living just five meters away, for firewood. To borrow would be to confess to dependency and inadequacy, and this would cause people to laugh and accuse him of not being a person (Bird 1983:106).

Yet the supremely competent hunter or the completely self-reliant individual is not held up as an ideal or rewarded in any way by others. On the contrary, in many of these societies the individual who boasts of his or her skill, of generosity, or of any achievements, is quickly put down in no uncertain terms. Arrogance among the !Kung is unforgivable and subjected to scathing criticism (Lee 1979:458). Independence and self-sufficiency seem to be what is expected of everyone and what everyone is capable of. It is not intended that individuals should live as islands among their fellows, however. Valued though self-sufficiency may be, the fear of abandonment and of an involuntary independence is deeply felt, at least among some such as the Inuit. To them, "one of the most frightening sanctions is abandonment, and—associated with it—death. A sense that one is vulnerable to that sanction is created by the everyday experience of comings and goings, which are the stuff of nomadic life" (Briggs 1982:120).

When Cephu, member of an Mbuti Pygmy camp, cheated on his fellow hunters by setting up his net ahead of them, he was punished by a temporary abandonment. Such a punishment was one of the most heinous crimes in Pygmy eyes, and the shame induced in Cephu by that punishment was so intense that it produced fears of death—transitory fears, it is true, but fears all the same (Turnbull 1962:106–8).

Self-sufficiency and abandonment are continuous but contrasting, yet both illustrate the social quality of life. Self-sufficiency, or independence, is admirable not because it allows one person to do without others but because it minimizes the demands of one person on another and thereby reduces the extent of intrusion and the accumulation of obligations. By reducing intrusion people gain authority over themselves, and by reducing obligation individuals reduce the degree of commitment and formality among themselves. One could say, perhaps, that commitment and formality are excluded as elements of social structure, and in this way issues of power in social relations are diminished, though not extinguished, in significance.

Such exclusion is further revealed when one examines what anthropologists of hunter/gatherer societies agree is a universal feature: the flexibility and fluidity of relations, especially kinship relations. The Hill Pandaram show "a general lack of emphasis of binding relationships; attachments are experienced at a very personal level, and as the needs and feelings change, so do marital parties" (B. Morris 1982:129). Ties between spouses do not seem to bind in any sense (ibid.:112). Those tying a man to his children are very loose (ibid.:113); by the age of five or six a Pandaram child has ceased to have close emotional ties with his parents, though there still may be affection between them, and "children are encouraged to express independence from the earliest years" (ibid.). The same pattern pertains among other south Indian foragers, while the Tanzanian Hadza are said to be "strikingly uncommitted to each other" and will change residence for no reason other than to satisfy the "desires and whims of the moment" (Woodburn 1968). The basic living unit of the G/wi is what Silberbauer calls the "clique," but the composition of a clique, which contains on average about seven households, is never constant, and the only criterion for membership that Silberbauer could discern was that "for the duration of the clique the members had preference for one another's company" (1981).

This seems to illustrate not that such people are callous and uncaring, selfish and individualistic, but that their commitments are personal, not formal, institutionalized, or rule governed. Relationships are activated and animated through proximity, and proximity is determined by affection and friendliness rather than any formal or even ideal "norm" of status. Neither

33

extreme competition nor extreme cooperation have any place in hunter/ gatherer social psychology because they require formal structure and rules, which are incompatible with a way of life that rides with the environment instead of attempting to control it. Hunter/gatherers are not selfish brutes in the Hobbesian sense; neither are they asocial and amoral in the Rousseauistic sense. When individuals cease to be attracted to each other they move away; intimacy disappears, and the composition of the camp, clique, or band alters. Hunter/gatherer nomads, having no or weak boundaries, are unconfined physically and unconstrained by categories.

Kinship works effectively only through proximity and intimacy. People who are kin render one another recognition, service, attention, and respect only when they live intimately as a household (though since houses are rare, this should perhaps be hearthhold) or as neighboring, extended hearthholds. The sense of kinship and kinship behavior weaken and attenuate as people become removed from the hearthhold to the camp to beyond, and this fading overlaps a fading of genealogical degree. Eskimo society, in which ties of kinship play a strong organizational role, tends to have a fade-out at the second or third degree of collaterals (see Riches 1982:105), and most hunter/gatherer societies do not reckon lineally above three generations. Beyond these levels kinship tends to be used as an idiom, a way of talking about relations in general. Ascending kin among the Naiken become "ancestors"; kin outside the circumference of the Mbuti hearthhold or nuclear family become more kith than kin, according to Turnbull (1966:270).

Camps, cliques, or bands, as I have noted, tend to have a fluid composition—individuals and hearthholds come and go. Such a unit cannot be said to have a total structure. As the !Kung exemplify, however, the camps are stable, because they revolve around a core of related older people, usually siblings and cousins. As these kin form the nucleus of a living group they are also identified with the focus of territory; they are the "owners," or K"ausi, of the water hole around which the territory is spread (Lee 1979:58). The kinship concept is isomorphic with the territory concept.

It seems to me, however, that the most important fact about kinship, or at least the one that contrasts most with kinship in sedentary societies, is that it does not impose status on a relationship and so does not constrain people. Duty is, as it were, owed between people rather than between their positions. The degree to which this is true probably varies among hunter/ gatherers, but, in contrast to sedentary societies, it is true of them all to some degree. The point can be made most explicit by considering the case of the Hill Pandaram. Brian Morris points out that "every Hill Pandaram with whom an individual came into contact was a relative of some sort" (1982:122), yet knowledge of actual relations rarely goes beyond an individual's father's relations (ibid.:124). Children, we have already noted, are free to leave the company of their parents after the age of about six years, and, what is more, spouses (that is, parents) are not bound by their relationship at all, only by their affection toward each other (ibid.:129). Thus even at the closest degree of kinship the idea that obligation attaches to the relationship, that there exists a duty independent of the person, is lacking. As long as people remain attracted to each other, as long as they are friends, they live intimately together and are kin. Then they owe and perform reciprocal obligations of deference and succor. Locality, and hence intimacy, are the terms on which morality is laid out, and together these constitute kinship. Without propinquity, intimacy, and deference, kinship is nonexistant or greatly attenuated.

Kinship terminology and the wide-ranging idiom of kinship, however, are used extensively to open up the possibly constricting and stifling nature of the camp or clique. Kin terminologies, for example, are highly general or classificatory and allow for great flexibility. In such societies as the !Kung, the Hadza, or the G/wi, one ideally marries outside the band or camp; the husband resides with the wife's parents and offers them services for a year or so; the two then return to the husband's band or join a group of their own choosing, providing of course that they are accepted. In this way active and performed relations are established, and a basis is laid for a network of ties that can, if necessary, be constructed into a basis for alliance or for social routes. To establish and claim kinship in the initial instance is to predict a friendly relationship, to offer an earnest of trust that will give a sense of security to those admitting new members to their company. But to claim kinship is not to assert a right; it merely justifies a preference.

Kinship, or claiming kinship, signals friendship, while friendship realises and confirms kinship. In the continuous pattern of coming and going that is signified by flexible social composition, there is bound to be a degree of uncertainty at the inauguration of a new proximal relationship. This uncertainty can be reduced through kinship. To claim kinship is to proclaim trustworthiness.

This does not mean that social life is anarchic. It means that when a relationship is mutually acknowledged and undertaken, that undertaking is constituted less by predetermined structural ties than by voluntary agreement to enter into obligations to share, to cooperate, to show deference, and, in some cases, to observe taboos and prohibitions. Even among the Hadza, where kinship relations are not load bearing, where they do not determine the organization of activities, some relations are marked by obligations. A man is obliged to live with his wife's mother and to provide her with beads, meat, and trade goods (Woodburn 1968:109). But this relationship is entered on by choice and may be dissolved by choice.

Resorting again to the metaphor of focus, kinship is clearly defined in the center: the hearthhold and the camp. Beyond, as the range increases, kinship is a reservoir of potential but undefined (or increasingly vaguely defined) connections. These may be brought to life and given precision according to circumstances—change of residence, search for marriage partners, desire for friendship, and so forth. When this happens, what was once the center shifts to the periphery. And those who were at the periphery move to the center. Another way of describing this is to point out that for most hunter/gatherer societies the entire dialect group is small enough for each individual to have some kinship tie with all the others. But of these possibilities any one individual will maintain vivid connections with only a fraction of the population at any time. These universalistic tendencies of what is usually bilateral kinship undergo a degree of ideological limitation through genealogical amnesia—as when people forget their father's generation's relatives or relatives three degrees removed.

Sharing

One way in which the loose discipline of kinship is countered in some hunter/gatherer societies, such as certain Eskimo groups or the !Kung, is by the practice of name sharing. Generally only a few names are used to identify individuals, and to these are added such qualifiers as nicknames, diminutives, and the like that distinguish individuals living in a small community. Among the Qiqiktamiut Eskimo, for example, children are sometimes given the name of an older, often prominent, individual—with the latter's agreement. Thereafter they enjoy a restricted and special relationship of namegiver to namesake (Guemple 1965:324). Between these two are general obligations that involve "helping," "looking after," and sometimes gift giving. This is usually a one-way traffic because of the difference in generation between namegiver and namesake, but the former receives a degree of prestige and social worth from camp residents (ibid.:327).

One of the effects of this name sharing is to skew kinship such that the namesake is engaged with the kin of the namegiver. Furthermore, as they switch to this, the partners become special kin (*saunik*) to one another, and this takes precedence over the other relations and over the terms of address and reference that might otherwise identify the individuals.

This practice of name sharing focuses a relationship in a way that differentiates it from relations in general. David Riches (1982:86) points out that it defines a degree of privacy and exclusiveness, because it is a special relationship between partners and excludes others. I find no mention as to whether namesaking is revocable, and I assume that once it is agreed on it persists and that people do not walk away from it, as they do from kinship relations. Among the !Kung namesaking works in the same way, except that it is revocable (Marshall 1976). It may define corridors of privacy or privilege that give partners a more certain chance of being welcomed and established in different areas and into different bands (Keenan 1981).

Among the Qiqiktamiut the exclusiveness of namesaking derives largely from obligations and especially from gift giving with its attendant insistence on recognition and reciprocity. In return for gift giving, the namegiver receives prestige and, possibly, return gifts. Namesharing also opens up the system and fulfills the more common effect of sharing, which is to disperse and distribute. The saunik system allows a namesake to haul into his kinship network anyone related to the namegiver and hence to identify as kin "persons to whom no known (or imaginable) genealogical connection can be traced" (Guemple 1965:331). Sometimes the Qiqiktamiut make a game of this. Lorna Marshall says that the homonymous kinship among the !Kung makes it possible to classify an entire population as kin, which in turn inspires confidence and trust.

Sharing among hunter/gatherers is ubiquitous, though the pattern may differ between societies. A virtually universal rule is the sharing of the meat of large animals. The obligation to share meat can, one may argue, have clear economic functions. One or two individuals can neither consume nor store a large animal on their own. Given the uncertainties of hunting, those who are successful one day may fail on another. By sharing each is assured of meat whenever it becomes available. Ways of sharing meat differ, but by far the most common among hunter/gatherers is to divide an animal into specific portions and distribute the flesh. Rarely is an animal cooked first and then eaten as a meal by a group. Among the Nyae Nyae, "Meat is not habitually cooked and eaten as a family meal. . . . When an individual receives a portion of meat, he owns it outright for himself. He may give and share it further as he wishes, but it never becomes a family or group property" (Marshall 1976:302). On one occasion Lorna Marshall counted sixty-three divisions of raw meat, and she adds, "doubtless there were more." Details of a typical pattern of meat division among the G/wi show sixteen individuals receiving 69.5 kilograms of meat, and most of these portions are further subdivided (Silberbauer 1981:234). Every household of a camp, and many of those in neighboring camps, end up with at least some meat from a member's kill. The distribution of portions varies with who is the hunter, who his partner, and, in some instances, who the maker of the arrow. These people distribute their initial portions among members of their households and then to kin and affines; meat traces out kinship connections and, in so doing, keeps them vivid and active. When meat comes into the community but the hunter is not a close or primary kinsman, people may well wonder whether they will receive meat and if so, how much (Shostak 1981:88).

A !Kung hunter who kills a large animal is "rigorously required" to be self-deprecatory about his "success." When he gets back to the village he walks in silently, sits down by the fire, and, after greeting people, waits. Slowly others elicit the information about the kill, but if he shows any sign of boasting or arrogance, "pointed jokes and derision may be used to pressure him back into line" (ibid.:86).

In the dispersal of meat and the downplaying of the success of the hunter there seems to be a conscious attempt to resist a convergence of possibilities that would introduce boundaries to the community. Specifically, the animal to be consumed by everybody is dismembered and distributed. And the identification between the hunter and the animal is forestalled so that, among other things, he cannot be identified as the distributor of the animal and thus claim recognition as a benefactor. That flesh rather than cooked meat is distributed is quite the opposite of the usual practice among sedentary peoples, where animals are cooked and eaten commensally by the assembled community or congregation. This commensality helps to define the social unity of the group, while the animal itself symbolizes that unity.

The idea of a donor or distributor of the feast is a performance of status in itself.

On occasions hunter/gatherers participate in a feast, and at these times participants explicitly affirm bonds of unity and repair strained relations (Silberbauer 1981:175). A feast is provided among the Mbuti at their *molimo* celebration, when special emphasis is placed on social solidarity, for example, after a death (Turnbull 1966:260).

Sharing forestalls accumulation, and this has practical advantages among nomadic hunter/gatherers. But it also militates against the mounting of displays. The hunter is not denied his skill by the rules that forbid boasting, but he is prevented from *making a show of it*. The dismemberment and distribution of the animal ensures that it cannot be displayed, that it cannot thereby be converted into a source of admiration and, thence, justify a claim to prestige and status (see chapter 5).

The obligation to share meat clearly has economic functions and helps to reduce risk and uncertainty of food supply. But I suggest, further, that it has a positive function in ensuring the continued openness of the society and its groupings. Sharing is generalized in that it does not confer or define exclusive relations or suppose an immediate, direct, and balanced return (Sahlins 1972:194). But the sort of exchanges that have an embryonic place in the saunik relations of the Qiqiktamiut take on a fully grown and central place in the system of *hxaro* Wiessner describes for the !Kung. These are relations entered into voluntarily by individuals who are most often also close kin. These relations are revocable, principally when partners move too far away from each other. Wiessner argues that the system greatly minimizes economic risk and reduces uncertainty: it works by "pooling risk through storage of social obligations" (1982:65). Hxaro relations seem to overlap close kin ties rather more than saunik relations; hxaro partners enjoy a degree of privacy of distinction from kinship ties, but not as complete a one. A hxaro relation is certainly special: "Once a relationship is firm, a person is said to '//hai' that person in his or her heart, meaning literally to hold and figuratively to be responsible for the person. A strong bond of friendship is solidified by the *hxaro* partnership" (Wiessner 1982:66). This points to a degree of privacy.

The essence of hxaro is the presentation of gifts and their return, and "because *hxaro* partnerships are not economic contrasts with set terms, but rather bonds of mutual help, it can be difficult for a person to avoid exploitation" (ibid.:68). This leads to a considerable degree of calculation and discretion: people are discrete about showing what they have and about the timing as well as the placement of their gifts. Correspondingly, a degree of anxiety may arise between partners (see Wiessner 1982; Shostak 1981). This may even include deceit and lying.

The pressures generated by exchange and gift giving may call on individuals to find some way to conceal something of themselves from their partners, to create for themselves a degree of privacy. This has to be obtained within the framework and ethos of an open society. It could be that, under severe conditions of deprivation, such a system of sharing and reciprocity will generate extreme pressures of privacy, so extreme that they will come into open conflict with the ethos itself and eventuate in frenzied efforts to evade scrutiny and to invade privacy, as Colin Turnbull (1973) has described for the East African Ik. Here was a hunter/gatherer society knowing no other ethic than that of the open society but so deprived and under such strain that people were in constant suspicion of one another, strove desperately to keep a permanent watch on one another, and, just as desperately, sought to evade one anothers' attention (Wilson et al. 1974).

The Hadza do not appear to entertain gift giving but achieve the same ends of redistribution by gambling (Woodburn 1982). Gambling away artifacts disperses them in the same way as an animal is dispersed after being killed. But there are hints, in Woodburn's account, of pressures. Losers sometimes pursue winners in the hopes of repossessing articles by renewed gambling (ibid.:443). The Naiken, by contrast, neither exchange nor gamble, and neither do they lend, borrow, or accumulate goods. Even when working on estates for wages they consume immediately (Bird 1983).

The Naiken, the Hill Pandaram, or the Hadza are examples of what Woodburn calls *immediate return societies*. They gather what they need and consume it immediately; they exchange services straightaway and employ a simple technology that involves a small investment. Some hunter/gatherer societies, for example the Mbuti, have elements of a *delayed return system*, since they use such items as nets for hunting on a large, cooperative scale. Investment need not be confined to material culture, though. The widespread practice of sharing among hunter/gatherers carries with it hints of investment—one shares to ensure a later return from someone else. This becomes explicit when specialized sharing relationships, such as the hxaro, develop. Wiessner (1982:68) writes that a !Kung hunter may pause after a run of successful hunting to enjoy some of the reciprocal obligations he has built up. When he does this he operates on the principle of "delayed return."

Social Circuitry

Hunter/gatherer life is by and large intimate and open to view. People are constantly exposed to each other's attention, though people do divert that attention at agreed upon circumstances. Even so, and even granted a limited material culture and a distribution process that reduces personal possession to a minimum, the exposure of people to each other, and of the individual to the group, seems extreme, and one wonders about the possible consequences of this for the integration of the individual.

On the surface the openness of hunter/gatherer life is reminiscent of the way in which Erving Goffman characterizes the degrading life of people in our own society confined to total institutions:

> The central feature of total institutions can be described as a breakdown of the barriers ordinarily separating these three spheres of life [sleep, play, and work]. First, all aspects of life are conducted in the same place and under the same single authority. Second, each phase of the member's daily activity is carried on in the immediate company of a large batch of others, all of whom are treated alike and required to do the same thing together. [1961:6]

The conditions are not identical, but the main point, that individuals have no physical and little psychological space for privacy, applies. As we have seen, many aspects of hunter/gatherer life are attempts to balance the prevailing openness.

A prominent way in which this is done, a probably universal practice, is to express criticism obliquely and to make one's opinions known indirectly. Disagreements and criticisms are potential grounds for disruption and for giving offense. If protest is not made, the individual continues to suffer, and to this suffering will be added frustration. Yet to criticize openly may offend and place further strain on a relationship. To criticize others is to assault their integrity, their self-mastery. Such an offense is avoided by obliqueness. The chief circumstance in which interpersonal friction is likely to arise among the Naiken is between the "host" and the "lodger"— the latter being a young unmarried person living in the hut of a married couple. Each often perceives the other to be failing in personal obligations, but when this occurs he or she does not complain directly. Instead, each

41

voices his or her dissatisfaction to others in the vicinity in the hopes that word will get back (Bird 1983:155). A public, direct complaint would result in the shaming of the accused, the forced exposure of a private relationship. Lorna Marshall (1976) describes a similar situation among the Nyae Nyae, who, when they have cause to complain, wait until the anonymity of darkness and then sing plaintively of their unhappiness. Neighbors mediate marital disputes tactfully and indirectly without seeming to interfere. Such obliqueness gives the plaintiff the chance to change the situation as if on his or her own volition, and this in turn serves to preserve a sense of individual integrity and separateness.

The issue of individual integrity becomes especially prominent in decisions likely to affect all or most members of a camp. The danger here lies in the competition of wills and the possibility that one person's integrity and autonomy may be violated by others. Integrity is preserved and disruption forestalled by general rules of procedure. For example, a Mbuti man who speaks from his hearth is considered to be thinking out loud and speaking solely for himself. If, however, he speaks from the "midcamp," he is "taking a band rather than an individual point of view" (Turnbull 1966:200). Space is used to define and express the "rule" that helps to delineate the individual as a private person from the individual as a public person. The Hadza make no such distinctions but maintain that all individuals are politically private. Community decisions are reached through a succession of individual, interpersonal discussions so that a final, concerted move or decision is, or appears to be, epiphenomenal (Woodburn 1979).

As among the Mbuti, the G/wi hearth may serve to demarcate a zone of privacy: political privacy. Around a hearth discussions bear only on those gathered. But this zone can be extended, without being disturbed, by people talking loudly enough for everyone else to hear, thereby forcing them to eavesdrop—comparable indeed to the Pygmy speaking from the hearth. In this way, Silberbauer (1981:173) suggests, people can criticize one another indirectly, without invading and challenging integrity. Subtly they transform the tacitly private into the emerging public. If these opinions gain currency and support, pressure mounts on the target to change and to accept the general opinion and decision. If the target cannot, or does not, accept the consensus, he or she is free, and encouraged, to leave for another band. Thus a private person is, by such pressure, gradually exposed as a public person: his or her privacy is stripped away. The art of indirect pressure that insidiously erodes an individual's self-control and social function is well detailed by Silberbauer:

> The offender's requests for goods or services are refused, with excuse being made for refusal. His suggestions are turned down or are so misrepresented as to make them ridiculous. Cooperative undertakings in which he participates are bungled. Much of what he says is misheard or not heard at all. . . . Such treatment is oblique and sometimes very subtle and amounts to a public conspiracy to keep the offender (or victim) on the wrong foot and engender the type of frustration of which he cannot legitimately complain. [Ibid.:174]

By this time, one would imagine, a person is virtually disenfranchised.

Analyzing further what goes on when such behavior takes place reveals more of how hunter/gatherer life runs without institutional differentiation and regulation. When people of a G/wi clique of a !Kung camp treat one of their members as Silberbauer has described, they are gradually disarming him or her as a social person within that group. They do so by "breaking the rules"—of reciprocity, of sharing, of cooperating, of listening, of conversation, of attention and company. When the majority "breaks the rules," they do so by commission and cut off the target individual from the grounds of identity. This is in response to the individual who has broken the rules by omission and who, by so doing, has fragmented the group through intrusions and corrosion of the links that bind everyone. In a sense the "rules" are brought into existence only to discipline the individual who has upset the group.

All of this, plus the fact that most ethnographers, particularly of African, Eskimo, and Australian aborigine hunter/gatherers, record occasional outbreaks of violence and emotion, attests to the presence of stress. This is despite the open intimacy of a life that provides little opportunity to hide. Even when public life makes it impossible for the individual to become introspective for a while or to seek quiet and solitude, it is clear that people either do, or are thought to possess, a degree of inscrutability behind which is believed to lurk their uniqueness, their selfishness, their cunning, their jealousies, their anxieties, their unpredictability, and their dangerousness. The Hadza have to assert their egalitarianism, presumably because it is too tempting to move to inequality (Woodburn 1982); the !Kung do covet meat and have to be compelled to share it (Shostak 1981), and !Kung men are sometimes jealous of their wives. In some ways the acknowledgment of these inclinations in a society where life is perpetually open and where attention is constant is even more threatening than in societies that are more closed to view. Such inclinations and the outbursts to which they may give rise are less expected, so more frightening when they occur. Emotional outbreaks are what many hunter/gatherers fear most for themselves.

Because the danger of human inclinations erupting looms so large in the minds of hunter/gatherers I suspect that any camp or clique or group must look in on itself and carry out constant inspection. I have no direct evidence for this, but this is the slot into which trance possession and shamanism would seem to fit, because these are extreme forms of transcendental examination and inspection. And shamanism, trance, and possession are typical of many hunter/gatherer societies.

Possession trance occurs many times a week in a Bushman camp, and the majority of adult Bushmen are capable of becoming possessed. Among the Hadza or Naiken, by contrast, only some individuals are occasionally possessed by trance. Recall that the !Kung live in camps that have a fluid composition but are stabilized around a core of kin; the Hadza live in camps without such a core, and the Naiken do not rely on a community life at all. A !Kung is never alone, but a Hadza may often go walkabout in the bush on his/her own for some time (Woodburn 1982:438), and the Naiken live their lives mostly in the company of a spouse with occasional, often disinterested, contacts with others (Bird 1983). This crude comparison suggests that possession trance, or its frequency, relates to the extent of community life and hence may be involved with the increasing intensity of problems that emerge with daily group life.

My chief suggestion is that all the studies of shamanism I have consulted characterize it as, among other things, an exercise in the art of "seeing"; through possession the human being can perceive things, people, and the world *as they really are*, not just as they appear to be. The first, vital stage of !Kung trance healing is "seeing properly," and proper seeing becomes more general as the healer becomes more powerful:

A healer can begin to see into and beyond many material manifestations. . . . As a healer in *kia* you see everybody. You see that the insides of well people are fine. You see the insides of the one the spirits are trying to kill, and you go there. . . . Others describe how they can see at a distance, or see what the gods want to tell the !Kung. . . . Proper seeing is a transcendant function and is itself a transcendant experience. The literal or physical act of seeing may or may not be involved. The eyes may be open, they may be closed; it is not crucial. The experience remains one of enhanced perceiving and knowing. [Katz 1982:105–6]

It often happens that the best, most powerful healer is blind yet is able to see further and better. The blind Kau Bua was one of the strongest !Kung healers (ibid.:211).

The object of *kia* is to heal. Sometimes the individual or everyone present has the sickness pulled out of them—sickness of which they may have been unaware. Although one or two individuals may go into a trance, a number of coresident people participate and assist at the seance, and since sessions last through the night and often into the following day until everyone is well nigh exhausted, in the end occurs a catharsis in which any tensions that might have existed between people are overcome.

Possession and trance also entertain; among other things, they provide a spectacle, and individuals may perform such extraordinary deeds as working with fire (ibid.:120–22). Such an entertainment, in which everyone is involved as performer as well as spectator, may reinforce a sense of good company. It also appears that engagement in possession fulfills individual demands for privacy, for establishing individuality and power amid an open, public, and egalitarian life. Writing in general of !Kung shamans and drawing on their own descriptions, Katz says that "they experience themselves as beyond their ordinary self by becoming more essential, more themselves" (ibid.:53). Given that so many adult !Kung enjoy possession at some time (and hence become more themselves), they clearly enjoy a sense of existential privacy even amid an active, public gathering. Wherever shamanism occurs some practitioners are acknowledged to be "better" or more "powerful" than others or are taken over by more powerful spirits. This confers on a person a degree of distinctiveness and status in a highly valued or esteemed social process, that concerned with illness and healing. The hierarchical nature of shamanism is apparent in the fact that healing is often achieved as a victory over malignant spirits by the shaman (or his spirit) in a battle. This "ranking" transcends the day-to-day social life of the camp or the band and can exist parallel to it without corrupting the camp's egalitarian ideals. Even so, highly gifted shamans, those who can see better than anyone else, do enjoy a special reputation, for they are expert in a transcendant (yet socially necessary) skill. Among the !Kung, however, they enjoy no special status or authority in everyday affairs.

The ability to see properly comes from outside the person, so the responsibility for seeing is not attributed to the individual shaman. In possession trance he or she is simply the vehicle through which the spirit, the power of perception, works. So what is being demonstrated during trance is the principle and importance of perception itself in the pursuit of social and individual life. If ordinary people during their ordinary waking lives find difficulty in seeing people and things as they really are, then this deficiency can, and must, be made good by making present an "all-seeing eye." Knowing that an all-seeing eye exists and that its perceptions can be consulted helps to monitor and regulate social life, its tensions and its tendency to inequality. Through possession the all-seeing eye becomes manifest and reveals that nothing can be hidden—not things, not intentions, not moods, not facts. At the same time, knowing that the shaman can see properly and can heal inspires confidence, for here is a guarantee of the integrity of companions. They are under shamanic surveillance.

Open Society

Even in such small-scale societies as those mentioned here, where economic scarcity is rarely a problem, social equality must be actively sought after and maintained, even asserted. A constant vigilance is maintained to ensure that individuals and groups do not "acquire more wealth, assert more power or claim more status than others" (Woodburn 1982:432). Woodburn, Silberbauer, Lee, and others describe in their ethnographies how such assertions are made and how such practices as mobility and the exercise of the exit option serve to trim inequalities. Woodburn (1982) suggests that the most basic leveling process is to ensure that all subsistence and economic practices are based on immediate rather than delayed return. This minimizes the chances of accumulation, of investment in long-term, elaborate technology and in extensive cooperative labor. These practices make it difficult for individuals to achieve powers of debt and credit over their fellows. Like the Hadza, the G/wi arrive at consensus decisions of public policy through individual discussions, through airing their opinions, testing the wind, and gradually adjusting points of view. But attempts to impose a viewpoint and arguments where emotions run too high are defused by a withdrawal of attention: "Members signal their lack of sympathy with the heated mood by affecting preoccupations with other matters" (Silberbauer 1981:171).

But there are leaders, individuals toward whom deference is shown, whose example is followed, whose decisions are authoritative. Lee mentions four possible criteria for leadership among the !Kung: seniority, n!ore ownership, marriage to a n!ore owner, and personal qualities. But none of these singly or in combination automatically qualify an individual to be a leader. "If anything," writes Lee, "the leaders share an absence of traits in common" (1979:345). And so is it the case among the G/wi, where leadership shifts unpredictably among acknowledged experts with the occasional inclusion of a "dark horse" (Silberbauer 1981:170). There is no spillage from one field of expertise to another such as might consolidate an individual's position of overall superiority. Discussing Eskimo leadership, Riches (1982:82) makes the point that for leadership to consolidate, food supply must be reasonably certain so that a hunter can show *sustained* leadership.

This emphasis on compartmentalization, where expertise is one activity segregated from other activities seems to clash with the avowal of an open, egalitarian society. Denying the claims of a person to status by virtue of accomplishment is only one side—the negative, reverse side—of the process. The important feature of these societies, the feature that ensures ongoing freedom, equality, and openness, is that no one is *disbarred* from assuming a position of authority by their prowess or lack of it in any activity. Being a good hunter may not serve as an a priori qualification for giving advice on moving camp, but neither does it prevent anyone from giving such advice.

If we look at matters from this point of view then the openness of the society becomes apparent and so too can we offer a clearer picture of what comprises a simple society. A simple and open society is one in which reputation is not acknowledged as the grounds for a relationship or status. A characteristic of such societies as the !Kung, the Hadza, the G/wi, the Naiken, or the Paliyan is that a "good hunter" is not necessarily thought of as a "better hunter." A Hadza man may say aloud that he is going hunting the next day, and others may or may not decide to go as well. If he is a good hunter and the chances are better that by going in his company one may find game, well and good, and to go with him is a rational decision. But to accompany is not the same as to follow, and no relationship other than that of association is established. The relationship between individuals is founded on their compatibility and not on the relativity of their reputations, real or inferred. It is entirely open for the less skilled hunter to initiate an expedition, just as it is entirely open for both hunters to make suggestions for moving camp or for reforming a dispersed band.

It now becomes possible to resolve what otherwise seems a contradiction in !Kung society, in which arrogance and boasting of one's accomplishments is treated as heinous (Lee 1979), yet men adopt epithets that praise their prowess in hunting (Marshall 1976:226). /Ti!kay, for instance, praises himself by calling himself Sharp Edge of the Arrow Point, and he calls himself this because he is very good at shooting. Other nicknames are bestowed by a person's companions: /Toma was nicknamed /Toma Word because of his outstanding ability to guide people by talking with them and to persuade them to do the right things (ibid.). Such epithets do not imply relationships or statuses; they are not titles in the sense that *chief* is a status term implying *follower* or *subject*. Their reputations are, in a sense, private rather than social phenomena and are to be measured by reference to the possibilities inherent in the actions themselves rather than the capabilities of others. Kau Dwa was a "strong healer" and Wa Na is a fantastic healer (Katz 1982), but their abilities do not put them in a hierarchy, nor are they indices of other skills and positions in community matters.

Leadership and hierarchic status does materialize in some hunter/gatherer societies. It may be found among some Eskimo peoples, for example. In these societies, as in African cases, men attract followers rather than command them, and they do this by providing highly visible indices of their suitability to lead. These indices become attached to the individual as a permanent, ongoing, visible aspect of his status, because their presence draws from others admiration and hence prestige. Among the features of display that indicate leadership are: having many wives and children, owning many dogs, and maintaining a superior and well-maintained technology, all of which result from superior economic prowess (Riches 1982:139). An individual's reputation materializes in objects that become part of his demeanor. This draws deference from others and places them in a status relationship (see Goffman 1967).

Anthropologists, working in a tradition of social theory based empirically on domesticated agricultural, tribal ethnography, have often found they had to portray hunter/gatherer social life through negative description. A typical example is Holmberg's summary of the Siriono:

> Generally speaking there are no formalized, obligatory patterns of kinship behavior. Brother-sister avoidance, parent-in-law taboos, joking relationships are lacking. . . . Beyond the stratification of sex and age, Siriono society is little differentiated as to status. A form of chieftainship does exist, but the prerogatives of office are few. . . . The legal system by means of which the relations between band members are governed is not an elaborate one. [1969:140]

Such descriptions give the impression of a deficient society, impoverished and without visible means of social support. Those sedentary tribal people who live as neighbors to hunter/gatherers seem to have a similar view, regarding them not just as lacking in structure, order, and culture but as less than human. African villagers equate the Pygmies with animals (Turnbull 1962:3), and the South American Cubeo likewise regard the nearby Macu as not being people at all but *filhos da onca,* or children of the jaguar (Goldman 1963:97). But then the Macu and the Pygmies tend to pity the poverty of their neighbor's static, rule-bound life in return.

In purely social terms the difference between a sedentary agricultural society and a nomadic gathering society is that the former sees itself, and is seen by such observers as anthropologists and nomads, as organizing social life with reference to a social structure, while the nomad organizes activities piecemeal, without a structure. Brian Morris says as much for the Pandaram when he writes, "It would not be stretching our point too far to suggest that the Hill Pandaram has little social organisation, or rather, to employ a useful but difficult distinction of Firth (1969), they have social organisation but little social structure" (1982:114).

Nomadic hunter/gatherers do not live in a state of anarchy, but neither do they live in organizations permanently structured according to social principles. There are, as we have seen, agreed or regular procedures for making decisions, and these rules ensure the smooth course of the procedures and do not specify the decision: no authority is designated, for example, by assigning precedence to age, sex, birth, expertise, or wealth—that is, by specifying a structure relevant to decision making. The existence and maintenance of the exit option is likewise a sort of metapractice that ensures the existence of conditions for organization without specifying what is to be the nature of the organization or whether there need be *an* organization. The exit option neither favors nor disadvantages hierarchy, for example, but if hierarchy exists, the exit option keeps it up to scratch.

The stress placed by some peoples on egalitarianism often appears in a negative manner as the avoidance of hierarchy and status. The culturally prescribed reaction of indifference and belittling to the success of a hunter or the deliberate withholding of gratitude suggests that such people as the !Kung or the Pandaram realize they have to fight against a tendency that could eventuate in hierarchy. Whether this tendency to stratification or status is natural or learned by example from sedentary neighbors is not apparent, but the ethnography clearly points to a self-conscious awareness of the dangers of arrogance and accomplishment and their relation to hierarchy. Egalitarianism is thus ruled or structured by prescriptions and pro-scriptions aimed at securing and upholding it and above all by insisting on universal entitlement irrespective of qualifications.

This glimpse of structure is subsumed within the more abstract direction that pervades nomadic hunter/gatherer society, the guidance by focus rather than by boundary, as is the case among sedentary agriculturalists. Without an emphasis on the very concept of the boundary the possibility of property—of clearly defined exclusion and inclusion, of the demarca-tion necessary to status—can never be properly realized. The hunter/gath-erer's landscape is open; people may spread their connections endlessly across it, just as they may move freely. Without boundaries and without the *concept* of the permanent boundary, people are not conceptually locked into their relationships or surroundings. Nomads focus on the landscape and its features: sites, tracks, water holes, lairs, sanctuaries, birthplaces, landmarks. Such a focus becomes clear or fuzzy according to distance and interest. Nomads focus on one another in the same way, keeping those in clearest focus who live in intimate proximity and for whom, at the time, they have intense feelings. Others who are spatially or emotionally farther distant are less in focus but can easily be brought closer, for no boundaries, geographical or conceptual, hinder physical or emotional movement.

The hunter/gatherer pins ideas and emotions onto the world as it exists: the landscape is turned into a mythical topographical map, a grid of ances-tor tracks and sacred sites, as is typical among the Australian aborigines (Munn 1973). A construction is put upon the landscape rather than the landscape undergoing a reconstruction, as is the case among sedentary peoples, who impose houses, villages, and gardens on the landscape, often in place of natural landmarks. Where nomads read or even find cosmolog-ical features in an already existing landscape, villagers tend to represent and model cosmic ideas in the structures they build.

The same is true of relations between people. Nomads organize their social lives through focusing attention rather than referring it to a rigid structure. Kinship, for example, which leans toward invariance and pre-scription in sedentary society, is assumed or dismissed by nomads and for-gotten according to how people feel for each other or to their proximity. Where a person's identity might be defined primarily by kinship in tribal society, nomads tend to identify those as kin who behave like kin, regard-less of genealogical status.

The obligation to share among hunter/gatherers is also evolutionist or anticonstructionist (Hayek 1973), because it distributes the materials of social (and physical) construction and accumulation. Unlike the contributory behavior of sedentarists when they hold feasts and displays, the sharing by nomads of food and articles, like the belittling of accomplishment, quashes the conditions for an enduring organization while allowing activities to be organized as and when convenient.

Violence is not unknown in nomadic societies and is greatly feared. Fights occur, and excessive, abnormal, or pathological violence tends to be countered by violence: men whose violent dispositions make them a threat to the peaceful life of a camp are reported as being ambushed and killed. But no modern ethnography gives any indication of such violence either being organized permanently or getting out of hand. Revenge, feuds, rioting, warfare, and battle seem to emerge among, and to be typical of, domesticated peoples. In small, intimate, open hunter/gatherer societies the control of force is not organized or delegated to agents. Force is universal and thereby confers no authority. The fear of force and violence is also universal, and this serves as a sufficient sanction against it running out of control. A companion is always at hand to step in when tempers explode. And if eruption seems imminent or inevitable because of a deteriorated social life there is always the exit option.

Violence aside, what of the demands of "justice"? What is done to ensure that people's survival and welfare needs are met, that people get what they deserve, that people do not cheat one another? In the open societies we are discussing, these questions cannot be isolated as reflecting articulated concerns of the people. Such matters become identifiable when they become problematic, and this begins in domesticated societies. In open societies the conditions for unjust behavior are minimal: people can keep one another in more or less constant focus, they can pay attention to one another, and they can, if they wish, escape the glare of too insistent a scrutiny. Justice does not have to be done, for in a sense it does not exist as something to be done: it occurs as a normal, integral part of everyday life. This does not mean that in open societies the differences between people are disallowed; it means that whatever differences are admitted are done so as equivalences and by common consent.

Beneath the easy smoothness of generalizations are, however, the qualifying uncertainties of the human being. No one can be sure of another's intentions and feelings, not even members of the open societies we have been describing. Marjorie Shostak has recorded the anxiety and uncertainty felt by Nisa about her husband and about the willingness of members of her camp other than her father to share meat fairly; Colin Turnbull described the unfair behavior of Cephu, who tried to steal a march over his net-hunting companions. The perpetual uncertainty of the human condition—an uncertainty that is not permanently uppermost but is always there—is met and dealt with in open societies by the transcendent, disembodied inspection and remedying of shamanism and trance possession.

Common to these focused open societies, though not emphasized to the same extent by all of them, is an ethic of independence. It seems to be an ideal of hunter/gatherers to strive at all times to achieve and maintain their independence. To put this a little differently, in answer to the Socratic questions "What should I do?" and "How should I live?" the hunter/gatherer can answer in Kantian fashion: Strive always to be independent. In this way an individual can further not only his own independence but also the independence of others. This will ensure that neither competition nor cooperation will become significant features of social life. It will also generate other regular features of hunter/gatherer life: the prevalence of the exit option, the reliance on affection to sustain and disaffection to terminate relationships, the abandonment of the lame, aged, and infirm, and the making of public decisions by tacit consent.

Modern ethnography suggests that it is *possible* that Paleolithic societies might have been founded on a principle of focus and an ethic of independence. This contrasts starkly with the principles on which nonhuman primate societies and, by implication, protohuman societies, are founded. As I have discussed, primate societies are founded on dominance and subordination, and dominance is the subject of competition. Human society could have begun, therefore, by refuting hierarchy and dominance and establishing in their place what John Stuart Mill considered the only true form of liberty, liberty from the interference of others. Ironically, perhaps, Isaiah Berlin thinks such a freedom unlikely ever to have been achieved, except "by any but a small minority of highly civilized and self-conscious human beings" (1969:161).

Appendix to Chapter Two

Any critical reader will note one glaring omission from the hunter/gatherer peoples considered in this chapter: the Australian aborigine. This omission is the outcome of a long-pondered choice. I think, though, that I owe the reader my reasons for this choice, as briefly as I can make them.

From its earliest days, speculative anthropology has seen in the aborigines the archetype and prototype of human society. Because nineteenth-century aborigines lacked all but a few items of material culture it was thought that all other aspects of their thought, belief, and society were equally primitive and primordial. The Paleolithic world, for example, was thought to have been totemic because the Australian aborigines were totemic. To understand totemism was to understand the origins of religion, and to understand origins was to be able to grasp the essence of religion, or kinship, or group life. Present-day reasoning no longer allows much scope to the ethnographic analogy and is especially restrictive as regards the aborigines. In particular it is pointed out that aborigines have inhabited the Australian continent for perhaps as many as thirty to forty thousand years, and until the nineteenth century enjoyed little contact with the outside world. They have pursued their own, independent lines of social change and evolution, and what we perceive now is the outcome of independent development. As Kenneth Maddock writes, "Aborigines, then, typify neither early men nor modern hunters and gatherers. They are properly to be regarded as having a distinctive and specialized culture" (1972:22).

The same must also be true, to some extent, of other extant hunter/gatherer people in other parts of the world, except that we can be sure the aborigine culture did not give rise to domestication, whereas it is slightly more likely that a form of hunter/gatherer society similar to the modern African or Indian ones generated domestication. I would not, however, like to defend this thesis too strongly. It can be argued that aborigine society was well adjusted to a relatively unchanging environment and had neither impetus nor inspiration to change. However, on the slender likelihood that other hunter/gatherer societies may have developed domestication and have almost certainly lived closely with domesticated people and the Australian aborigines did not, I have omitted the aborigines. This, however, was the weakest reason for my choice. The main reason was that aborigine ethnography and the theory that both guides it and stems from it is so divided in the interpretation and description of fundamentals that I, as an outsider, do not know what to think. What is more, because I am claiming to make a contribution to the interpretation of hunter/gatherer ethnography, I do not want to get tangled up with one side rather than another. In some ways aborigine ethnography and its attendant theory is a highly specialized discipline in its own right, and anyone daring to pronounce on the subject from outside, from even as close as New Zealand, is putting his head in the noose. Furthermore, one side of the debate furnishes more support for my ideas than the other, so it would be tempting to cite only work favorable to my way of thinking.

Stated in its most general terms, the debate is between (1) those who think that aborigine society possessed an intricate and far-reaching formal structure based on bounded groups and their subdivisions and (2) those who maintain that much of this complexity is culturally (that is, cognitively rather than socially) constructed from a fairly narrow and straightforward kinship base.

One side argues that the tribe is a clearly defined socially and territorially bounded unit, often based on different but adjacent ecological factors (Tindale in Peterson 1976). Peterson himself thinks that many Australianists would be inclined to agree with R. M. Berndt that there is no advantage to speaking about such units as tribes. So-called boundaries are really gradients, clines, or areas of integration (ibid.:6). Instead of bounded regions some anthropologists suggest that aborigines observe "overlapping gravitational fields," which are defined as being centered on religious sites (Piddington, cited in Maddock 1972:33). This notion coincides perfectly with my argument for definition by focus, and it is echoed by more recent students of aborigine social identity (e.g., Gumpert 1981). I am tempted to agree with and cite the work of such people as Piddington, Peterson, and Gumpert and to overlook the arguments of the likes of Tindale and Birdsell.

I am similarly tempted to side with those such as Harold Scheffler, who defends and advances the thesis that "Australian social categories are virtually exhaustively kinship categories" (1978:1) against those such as David T. Turner, who argues for descent groups, territorially defined land-owning groups, and reciprocal marriage exchanges between groups (1980:ii). For example, Scheffler, quite convincingly to my mind, shows that Walbiri patrilines and patrilodges are named only so by their ethnographer and states that "there is no evident necessity to conceptualise these Walbiri ideas in terms of descent and descent groups" (1978:517). The Walbiri claim only patrifiliation, and the groups function only to execute certain rituals associated with the Dreaming. The continuity of the patrilodge depends solely on the continuity of the Dreaming, not on any notion of descent (that is, it is cognitive, intellectual, and cultural). Scheffler argues that kinship terms are basic but are extended metaphorically to designate and classify people who are "like" kin (social categories) and those who can be likened to kin (cultural categories). Classes of persons of the same kinship category can easily be "read" as being a group that has real social existence and definition. I might add that this is especially true if most of the information anthropologists work with is oral rather than observational. And it is true of all those who would study the traditional system—they can only reconstruct rather than record.

Scheffler, only too aware of this, firmly asserts that his study of Australian kinship is strictly semantic. But to my mind it produces a plausible and economical foundation for reconstructing social structures. I would say this, of course, because the end result would probably fall more closely to the interpretation of hunter/gatherer society I put forward in this chapter.

David Turner offers an analysis based on what aborigines "do" instead of what they say. Rather than posit possible social analogues of semantic sets and classes, Turner (1980:vi) proposes that a social group, the patri-group family, is the irreducible unit with which analysis of Australian social organization should begin. Turner argues against the extension of meanings and classifications from the individual and in favor of bounded groups. He writes: "In short, genealogical reckoning beyond a certain range does not appear to be what Aborigines themselves *do* when they classify relatives. They seem as much interested in collectives as individuals, and even recognised genealogical paths to individuals are also paths to groups" (ibid.:132).

But the basic patri-group is not, to my mind, a clear-cut collective. Though land owning, it is not territorially bounded; though it hints at being a descent group, membership is gained through the father—that is, through patrifiliation. Though it is divided into "bands" of brothers and their wives and children, these mingle with other bands, often in other territories (ibid.:122). Even Turner must admit that at times the recruitment by "descent" is varied by residence and membership by consent (ibid.:iii). Eventually the clean definition of the basic patri-group is thrown into complete doubt, and a model that resembles more the focused company vaguely emerges:

> Common residence seems to have been a sufficient condition for incorporation into another patri-group under traditional conditions, if those concerned were not in opposite moieties. Ambiguities over the statuses of people resident in more than one patri-group country are well documented as are cases of transference of membership from one patri-group to another. [Ibid.:131]

I sense here all the indications of "looseness," "fluidity," and flexibility characteristic of traditional analyses of hunter/gatherer society. But then, it is clear, I am biased. I suspect that under traditional conditions, before the onslaught of white colonial society, aboriginal hunter/gatherers favored freedom and autonomy as well as the exit option and the right of entry. I do not say that they did not live in groups but rather that they used groups opportunistically and emotionally and that they may not have been the prisoners of a rigid social logic and structure.

My bias would further lead me to argue that, like the Bushman name sharing or the Hadza gambling, aborigines had a dispersal or a randomizing mechanism or mechanisms. One of these was what Maddock calls the "conception clan." Membership is gained by conception filiation in the following way: A pregnant woman looking for food feels a pain. This signifies a power, and her husband diagnoses the power. The power, a species for example, is responsible for the condition of pregnancy, and the child "belongs" to that species. The site where the woman first felt pain (or something else) is the child's "conception site." "The clan formed by this principle consists of all those persons whose mothers were spiritually fecundated by contact with a power of the same species, for example, euro, honey ant, native cat. Clans of this type are not exogamous" (Maddock 1972:31). Maddock argues that such "conception clans" provide people with an entrée to areas and people scattered far and wide. They are universalistic, as opposed to the parochialism of patricians (Maddock 1972:42). But why does Maddock call these *clans,* a term that implies in-depth descent? Nothing could be more alien to such recruitment than descent. Why not use some such term as *club* as, for example, in our own societies *twin clubs.* Certainly the idea of *clans* furthers the notion of a highly structured society—which I do not favor!

What I do favor is an analysis of traditional aborigine society that suggests that they were less inclined to be constrained by boundaries and more inclined to identify themselves by mechanisms which focused on a center such as a sacred site, a track, or a topographical feature and which guided rather than ruled them. It is abundantly clear from most of the literature that individuals achieved some of their identity through such focusing by "being born at a particular place, near a water hole on the track of a particular totemic ancestor" (Hamilton 1982:102). People moved freely over the landscape and were neither contained nor excluded by boundaries of territory or language. The landscape was "a sort of spectrum where a man moved gradually out of one district into another as he passed from one horizon to the next" (Hart and Pilling 1960:12). Many aborigines are bilingual or multilingual, especially where two or more language groups are neighbors. Maddock's brief and general reference to traditional politics suggests a situation in which no individuals held a hierarchical position but people who had special abilities or rights could exercise them in the relevant context and could not transfer them or use them for a general power base.

But then there are descriptions of aborigine society as a rigid gerontocracy. If I begin to discuss aboriginal gift exchange, sorcery, and beliefs and practices concerning death I shall defeat the purpose of explaining why I have not discussed Australian aborigines in this chapter. As it is, in making my excuse I have given more attention to arguments and evidence that fit more neatly with the viewpoint I have espoused in this chapter. Perhaps someone with far more expertise in Australian ethnography than I possess may be moved to consider that literature in the light of this book and, vice-versa, may be moved to consider the thesis of this work in the light of Australian ethnography.

3

The House in Order

For our house is our corner of the world. As has
often been said it is our first universe, a real cosmos in every sense of the word.

—Gaston Bachelard, *The Poetics of Space*

One of the most striking, and vis-
ible, differences between the open societies of hunter/gatherers and all
other human societies is that the latter live in an architecturally modified
environment. Hunter/gatherers create for themselves only the flimsiest architectural context, and only the faintest line divides their living space
from nature. What we know of prehistoric hunter/gatherers is entirely by
accident and good fortune, but what we know of prehistoric villagers is
partly by design, for it was part of the function of their architecture to
create a sense of permanence and continuity, to build resources for their
heirs and to commemorate their ancestors.

Ethnoarchaeologists who try to reconstruct the life of hunter/gatherers
from material remains find little if any remnants of a camp a week or so
after its abandonment (Yellen 1977; Gould 1980). But archaeologists of
prehistoric village societies can reconstruct entire settlements thousands of
years after they have been deserted.

Given this visible, substantial difference of architecture between open
hunter/gatherer societies and the rest, we may wonder what other fundamental changes arise from (or may be correlated with) the transition from
open to domesticated society? What aspects of human behavior, and especially what aspects of the ordering of human behavior and activity, have
evolved directly from the adoption of the house and the village as the
primary context of social life? In particular, can we attribute the adoption

57

of an architectural environment to the transition from a social order founded on a focus to one founded on the boundary?

Although the extent and depth to which the house is cited as a key vehicle of symbolic and systematic thought by ethnographers of domesticated societies varies, it is clear that the house and the village plan provide people the world over with an instrument, and a model, for conceiving the world in a complex, comprehensive way. The house and the village are not only an order constructed out of walls, boundaries, and fences; they also serve as smaller-scale reproductions of the structure of the universe. They do this because the house and village are geometric constructions and can therefore represent relationships irrespective of scale and the nature of the parts.

Whereas Paleolithic and modern hunter/gatherers were and are technically competent to build dwellings of a permanent nature, the conditions of their lives preclude settlement as a way of life (except in the case of Mesolithic collectors and such modern collectors as the Indians of America's Pacific Northwest). This means that the nature of their thinking and symbolic representation cannot call on or be furthered by the house. So not only does domestication occur as a historical development, but the frames of mind that rely on architectural structures for their articulation are also historically developed and cannot be biologically determined human universals—as generalizations of certain psychological theories have implied.

The adoption of the house as the permanent context of social and economic life also marks a major development in cosmological thinking. Open societies have available to them as tools for thought language and such features of the natural environment as animals, landmarks, topographies, and the like. But their artifacts are limited by the need for portability, and their nomadism restricts the range of communication of their art somewhat. With settlement comes a proliferation of material culture, and with the house is made available what has proved to be the most powerful practical symbol until the invention of writing. In many domesticated societies the house is appropriated to mediate and synthesize the natural symbols of both the body and the landscape. At the same time it provides the environment and context for social life. The adoption of the house and the village also ushers in a development of the structure of social life, the elaboration of thinking about the structure of the world, and the strengthening of the links between the two.

Prehistory

The earliest evidence of housing construction comes from deep within the Paleolithic, from the site of Terra Amata, which dates back to about 400,000 years ago (de Lumley 1969). Here were found the remains of postholes suggestive of a large building that served as a seasonal shelter. Even more tangible evidence of the technical ability of hunter/gatherers to build comes from the Later Paleolithic sites in colder regions. At Dolní Věstonice are the remains of substantial stone-built houses arranged in a village that had been divided into areas for dwelling, toolmaking, and animal preparation (Klima 1954).

Though construction and architecture were obviously within the technical abilities of Paleolithic people, permanent settlement as a way of life seems to have become widespread just twenty to fifteen thousand years ago. During the Mesolithic period an increasing number of populations settled into more or less permanent sites and constructed a careful, substantial architecture. The probable reason for this change was an alteration in environmental conditions, which reduced the herds of larger animals on which Paleolithic hunters had relied (Cohen 1977:83). Most Mesolithic settlements were built by the shores of lakes, rivers, streams, and the sea to take advantage of large reserves of seafood. But some of the earliest settlements, such as the first southwest Asian village sites of Mallaha, Suberde, and Mureybit, relied on harvesting wild grasses and seeds (Clark 1977:50–51; Redman 1978:142). Some of the earliest village sites have proved to be quite substantial and indicate a large population skilled from the beginning in construction techniques and well versed in a knowledge of architecture. Grahame Clark estimates the population of Jericho to have been as high as two thousand (1977:54), and it has been suggested that Jericho's inhabitants may have had a stratified social structure (Wright 1978:218).

Archaeological evidence clearly indicates that agriculture was not a prerequisite for sedentism and that human domestication occurred independently of plant and animal domestication (Redman 1978:142). A stable settlement does, however, seem to be an advantage, if not a necessary prerequisite, for the development of horticulture and agriculture, while a stable and cohesive population is an advantage in herding, even though neither animals nor people need remain settled. These considerations suggest that, to some extent at least, sedentism is independent of the mode of subsistence and thus that it might be more closely bound with more purely social factors whose realization could have provided the motive for establishing sedentism and domestication as a way of life. One such possibility is that village life provides the facilities for an enriched or heightened social life at the same time as it offers the means and instruments for keeping that social life under control, preventing it from getting out of hand by assembling people within boundaries and separating them by partitions. Modern hunter/gatherers in many parts of the world often assemble in large numbers at certain times of the year in a particular spot, usually when specific animals or insects swarm. During such occasions social life rises in tempo and pitch, major ritual takes place, marriage partners are selected, and people feast together. As ethnographers note, this is also the time of flashpoint tensions and conflicts: people are soon glad to depart and continue life in small, wandering groups. Domestication permits larger populations to live together and thereby provides individuals with greater social satisfaction. It increases the risks of conflict but provides basic, inert structural conditions, which, when taken up, can be used to impose order and discipline.

The earliest dwellings found in village sites in the Near East were circular. In Beidha, round houses were arranged in clusters and connected by rectangular passageways; walls surrounded each cluster and the village itself (Redman 1978:147). Later structures, both at Beidha and elsewhere, tend to be rectilinear and provide increasing evidence of task specialization.

As archaeological evidence suggests, the buildings in these early settlements were substantial, carefully constructed, and, in some cases, varied. They were meant to last. Settlements were often built atop each other, or as a house decayed a new one was built on the same site. Decay did not necessarily lead to termination; as a result, many of the earliest community sites were continuously occupied for hundreds of years. Whether or not it was intended, time became anchored in space.

By their very architectural and structural nature, houses represent plans, and at a minimum it seems reasonable to propose that people recognize an association between particular groups and particular sites, as between the house and the household, the [architectural] structure of the one providing an analogue to the structure of the other. In much the same way, delimiting the village in space, planned or not, offers boundary analogies for the definition of a community. The social relations between people receive an increasingly precise spatial—hence visual and material—definition: structure becomes more explicit. Social activities likewise become more placed since in many cases artifactual remains indicate that specific activities were carried on in specific places. Included in the architectural structuring that creates domestication is the enclosure of the yard, often as an adjunct to the enclosure of living space. This yard may enclose plants and animals, and in some societies yard, cattle or pigs, and people are all enclosed within a perimeter fence. In ancient Greece, "The sacred enclosure, which the Greeks called ʽεοχος, and the Latins *herectum*, was the somewhat spacious enclosure in which the family had its house, its flocks and the small field that it cultivated. In the midst rose the protecting firegod" (Coulanges 1969:63). The enclosed yard or garden was in many parts of the prehistoric world the primary mode of economic domestication. In most New World areas gardening preceded agriculture and, as in the island civilizations of Polynesia, was the primary subsistence mode (Forde 1985; H. M. Leach 1984).

Little can be said about the importance of the prehistoric house (and yard) for symbolic thinking, since verifiable evidence that the house had symbolic meaning is well nigh impossible. Distinct spatial arrangements do indicate structure, and structure is capable of bearing symbolic loads as well as being suggestive of symbolism, but, as Mary Douglas (1979) has pointed out, similar structures discerned in contemporary societies may have very different symbolic connotations or, as Holy (1983) has indicated, no symbolic connotation at all. On the other hand such distinctive variations of architecture within the same settlement, together with elaborate decoration—such as has been unearthed at Çatal Hüyük—strongly hint that architecture and symbolism were closely associated. Finally, although not in itself evidence of prehistoric symbolic thinking, it is worth noting that our own Judeo-Hellenic tradition prizes the walled garden, the Garden of Eden, as its most appealing symbol of paradise and the architectural city (sometimes walled) as its ideal and model of utopia (McLung 1985).

The adoption of architecture as a living environment occurs as a distinct moment in human prehistory, in most cases preceding the human domestication (or enclosure) of plants and animals. Architecture is a materialization of structure, and the adoption of architecture as a permanent feature of life introduces spatial organization and allocation as an ordering visual dimension. Some circumstantial evidence of the transfer of spatial struc-

61

ture to the structure of human activities is present from the beginning, but the transformation of spatial structure to social structure and its application to symbolic thinking, though more than likely in Neolithic times, must remain strictly conjectural.

Architecture in the Open Society

Mobile hunter/gatherers live in the open and are open to one another's view. But many of them build huts that are intended to last from a few days to as long as several months. Architecture is by no means beyond their demonstrated capability. The Naiken hut, though flimsy, has a plan and is divided into compartments, one for the resident host family and another for the visiting lodger. The Mbuti orient their huts toward or away from neighbors as a reflection of their friendliness and in so doing perform an elementary exercise in spatial communication. Some people, the Macu of the Amazon, for instance, raise no architecture. They erect a flimsy canopy over their hammocks but build no walls, and they allow rubbish to accumulate beneath them until the floor is no longer habitable (Silverwood-Cope 1972). But for the most part, open societies produce a temporary architecture that clearly indicates their ability to develop a domestic geometry. Thus when he speaks from his own hearth a Mbuti hunter is understood to be simply airing his thoughts and testing the wind of public opinion, but when he speaks from the "midcamp" he is pronouncing his considered, final opinion, his contribution to the public domain. Silberbauer describes a similar use of space to frame and announce politics for the G/wi. In a sense space is used as an elementary tool for the making of political structure and is, perhaps, to politics what the Acheulean hand ax is to technology.

When many hunter/gatherer societies gather in large numbers at one spot for a while they build their huts more carefully and solidly, and the settlement assumes a more structured appearance, all of which shows how the shift to permanent settlement by hunter/gatherers could be smooth and easy, should circumstances demand. Only a relatively brief extension of time would be required to convert a hunter's seasonal camp into a permanent sedentary village. The !Kung live near water holes in dry season villages that consist of between eight and fifteen well-constructed huts (Lee 1984:29). Each "village" is usually built on top of or near the previous year's settlement but not, it seems, as a total unit. From Lee's account it would appear that the village is built as an accretion of separate huts rather than a community. Each hut is located according to an individualizing rule—namely, that siblings (and their families) of the senior couple build their huts on either side of the couple in such a way that they can all *see* one another. This results in a semicircle of huts. In-laws of this core group set up house facing the siblings, and they, too, follow the rule that they must be able to *see* one another. This leads to another semicircle. The principles on which the village is founded are affection and mutual accommodation expressed through kinship and "government" by attention. But the appearance of the village as a whole, as it rises out of the landscape, is of a roughly circular structure divided down the middle between affines or between hosts and in-laws. Each hut follows a certain hygiene routine based on space: in linear arrangement there is the hearth, the hut, the ash pit, the cooking pit, the empty zone, the defecation zone, and, finally, the bush. Assembled together, the huts produce a village structure of concentric circles. So, although unintended, the !Kung village displays in pristine form the paradigmatic characteristics of Lévi-Strauss's (1963:135) structuralism: concentric structure, and diametric structure. Lee gives no indication that such a "structure" is at all relevant to the !Kung, either in the sense that they deliberately set out their village to symbolize aspects of their social or cosmic order or that anything in !Kung society would justify an observing anthropologist to impute symbolic functions to the village pattern. Patterns promising for symbolism can emerge, even though they are unintended and unrecognized. The !Kung themselves, where they have chosen to settle as herdsmen and work for their Herero or Tswana neighbors, construct crescent-shaped villages that facilitate *overseeing* their herds. The symbolic potential of their original dry season villages is, apparently, passed over, but they have maintained the connection between spatial layout and the demands of attention.

The case of the !Kung dry season village is instructive in other ways. The huts "tend to be well constructed" and the "site is cleared with care"— good construction and careful preparation, then, are activities that intimately bind space with time: the huts are intended to last far longer than the flimsy shelters of camps. For most of the year nomadic hunter/gatherers chase time by moving from place to place to follow ripening schedules and animal migration timetables, watering habits, and seasonal availability. But when they settle, time passes through place, place receives time, and the two merge. The buildings of a domesticated village, by virtue of

63

their careful and often complex construction, are intended to stand for at least a year in most agricultural and horticultural societies, and so they embody time as well as occupy space. People wait in one spot for the seasons, growth periods, and stages to come to them, as it were, and instead of following grazing animals, they keep beasts in the pasture. The relationship between time and space thus changes once people settle in the sheltered stability of architecture: time becomes repetition and recursiveness—the same things happen at different times in the same place— birth, death, growth, decay, ripeness, seasons, comings and goings. Seasons and growth cycles are not lost on hunter/gatherers, far from it, but for sedentarists they are marked, concentrated, confined or bounded, and given spatial, hence visible, form. In this way the idea of continuity and stability may become an explicit feature of domesticated life, an idea manifested in different ways and levels of activity: daily routine, timetabling, seasonal routines, traditions. Although hunter/gatherers carry out a round of similar activities, the ethnography gives the impression that they do so not so much on a regular as on a convenience basis: one hunts when one wishes or when people agree it has been a long time since there was any meat to eat. Naiken who work on estates do so when the mood takes them; Mbuti arrive at their Negro master's villages unexpectedly and depart without warning. But people who live in villages and who cultivate organize their lives with much greater reference to time and place: events must be carried out at propitious times, whether these be ritual or economic. Where learning among hunter/gatherers is left mostly to observation and imitation, sedentarists place greater emphasis on instruction by prescription, proscription, initiation, and the insistence on traditional, conventional ways of doing things "at the right time in the proper place." Such techniques ensure continuity through repetition by making sure that what people do at different times in the one place remains the same. This welding of time and place that settlement and architecture represents helps to explain the explicitness of a structured life among domesticated people when they are compared to members of open societies, who, as we have noted, are usually described as lacking or having loose, flexible structures. As Giddens has put it, "Routine is integral both to the continuity of the personality of the agent, as he or she moves along the paths of daily activities, and to the institutions of society, which are such only through their continued reproduction" (1984:60). One must point out, however, that there is no evidence that hunter/gatherers, whose routines are vague and underdeveloped, display any discontinuity of personality. Repetition and recursiveness build, sustain, and reproduce the institutions that become so central to the life of domesticated societies (ibid.).

The rough diametric and concentric pattern of the !Kung dry season village is neither conceived nor constructed as an entity but emerges "fortuitously" out of a series of individual activities more or less identical with (that is, repetitions of) each other, in much the same way in which Lévi-Strauss (1973:191) shows how Caduveo designs of great intricacy emerge from the repetition of singular motifs. Whatever the overall pattern of villages—circular, rectangular, parallel rows, or even higgledy-piggledy—it is striking that in domesticated societies each house as a unit is a repetition of its neighbors. In the case of longhouse villages a single, large building is divided into identical—that is, repeated—sections or apartments. True, size and decoration may vary between dwellings, these reflecting status (larger house = chief and/or wealthy person or men's house) or function (storage houses, separate kitchens), but these are invariably scaled repetitions of the basic structure. Not until the advent of the city is more than one style of unit repeated within the same territorial space. And if one takes a closer look, the house itself is usually divided into repeated sections (rooms), and even the walls are the product of repeated elements: bricks, ice blocks, boards, saplings, reeds.

Of course the flimsy shelters of hunter/gatherers are made up of repeated elements by repeated actions, but the *principle* of repetition and recursiveness is not insistent simply because the structures are temporary. With permanence, what people do takes place within a setting and is dispersed into separate regions which may be allocated to various zones (Goffman 1959). Much of what people do with one another in pursuit of their daily round, and more, their annual and life cycle rounds, has its proper time and place, these being mutually allied into what have been called "time-space paths" that run along "time-space maps" (Giddens 1984:110–16). Even when individuals change villages they move to identical or repeated general structures: even when a village is abandoned new ones are built on the same pattern. Members of domesticated societies, then, are born into and surrounded by visible, material elements that not only are themselves arranged as structures but serve as the bases for social structures. Through settlement and architecture the *principle* of pattern and structure is embodied in the atmosphere, the very environment and context of living, a situation rather different to that of the individual living in the open society. In

65

this sense, irrespective of the activities pursued by individuals, the idea of organization is ever-present in the social and psychological background of life. And because it shapes and frames activities and relationships, every act or relationship is a reproduction at the social level of the conditions of structure: by cooking in one place rather than another, the place is reproduced as a kitchen. When this does not happen there is "matter out of place," or pollution, as Mary Douglas (1966) has explained at some length.

Houseplans

Throughout the domesticated world the house, and often the village, serves not simply as a dwelling, shelter, and spatial arrangement of activities but also as a central instrument through which people record and express their thoughts. Furthermore, it, or its derivatives, embodies the spiritual beliefs of people and contributes the setting, and sometimes the text, of their religious lives. The house is "one of the best modes available to a preliterate society to encapsulate ideas, given the absence of literature and the sporadic occurrence and varying degree of participation in ritual. In addition the house illustrates more than particular principles of classification: it illustrates the value of classification per se" (Cunningham 1973:235).

This imaginative use of the house (and the village) to further knowledge, to shape ideas, and to express thoughts of the unknown must count as one of the major cultural achievements of the era of domestication. It makes its own contribution to expressive culture and has evolved from the multipurpose dwelling to the exclusive sacredness of the temple, from the occasional display of facades to the permanent exhibition of palaces. The character of the house as an instrument of thought as well as a vehicle of power has persisted into recent times and is still a feature of the intellectual and ritual life of many of the domesticated peoples studied today by anthropologists. The house begins to lose its power when printing, in particular, penetrates a culture and when villages become large cities, for "a house in a big city lacks cosmicity. For here, where houses are no longer set in natural surroundings, the relationship between house and space becomes an artificial one" (Bachelard [1964] 1969:27).

The house is a geometry, a series of relationships between objects rather than a collection of objects. The house that loses its geometry simply falls into ruins. Because it is a topography the house may be a model or map for any other structure irrespective of materials, appearances, and location, and the house may equally be understood as a model of any other phenomenon. Dogon homesteads and villages in West Africa, for example, are built according to a plan of the human body and consequently are recognized as representing the body. Although the village shape may be square or oval, relations between the constituents are invariant; they are the geometry that models the body—"a person must live in a north to south direction" (Griaule and Dieterlen 1954:96). Villages are always built in pairs to reproduce the relational property of twinness, and thence of heaven and earth. The homestead itself is laid out as if it were a procreating man lying on his right side whose other limbs also have architectural counterparts. As such, the house/person "is" Nommo, son of god, who in turn "is" the "appointed model of the universe" (Griaule and Dieterlen 1954:97). Individual human beings, ancestors, spirits, and the earth itself can be located in and identified with the house, which becomes their common meetingplace.

In other instances it is not so much that the house is laid out according to the plan of the human body as that the house *is* a body (and a body is a house) and becomes so at certain times, on certain occasions, in certain contexts. Thus among the Para-Pirana of Colombia the longhouse is, much of the time, a dwelling place with an interior layout that provides an arrangement for daily intercourse. A linear male-female axis runs between the two doors and activities occur around a concentric pattern in which the periphery represents private family life and the center public, communal life (Hugh-Jones 1979:246). But on ritual occasions, or for purposes of conveying myth, the "house is a person, a mythical figure called Roofing Father, who is an enormous bird. . . . The different species of palm leaf used for roofing grow as feathers from various parts of his body. His head is at the male end of the house, his anus at the female end, and the sides of the roof are his rib cage" (ibid.:248). The male-female axis between the doors becomes the digestive tract, and the two doors reflect the ingesting and evacuating functions of the human orifices.

In yet another sense the Para-Pirana house is a womb where the men's door is the vagina—the entrance for semen, the exit for birth. The women's door "is an internal passageway to the manioc gardens, the nourishing base of the home community." The patterns and analogies are deepened by the relation of the longhouse to its setting and, as these representations, to mythical concepts: "The analogy between the universe and the womb may be described in the same terms, with the Milk River representing a pathway into the womb up which the inseminating anacondas swim" (ibid.:249).

In many domesticated societies the house is the prism through which both conceptions of the universe are concentrated and projections from everyday life are dispersed. The house, the village, and the areas within and immediately bordering them, concentrate and miniaturize the universe, making it manageable and, it is hoped, controllable. This is particularly so in ritual contexts. Writing of the Para-Pirana of Colombia, Christine Hugh-Jones explains:

> People must transpose the system of the universe with its creative processes onto the concrete systems which they are able to control, or at least change, through practical action. To do this, they construct their houses to represent the universe. They also conceive of their bodies, their sexual reproductive systems, their natural environment known through direct experiences and the sructure of their patrilineal descent groups in such a way that these too correspond to the structure of the universe. [Ibid.:235]

Houses may represent the universe because they and the universe are built according to the same principles of structure: the house is itself a universe representing each, and any, universe. To put it another way, the same principles are employed by people to build houses as they think are used in the structure of the universe. The house they build materializes out of what they know (or believe), though the anthropologist usually has to work from the house which he or she observes to what people know (see ibid.:244).

A good example of this is Cunningham's (1973) analysis of the Atoni house. The Atoni house is characterized first by a cross pattern built up in different ways out of four elements:

1. The four points of the Atoni compass
2. The four corner "chicken posts"
3. The four points of emphasized order: water jar, sleeping platform, door, and great platform
4. The four mother posts
5. The central hearth

The configuration of these may be represented as (1) concentric circles and (2) as intersecting and arranged crosses to form + and ×. The second feature is the divisions with units that are halves of greater wholes. This division applies not only to the house but also, according to the Atoni, to the cosmos:

> The Earth . . . is divided into the "dry land" . . . and the "sea" in opposition to the "sky," which is conceived as a dome over them. . . . The sea, in turn, is conceived to be in two parts. . . . Both parts stand opposed to "dry land." In all of these oppositions—dry land and sea to sky, male sea and female sea to dry land, right and left sides of the "house center" to the yard, right and left sides of the inner section to the outer section, and inner and outer sections of the house to the attic—a conceptually subordinate pair as opposed to a superordinate unit. . . . I noted that the attic is ritually proscribed and access is allowed only to certain persons. Atoni conceive the Divinity also to be isolated from man and approachable only through prayer and sacrifice at designated places. . . . It is not fortuitous, or merely practical . . . that the attic of a house is devoted only to rice and maize, produce of the fields; that the altar stone for agricultural ritual is kept there; and that entrance is restricted in a ritual idiom. Dome-shaped as it is, it represents *neno* (sky) and all that it implies.
>
> In one sense, therefore, the Atoni house is a model of the cosmos. However, it is more than simply analogous to the universe; it is integrated within it. Prayers are made to the Divinity facing sunrise from the *hau mone* (male tree *or* outside tree), a ritual post set in the yard. . . . These reasons, or better, symbolic statements express the notion that the house is set in opposition to the sun, sky or day (all *neno* in Atoni). [Cunningham 1973:216–21]

House and cosmos are homologous in structure, so the house represents and models the universe. The universe is not the same as the house as far as materials and components are concerned, of course, but it embodies the same principles (of cardinal points in cruciform and concentric structure, of contrastive opposition by division). The house and/or its parts are homologous with the universe and/or its parts: the dome shape of the roof is homologous with the dome shape of the sky, and the relative position of attic to roof is analogous to the position of divinity to sky. But the house is also an integral part of the universe; because it is in the house that one approaches and communicates with the divinity, so the house serves as a sign of the cosmos. Presumably every Atoni assimilates the relation between house and cosmos into his or her thinking during the course of socialization, and the house depicts ideas not only "symbolically" but "vividly for every individual from birth to death" (ibid.:204).

The house, then, may symbolize the human body and its processes and the cosmos and its processes. It abstracts both body and cosmos and fits them within a single thought-system. At another level, the house mediates between the natural symbols of the body and its processes and the cosmos, miniaturizing the world without changing it or taking anything from it. The house also materializes another layer of the universe or serves as the screen onto which may be projected otherwise invisible realities.

The house may depict a purely social structure, and since such a structure is depicted in the house, which may also be used to model the body and the universe, it can make of a "social" structure a natural one. Marshall Sahlins (1976) presents a succint example of this in his argument in favor of the determining influence of symbols on human social life. The Fijian house is, in effect, a map of Fijian hierarchy and etiquette: "The side of the house towards the sea was called the noble side and with it went the east end or, if the house were perpendicular to the seashore, the east side was the noble one, and with it went the sea end" (1976:33, quoting Hocart 1929).

The entire topology of the house situates and maps formal behavior and the disposition of people vis-à-vis one another. I shall *italicize* dimensional or spatial terms and CAPITALIZE the notions of social order they embody in the following quotation.

> The *upper end* of the house is *separated* by a bark cloth curtain and is *restricted* to FAMILY MEMBERS and *reserved* principally to the CHIEF and the CHIEFESS. In it are stored valuables, weapons, tools, and the sleeping platform is situated here. The *lower end* of the house is associated with the WOMEN's hearth, culinary utensils and cooking. The *upper end* is PRIVATE and the *lower end* is PUBLIC. *Between* the two *ends* is the *central* section, the common ground where men, women and children congregate on EQUAL terms along with visitors. . . . It is *framed*, however, by *longitudinal* and *lateral* coordinates of RANK, set out by the value *opposition* of *slides* and *ends* of the dwelling. [Ibid.:35–45]

Essentially, then, the geography of the house is used to depict the contours of social rank, and the Fijian house "functions as a medium by which a system of culture is realised as an order of action" (ibid.:36).

Who one is in domesticated society is largely a function of where one is—"the important aspects of an individual's identity are not names but houses" among the Toraja (Volkman 1985:48). Houses for the Toraja record a person's genealogy, ancestry, and history (ibid.:53). In a comparable way, though by different means, the Maori meetinghouse is the symbolic body of the founding ancestor and the genealogical history of those who gather there (Metge 1967:230). In domesticated society the sense of place, of belonging and of owning, becomes the key to a person's legitimacy and relation to others. The right of a Maori man to speak in public on the *marae* depends, in part, on his being able to establish the right to do so because he belongs there (he is *tangata whenua* on his *turangawaewae*). In much the same way the right of a man to participate in the public life of the ancient Greek polis was determined by whether he owned a house. Without a house a man could not take part in the affairs of the world "because he had no location in it which was properly his own" (Arendt 1958:28).

In many domesticated societies such as those of Indonesia or ancient Greece the house serves as the symbol of the perpetual lifeline that connects ancestors and descendants and as the spatial focus that binds generations. Among the Indonesian Toraja and Atoni as well as the ancient Greeks, the hearth served as the center, the still point around which the house, the household, and their cosmic associations revolved (Volkman 1985:47; Cunningham 1973:208; Coulanges 1956:61). According to Coulanges, "When they [the Greeks] establish the hearth, it is with the thought and hope that it will always remain in the same spot" (1956:61).

To protect this permanent, sacred spot a permanent dwelling was needed, because "the family did not build for the life of a single man, but for generations that were to succeed each other in the same dwelling" (ibid.:63). Within the house itself the hearth was specially enclosed, and beyond the house, the fields were enclosed by a band of soil that was regarded as sacred and was marked, at certain points, by *termini* (ibid.: 67–68).

The anchoring of a person that comes with domestication results in the identification of person with location and location with person, a merging of person and place which differs from the idea of focus that specifies the relation between hunter/gatherer and location. The merger of person and place and their reciprocal identity is the essence of property, of ownership, the right to exclude others. From this identity and its expression springs the sustained sense of a person's political character, in contrast to the fleeting, ad hoc political participation of the open society member.

Houseplans become ideological tools in their own right. They are practical symbols mediating between the natural symbols of the body and the environment, transforming the one into the other or creating the link between them. To the extent that this is so, and to the degree they serve to record thought and depict it in a more permanent form, houses make for more extensive and structured thinking about the world than in societies without architecture.

To some degree the contribution of the house to the ordering of thought

71

and its recording is echoed in the way in which village sites may be used to symbolize and locate varieties of structure. Christine Hugh-Jones (1979) concludes that the Para-Pirana longhouse as a symbolic structure is integrated with its setting into a broader cosmological symbolism, where the longhouse as body is connected, via the path, to the river—that is, the path becomes the umbilical chord that connects the souls (the longhouse communities) to the Milk River. In sum, the river is conceived as "a spiritual power supply connecting the longhouse community with the ancestral powers to the east" (ibid.:244). In other examples, such as Lévi-Strauss's (1963) well-known suggestion for reinterpreting Trobriand village structure, the concentric pattern reflects and marks hierarchy and gives material, spatial dimension to the distinction between sacred and profane. The position of the chief is marked by his presence in the middle of the village where other such activities as burial rituals and yam storage suggest a sacred character. This contrasts with the location of domestic activities and the situation of women and commoners in the outer circles. A more elaborate and extensive example of the reconstruction of architecture and landscape into a symbolic universe is described by Alfonso Ortiz, analyzing the Tewa world:

> All human and spiritual existence is classified into a hierarchy of six categories, three human and three spiritual, and . . . the spiritual categories are further associated with specific geographical points in the Tewa world. Moreover these six categories are linked into three pairs; that is to say, the spiritual categories represent counterparts of the human categories. [1969:9]

These fundamental categories of Tewa thought have their counterparts in the physical world. Thus the Tewa landscape is bounded by four sacred mountains, the same mountains that in the origin myths were seen by the first four pairs of sibling deities as they were sent out to explore the world. With each mountain is associated a lake or a pond in which live the category of beings *Dry Food Who Never Did Become*. Atop each mountain is an "earth navel," a special arrangement of stones in which dwell the *Towa e*, who stand watch over the Tewa world. Then come the sacred flat-topped hills with their caves and tunnels in which dwell the "masked supernatural whippers." As the circles close in toward the village the markers become shrines of stone, of direction, in which live the souls of a large category of spirits and objects associated with men, such as tools, weapons, and bones. Finally, within the village are the dance plazas where public rituals are performed. In the center of the village is the *Earth mother navel middle place*, which is the sacred spot where all rituals are initiated. This is the center of centers, the navel of navels, and it is here, for example, that at the beginning of the year the medicine men of the village plant the seeds of all the crops used as food, thereby reawakening nature. The actual village is quartered in the same way as they conceive of the physical world in quarters. The Tewa world of the unseen and the unreachable, the cosmos, is thus mapped onto and symbolized by the seen, physical, geographical world of natural and constructed features, which can be represented in somewhat simplified form (see accompanying figure).

In domesticated societies the house and the village are the fusion of microcosm and macrocosm, body and world, individual and collective, and at the same time, they are the presentation of these abstractions to everyday life. One of the most startling illustrations of this is reported by Lévi-Strauss (1973:220) for the Bororo of Brazil. Their villages, circular in form, revolved around a central men's house and had paths crossing the village so that "seen from a treetop or a roof, a Bororo village looks like a cartwheel." The Salesian missionaries persuaded the Bororo to abandon their circular villages in favor of houses set out in parallel rows. This completely disoriented them, and

> once they had been deprived of their bearings and were without the plan which acted as confirmation of their native lore, the Indians soon lost any feeling for tradition; it was as if their social and religious systems . . . were too complex to exist without the pattern which was embodied in the plan of the village and of which their awareness was constantly being refreshed by their everyday activities. [Ibid.:221]

In his more recent work Lévi-Strauss has tried to introduce the concept of "the house" (as in the idea of the "noble house") to the domain of structural discourse occupied by clans and lineages and by kinship and descent. The house is a unit of social structure where clans, families, and lineages are inappropriate but where fictive kinship, based on alliance or adoption, is taken up as a means of organizing estates, rights of inheritance, and the transfer of power (1984:189). Cleaving to his central idea that all human society revolves around the exchange of women, he suggests that in societies where the "house" is the unit of social structure it is so because it serves as a "fetishization" of these exchange relationships (ibid.:195). For Lévi-Strauss, kinship is ontologically prior to all else in human society, so he makes the weak suggestion that the social concept of

73

A RENDERING OF THE TEWA WORLD

WHITE

BLUE-GREEN

TOWA E

DRY FOOD WHO NEVER DID BECOME

TSAVE YOH IMPERSONATED BY TOWAE

SOULS-DWELLING MIDDLE-PLACES

NAVEL OF NAVELS

DANCE PLAZAS FOR RITUALS

RED

YELLOW

the house originates in societies where political or economic interests tend to invade the social field but, lacking a distinct terminology of their own, must borrow from the discourse of kinship. Inevitably this subverts those interests (ibid.:191). It seems to me that there are no incontrovertible grounds for this and that, on the basis of the present argument, the house, in all its structural ramifications, is equally likely to be a sociological precursor and foundation of social systems founded on such abstractions as descent, lineage, and clan. In any case the incorporation of the house into the concept of domestication leads into areas of social life relatively unconsidered in the structuralism of Lévi-Strauss.

Although I am concerned in this book with domesticated society, essentially people who live in villages, it is important to note that the themes outlined in the present chapter are developed with greater precision and elegance in the growth of ancient towns and cities. The Greek city (Foustel de Coulanges 1956), the Roman town (Rykwert 1976), the Indian city (Rowland 1953), and the Chinese city (Wheatley 1971) were all planned representations of microcosm and macrocosm, projections of the human body and distillations of the universe, as were the prominent public buildings within the city's boundaries. The building of houses, towns, and cities was inextricably bound up with the performance of rituals and, later, with the existence of texts, each presenting the same vision of the world in its own medium. To live in the city was simultaneously to have all cosmological knowledge presented to the senses, especially to vision, and to have the structure of the universe represented. The city dweller was integrated, at one with the world.

> A thoughtful Indian, even obscurely aware of the terminology of yoga, can, by looking at a temple, infer the *vastupurusamandala* from it, and identify his body, limb by limb, with its different parts and so with the whole universe which it represented. In a similar way a Roman, however cursorily acquainted with traditional cosmology—certainly without going into any of the finer points discussed by philosophers—should certainly have been able to infer the *templum* from the layout of the town and so have situated himself securely in the world. [Rykwert 1976:168]

The idea that the city paralleled the cosmos in its layout, in its orientation, and in the way it transmitted the continuity between the body and the world has survived into comparatively recent times. Roman temples were "planned in accordance with the *fabrica mundi*, to reflect the propor-

75

tions of the world" (Yates 1969:343), and it is possible that, through the writing of the Hermetic philosophers, this plan carried over into the construction of the Elizabethan theater. Yates suggests that Shakespeare's Globe Theatre "with its 'heavens' over part of the stage, would also have been planned in accordance with the *fabrica mundi*"(ibid.).

Yates has also brought to modern notice the critical function of architecture as a memory mnemonic in the ancient art of rhetoric. As discovered in Greece by Simonides and widely publicized by Cicero, the art of memory, so essential to oratory and rhetoric, was greatly enhanced by transplanting the facts and the order of their connection onto a sequence of places in a building, thereby making of the architectural structure a metastructure. The repetition and seriality of architectural parts provides the model for situating thoughts in time (sequence) and place (disposition) to create of them a system that can be manifested where it would otherwise evaporate due to the weakness of human memory.

In many ways the memory system of Cicero is a reversal of the "order" of events in which architecture serves people. The memory system pins facts onto buildings, but in everyday life buildings present, represent, and commemorate facts of the world to people. When Clark Cunningham was studying Atoni houses he was told "how parts, sections and appurtenances are made and used. Villagers are equally explicit, however, concerning another aspect of the house, the *order* in which things are placed and used. To the question why a particular order is necessary, one simple answer predominates: *Atoran es ia* ('this is the atoran', the order of arrangement)" (1973:204).

In other words, the architecture speaks for itself, and there is no other way in which it is spoken for; it is a means of symbolic communication, a "material representation of abstract ideas" (Leach 1976:37). Instead of being the mnemonic for memory, the Atoni house is memory itself and what is to be remembered. For domesticated societies such as the Atoni this mode of visual systematization and expression serves as the principal mode of recording and communicating cosmic ideas (together with ritual) until the coming of the anthropologist with notebook, tape recorder, and camera.

Bear in mind also that this association between cosmic symbolism and architecture is not a human universal, since open societies of hunters and gatherers lack an architecture substantial enough to serve symbolic functions. The widespread recurrence of symbolic patterns to be found in constructions and layouts—particularly the pattern of concentric circles with its powerful middle, the circle quartered by the cross, and the orthogonal layout—is something particular to the epoch of domesticated culture, something of little moment to hunter/gatherers or to urban industrial cultures. Bachelard's contention at the epigraph to this chapter is an echo of psychoanalytic thought, and its claim to universality is false; houses may be of cosmic import, but only to those who live in them. By far the greater part of humanity has lived without houses and hence without the props of such symbols.

Similarly, those who have studied *topophilia*, "the human being's affective ties with the material environment" (Tuan 1974:93), frequently conclude that the manifold functions of architecture, and of domestic architecture in particular, allays individual anxiety by providing a womblike security. To be able to see the cosmos represented and to be able to move about in it is to place oneself exactly in space and time and to have answered all the mysteries of existence, of life and death. Rykwert's conclusion to his investigation of the idea of the Roman town is a case in point:

> It is difficult to imagine a situation when the formal order of the universe could be reduced to a diagram of intersecting coordinates in one plane. Yet this is exactly what did happen in antiquity: the Roman who walked along the *cardo* knew that his walk was the axis around which the sun turned, and that if he followed the *decumanus*, he was following the sun's course. The whole universe and its meaning could be spelt out of his civic institutions—so he was at home in it. We have lost all the beautiful certainty about the way the world works. [1976:202]

Rykwert is clearly indulging in a certain amount of sentimentality as he concludes his disciplined work. But the comparison he makes, between ancient Roman society and modern Western society, is conventional. I doubt whether a less conventional, but just as valid, comparison with nomadic gatherers would yield the same contrast between security and insecurity. Rather, the most obvious difference would be the containment of Roman life versus the freedom of nomadic life: the inner complexity of prescription, proscription, and hierarchy in a Roman community contrasted with the spontaneity, immediacy, and voluntariness of the open society.

This at any rate is the point I want to emphasize. The most far-reaching difference between open and domesticated societies, between Paleolithic and Neolithic societies, between hunter/gatherers and agriculturalists, be-

77

tween nomads and sedentarists, is that in the former the sense of structure and constraint is tacit, subjective, personal, and focused, whereas in the latter it is explicit, embodied, objective, and externally bounded. The source of this difference, its origin, lies in the adoption of architecture as the permanent living environment. The influence by suggestion (or metaphor) of architecture on human thinking as well as its more direct and practical use as an instrument of organization opens so many possibilities for people to structure and objectify their social lives, their communities, their thoughts, their activities, and the world about them. In a very real and literal sense the adoption of architecture is an acceptance of structure and constraint.

From a sociological point of view this difference between open and domesticated society is revealed by the prevalence of formal, structured institutions in the latter and is reflected in the emphasis placed by anthropologists on the social structure in their studies of domesticated societies in contrast to the negative description that characterizes so many studies of hunter/gatherers.

But this difference does not mean that informal behavior and relations are superseded or canceled. It seems rather that they come to be conducted in the shadow of the social structure, to the extent that ordinary, daily, routine behavior often passes beneath the notice of anthropologists. It seems that day-to-day activity, the intimate, affective interaction between individuals, is encroached on by the various forms of structure that impose on a community. It means also that the social structure of a community, the formal, institutional arrangements, activities, and relationships, are affected by, as they affect, the informal routines and emotions of people. The result of this construction of domesticated society is the growth of certain beliefs and practices that occupy a region between informal behavior and institutional behavior. It is to this nether region that I now propose to turn.

4

Open House

> Moreover, these institutions have an important
> aesthetic side which we have left unstudied.
>
> —Marcel Mauss, *The Gift*

Generalizing largely from the work of Malinowski among the Trobriand Islanders, Karl Polanyi gave a succinct formulation of the essential difference between traditional and modern societies that has come to serve as the foundation of modern social theorizing. Polanyi wrote:

> The outstanding discovery of recent historical and anthropological research is that man's economy, as a rule, is submerged in his social relationships. He does not act so as to safeguard his individual interest in the possession of material goods; he acts so as to safeguard his social standing, his social claims, his social assets. He values material goods only in so far as they serve this end. Neither the process of production nor that of distribution is linked to specific economic interests attached to the possession of goods; but every single step in that process is geared to a number of social interests which eventually ensure that the required step be taken. . . . the economic system will be run on noneconomic motives. [1957:46]

Much the same conclusion may be discerned amid the terminological jungle of Marxist theorizing. Summarizing the state of Marxist anthropology in relation to segmentary societies (roughly the same as domestic societies), Joel Kahn concluded:

> Quite simply all the writers agree that while the property relation between worker and capitalist may actually be the key to uncovering the secret of capitalist formations, such is not the case for pre-capitalist societies in general, and segmentary societies in particular, where there has been no separation of

the labourer from the means of production. The key must therefore lie, they conclude, elsewhere—in social ties which are more directly personal. Whether these ties are taken to be basically egalitarian . . . or inegalitarian . . . they must nonetheless be personal. [1981:84]

Granted, then, that precapitalist economies are submerged in the social, they do not work by rational economic thinking and are not motivated by the desire for economic or purely material gain. Rather, says Polanyi, they work by reciprocity and redistribution. Reciprocity works "mainly in regard to sexual organisation of society, that is, family and kinship; while redistribution is mainly effective in respect to all those who are under a common chief and is, therefore, of a territorial character" (1957:47).

Polanyi and the Marxists would agree that domesticated people work and that they produce material goods but do not work for material gain. But they do work for gain, since what they seek to do by working is not only to feed themselves but to safeguard and further social assets and standing. This raises a problem: how do physical labor and the material products of that labor get converted to nonmaterial social assets, positions, and claims? Polanyi (1957: 43, 50) insists that precapitalist people show no evidence of Adam Smith's suggested universal propensity to truck, barter, and exchange, but he does not say how one might keep or augment social assets otherwise than by exchange in some form. Yet Adam Smith himself, in his early work on moral sentiments, suggested that the process of material production might be translatable into social assets through the medium of respect—that is, it is the *capacity* to work and produce rather than the product that might be the subject and object of exchange: "The desire of becoming proper objects of this respect, of deserving and obtaining this credit and rank among our equals is perhaps the strongest of all our desires, and our anxiety to obtain the advantages of fortune is accordingly much more excited and initiated by this desire, than by that of supplying all the necessities and conveniences of the body, which are always very easily supplied" (Smith [1759] 1976:212–13).

What we can do, then, is exchange material products in which labor is embodied for respect, credit, and rank—that is, for social standing and assets—instead of exchanging one product for another. But if this is the case, then a different sort of economic rationality is supposed than the Weberian concept, which holds sway not only in capitalist practice but also in social theory. Economic rationality may be stated as a process of production in which the most, or the best, returns can be secured for the least

80

effort or lowest cost. Applying this measure leads to a negative appraisal of precapitalist activities of production, especially gift giving and elaborate "redistributive" feast giving. Defenders of traditional economy seek to make sense of it—to make it appear rational according to Weberian criteria—by suggesting that such practices perform hidden functions, such as ensuring ecological balance (for example, pig feasts among the Maring of New Guinea [Rappaport 1968]) or covertly distributing protein on an even basis (human sacrifice among the Aztec [Harris 1977]). This approach keeps the exchange at a material level (ecology and protein) and retains Weberian rationality. But respect and social standing, which is what no less an economist than Adam Smith claims to be exchangeable, are not material. It is therefore perfectly possible and logical that the material product of labor is not the object or aim of the labor but the means. In other words, the important factor in precapitalist economies is that production is the means for labor rather than labor being the means for production: the more labor products represent, the more valued they are, because in precapitalist societies what is exchanged is *labor* (work) for *respect* (esteem or prestige). The tangible objects that might change hands (or more often, as I shall claim, the displays offered for consumption) are merely indicators of the real goods: labor, effort, ingenuity, talent, and skill. And these are exchanged for *commensurate* goods—prestige, reputation, esteem, rank, and so on.

Economic rationality is quantitative; literally, it is the ratio of cost to product measured in terms of numbers. Precapitalist or domesticated rationality is *qualitative*, and though numbers or relative size may still be a factor, it is as a qualitative factor in the sense that greater size or numbers is valuable for the impression it makes or for its contribution to an aesthetic whole rather than for its relation to costs. The objects produced under this form of rationality are more likely to stress quality, beauty, refinement, or whatever aesthetic properties are valued in a particular culture. Competition, instead of being based on the production of more for less, will be based on the idea of who can mobilize and put in more work, which will be measured and made visible by the more impressive product, a product that may be greater, more beautiful, more lasting than its rivals. Under such a rationality it is not material utility that really matters but the spectacle of beauty and awe the product presents, because this is not only admirable for its own sake, a thing of beauty being a joy forever, it is also the measure of a vast labor input, a demonstration of people's talent, skills, and knacks, evidence of the perfectionist ambitions and perfectibilist aspirations of human beings. Monumental and gargantuan aesthetic achievements, not profits, are the proofs of success in precapitalist, domesticated societies. And before steam the possibility that energy or labor was a "cost" and could be "saved" relative to production was not a practical or even a theoretical consideration. Labor, talent, skill, and artistic sense were the main human possessions that people had to create a world which could satisfy their senses and their social and intellectual ambitions. The more labor and so forth that was expended, the richer and more rewarding the world of sensual and intellectual products. In many ways the evolution of domesticated society is a record of the marshaling of human labor for the production of ever greater and more massive monuments on the one hand and an expansion and refinement of aesthetic activity on the other. In precapitalist "economic" thought the output was a reliable, accurate measure of the input, whereas in rational capitalist thinking success as profit is the extent to which the output or product disguises the input.

From this point of view we can see that capitalist, industrial society has different aims and produces different products than is the case in domestic society. The industrial economy circulates and exchanges material goods via a money medium, and the control of various material sectors of production (the land, raw materials, machines, and so on) contributes to the social or class ordering of the population. In the domestic economy we tend to find that the greatest prominence is given to the exchange of like material goods (food for food, shells for shells) in contrast to the capitalist economy, which exchanges unlike material products through the medium of money. But in the domesticated economy the exchange of material goods is only the *means* and not the *end* of transactions: such goods as pigs, shells, blankets, yams, and food in general are the medium through which one commodity (labor, skill, talent, knack, ingenuity) can be exchanged for or converted into another, different commodity (prestige, esteem, reputation, honors, titles, ranks). If this is the case, then the materials involved in the major "economic" activities of domestic societies have a conveyancing function; they convey and portray work, skill, talent, and aesthetic sense for the admiration of exchange partners who are less like customers and consumers than an audience. In return for being provided with this display of the exhibitors' powers the "audience" grants or confers reputation and esteem.

I do not want to give the impression that utilitarian production of goods

82

necessary for bodily survival has no part in the theory or practice of domesticated society. That would be nonsense. I am claiming that such production is subordinate in thought and practice to the "social production" of renown, prestige, and honor by means of display. For example, in the Trobriand Islands the staple is yams, and the gardens where they are grown are effectively worked. No doubt yams are appreciated as food. But as much if not more value is attached to the size and appearance of yams because they are critical items in the creation of displays, which in turn govern much of Trobriand interaction and social evaluation. When yams are dug up they are displayed then and there in the gardens; when they are sent to the sister's husband as *Urigubu* payments they are arranged in conical heaps for display; when guests are entertained the yams are first exhibited, then cooked. And when they have been harvested and transferred to the village to be stored they are carefully arranged in what Malinowski calls storehouses but which might more accurately be called galleries. These galleries are the only village structures other than the chief's house that are decorated, "framed in wood and decorated with paint" (Malinowski 1961:168–69).

This emphasis on the aesthetic value of food and other products dominates the value placed on food as a means to satisfy hunger. The same items of food can be appropriated for everyday, necessary consumption, in which case they are given everyday value. And they can be appropriated for the periodic but more spectacular and significant process of producing displays that are exchanged for prestige.

Nineteenth-century Maori society provides a good illustration of how everyday items may serve aesthetic as well as necessary functions. As in the Trobriands, the Maori storehouses were decorated whereas their dwellings were not. But on specific occasions when some villages hosted their neighbors, the display value of food was elevated above all others.

In the northern district of the North Island huge stages or scaffolds were built to support the food, and tree trunks of quite large size were used in their erection. Yate, Wade, and Thomson all describe such *hakari* stages, and it is obvious from their accounts and somewhat crude sketches that an *immense amount of labour* was necessary to construct them, measuring as they did upwards of 50 feet in height. Some were conical, while others were of the shape of a triangular prism. Colenso states that the food was generally piled up in the form of a pyramid 80–90 feet high, and 20–30 feet square at the base. A straight trunk of a tree was set up in the ground, strong poles were fixed around it, and a series of horizontal platforms was then erected to encircle the scaffolding at intervals of 7 to 9 feet. The whole of this structure was then filled in by baskets of provisions, and built up so as to *present to the eye,* when completed, one solid mass of food! . . . The *manifest purpose* of building such structure was to *impress the guests* and to give scope for the *display of food* to the best advantage. The effect was much more striking than if the provisions had been merely heaped on the ground. [Firth 1959:319–20, emphasis added]

European observers, including anthropologists, have been in the habit of describing such events as *hakari* as feasts, thereby emphasizing the eating function and the value of the goods as food. But it seems fairly clear that eating itself on these occasions was the last and least important procedure. People did not attend these events to have a good meal so much as to be given a rewarding entertainment, of which a meal was a part. In the hakari when the time came for eating the eatables were presented by the hosts to the guests in a way that drew further attention to the aesthetic quality of the offering: "Young woman [*sic*] advanced in line across the public square with a slow step, hips and bodies swaying in time to a *waiata,* each bearing in her hands a basket of steaming food. This custom was always made much of by the olden Maori, and it is picturesque even in these days when the feast is shorn of much of its former ceremonial" (ibid.:320). The actual handing over of the food was "fairly indiscriminate," and actual interest in the eating itself was often minimal. But to European observers of the time, looking at these events from within a rationalist economic point of view, these hakari were inefficient and irrational:

Thomson brings up the oft quoted simile from Montesquieu that like Indians who fell trees to gather the fruit, the Maori at these gatherings quite overlooked the future for the present, and to *have his fame spread abroad* would endure hunger for months without repining. Rev. J. Buller remarks that the natives often impoverished themselves for a while by their lavish expenditure on such occasions; T. Moser pointed out that the tribe which gave a feast nearly starved for some months afterwards in return for their "misplaced hospitality." [Ibid.:333]

Just as the rationalist can recognize the display function of the gathering yet criticize it as irrational or improvident, so presumably the Maori could acknowledge the expense involved yet regard this as secondary to the display function. The priorities are reversed.

The same relative priorities seem to exist wherever similar gatherings in domesticated societies take place. In contemporary New Guinea among the Melpa the climax of the *moka* exchange is the "concerted showing of gifts at the ceremonial ground" (Strathern 1971:177). For the Wola the display of pork (not the eating of it) is a "proud moment," and the exhibition is prepared with great care and precision (Sillitoe 1979:181, 260). In Wogeo food is "both for display and to eat. We like to see it all spread out before us" (Hogbin 1938–39:324–25, cited in Rubel and Rosman 1979:317). But not only food is exhibited. In the discussions of the *kula* all the emphasis has been placed on the exchange aspects and the enormous efforts of preparation that lead up to the kula voyage. But the gifting of valuables is but one act in the event, and not necessarily the principal one. Just before the voyagers return home all the valuables acquired on the trip are arranged and displayed for all to see and compare. In this *tanarere* the valuables are arranged in precise ranks, and the members of the expedition "walk up and down, admire and count them" (Malinowski 1961:375). In fact the entire kula cycle consists of a series of interlinked displays: voyagers adorn and display themselves before meeting their partners; canoes are specially decorated, and just before the expedition comes into view of the hosts the canoes are lined up in formation to display before the partners/rivals. Each major act in the kula event is in fact marked by a display of some sort (ibid.:388, 390).

While each individual kula or moka or potlatch has to be considered as a total display in which pigs, pearl shells, people, yams, or coppers are the ingredients blended to form the whole, each item is prepared individually for its demonstrative role. Shells to be displayed in the moka are specially mounted on leaves or resin boards and sprinkled with red ochre to highlight their iridescence (Strathern and Strathern 1971:20). When pigs are displayed by the Wola they are staked out according to their size "with the largest pig first . . . the next largest second, and so on down to the smallest pig which is the last in line" (Sillitoe 1979:181). People dance and parade up and down wearing elaborate decorations of wigs, feathers, and paint, which are "designed for effect, to impress others" (Strathern and Strathern 1971:20). The decorations, the arrangements, the presentation of pig or pearl—all are intended to carry and convey messages, all are symbolic: "The men walk in stiffly, each muscle and feather on rigid display, and their friends as well as their enemies size up their physical conditions as well as the splendour and correctness of their decorations" (Strathern 1984:100).

These displays are all, to some extent, architectural in form, they are constructions that require a considerable investment of labor and that have a conscious aesthetic aim. Their scale and style are intended first and foremost to express and impress. The hakari platforms and towers of the Maori or the Solomon Islanders (Oliver 1967) are literally architectural constructions to "house" the food. They are the monumental versions of the everyday decorated storehouses or galleries. Elsewhere in New Guinea actual houses are constructed whose prime function is display rather than shelter. The Abelam, for example, center their ceremonial life around two cults, the *long yam* cult and the *tambaram* cult. Each of these cults has an elaborate display as its center. In the long yam cult each yam is decorated and set out for display, while the tambaram cult "involves a series of displays of things all classifiable loosely as art" (Forge 1970:272). This culminates in the revelation of huge carved figures (*nggwalndu*), which are housed in huge structures distinguished by a triangular facade towering up to sixty feet. These can be seen for miles around and are decorated with elaborately carved boards and bands of polychrome painting.

While the displays of the moka and the kula do not call for special constructions, their geometrical arrangements of pigs, food, and shells and of people and canoes in formations are all architectonic. It is possible, and I think proper, to consider the form of such displays as two-dimensional architecture. The principal architectural motif exploited in these exhibitions and accompanying performances is the repetition of like units. In buildings, bricks, stones, planks, reeds, and other materials are used to build a structure by being repeated; in the majority of domesticated villages the settlement is a structure of repeated forms: identical dwellings. And so the impressiveness and solidity of exhibitions of resources is built up by arrangements comprising repetitions—of artifacts and items, in rows and columns. This is not a fortuitous or unconscious knowledge on the part of domesticated people. Captain James Cook was suitably impressed by the singing and dancing of people in the Melanesian and Polynesian islands he visited, and the focus of his admiration was the way in which great numbers sang and danced in unison, as one (Renfrew 1984). The striking thing about these displays, at least to observers from a capitalist society, is the huge investment of labor, time, and resources, bearing in mind that such expenditures appear to have little or no material return. Anthropologists, however, have stressed the returns in terms of prestige, sociability, and redistribution. I have reiterated and singled out the prestige aspect. I want also to suggest that in domesticated society "efficiency" (if I may use the term) is not measured as a ratio of labor input to product output but as the expenditure of what has little value on returns that are

86

highly valued, specifically labor for honor. The most readily available means whereby great quantities of labor may be used to convert to prestige, a means that is the great invention of domesticated society, is architecture in general and the house specifically. Human society did not come up with another "invention" that allowed for the expansion of investment and energy greater than the opportunities presented by architecture until the industrial revolution. Throughout the era of domestication, buildings and analagous architectonic displays provided the primary outlet and means of expression for human powers. What is more, architecture in the broadest sense spurred the development of those powers. In open societies of hunter/gatherers the opportunities and the means for large-scale mobilization, for extensive division of labor and for varied cultural expression, were severely limited by the conditions of life—such requirements as small groups, mobility, flexibility, portable material culture, and so on. I do not say that such people lacked aesthetic capabilities or were lazy; Paleolithic art refutes that suggestion. I suggest simply that human capabilities, potentials, and capacities were challenged and extended by the continued presence of architecture as the human environment. Huge displays and massive monuments are analogous expressions of the same ambitions. Consider the following:

- "It has been estimated that such causewayed enclosures as Windmill Hill represent 120,000 manhours, Avebury represents 1.5 million manhours and Stonehenge perhaps as many as 30 million manhours" (Renfrew 1984:234).
- "In 1844, at Remuera a feast with 11,000 baskets of potatoes, 100 large pigs, 9,000 sharks, liberal supplies of flour, sugar, rice and tobacco. There were about 4,000 visitors, the feast lasted nearly a week, the shed was nearly 400 yards long and was covered with Witney blankets and 1,000 more besides as presents" (Firth 1959:329).
- "The Aztec capital of Tenochtitlal centered on a ceremonial area measuring 500 square meters. On all sides of this were 78 monumental structures, of which at least 40 had towers. 'The eight or nine temples in the city were all close to one another within a large enclosure. Within this compound they all stood together, though each had its own staircase, its special courtyard, its chambers and its sleeping quarters for the priests of the temple. . . . How marvellous it was to gaze on them. . . . All stuccoed, carved and crowned with different types of

merlons, painted with animals, (covered) with stone figures'" (Berdan 1982:11).

These and the countless other examples that could be cited suggest people who, though culturally, linguistically, geographically, and historically quite separate, would all have shared a frame of mind and a sense of values. We have nineteenth-century English observers who, in spite of their bias toward rational economics, nevertheless concur with Polynesian performers in rating the visual appeal of monumental and gargantuan displays so impressive as to justify their exhibition; we have a twentieth-century archaeologist noting with awe the labor achievements of prehistoric people; and we have a Spanish priest speaking in admiration of the visual splendor of Aztec buildings. Although people eat the food displayed or live in the sumptuous buildings, the pragmatic, utilitarian function is secondary to the aesthetic function, and through that the political function. In one sense we have a common philosophy among domesticated people of reaching for glory through technology: architectural displays are constructed as a testament to the power, force, and energy people can muster and exert on the world. That power is "organized labor"—organized by division and by mobilization. The division of labor makes possible the specialization that produces the skill and refinement, the "workmanship" and the "grace"; the mobilization produces the scale and the might. It is not until mechanical labor became operationally independent of natural power that human aspirations for and claims to glory shifted from perfecting, enlarging, and extending architecture to developing transportation and firepower. In a second sense we have a common acknowledgment that the most telling and impressive aspect of architecture, both literal and metaphorical, is not the size and extent per se, or the sheer quantities of materials used in construction, but the arrangement of materials for visual display and satisfaction. Although buildings and displays of food may be analyzed in economic terms of exchange and redistribution, we are still entitled to ask why these essentially "economic" activities and achievements should (1) assume an architectural form and (2) lay so much emphasis on the visual appearance, on the display aspects of food, housing, persons, shells, weapons, and so forth.

In open societies labor power has little opportunity to embody itself in objects or products separate from the person. Implements and artifacts are few, small, and portable; such housing as there is is temporary; the killing of animals is restricted more or less to what can be eaten on the spot at any one time (though it is possible that the large-scale trapping of animals, for which there is some evidence in the Paleolithic, offered a means for expressing power); and people are always on the move. Labor power as productivity, to all intents and purposes, cannot be taken up as either a commodity or as a means in open societies. In industrial society labor power is the means harnessed for the production of the end, material wealth and profit. But in domestic society labor power is an end, a product produced by sociopolitical division, organization, and mobilization, embodied or objectified in its most spectacular product and "exchanged" for moral and political "goods"—honor, prestige, reputation, esteem—and the material signifiers of these—rank, office, and emblem. In other words, one of the main goals of people in domesticated society is to recruit and organize the labor power of individuals so as to create a great force and then to record that accomplishment through the production of a suitably vast and impressive monument, building, display, or performance. Labor power is not so much a cost that must be reckoned in manufacture but something that must be produced and maintained.

Is this process achieved by some sleight of hand? Does the "chief" hoodwink the people into thinking that he is the "great provider" when he gives them back their own produce that they offered him as tribute and that therefore they owe him allegiance and obedience, including their labor power? This seems to be how political anthropologists account for the achievement of rank through redistribution. Morton Fried argues that rank society rests on a domesticated food supply, which in turn allows for larger, more permanent communities that are organized with reference to a clearly distinguished descent principle. The system is fueled by an economy based on redistribution in which there is "a characteristic flow of goods into and out of a finite centre." "Invariably that centre is the pinnacle of rank hierarchy" (Fried 1967:115–17). Why is the influx of goods evaluated differently from the outflow of those same goods? Why is the influx a sign of inferiority and the outflow (redistribution) a sign of prestige? Fried cites an example from Fiji where the chief has the right to summon labor to gather the greater portion of the first fruits of the yam crop, which he later distributes in the general welfare, a procedure that confers prestige on him and bolsters his status. But why do people attribute this power and benevolence to the chief when they know full well it was *their* labor that gathered *his* crop? If it was a matter of simple redistribution, which had the effect, say, of ensuring equal access to resources or which spread out supplies over the year so people did not go hungry, then we could perhaps appreciate that the chief's wisdom as a redistributor gave him stature as an upholder of justice or prudent manager. But in most cases this simply is not so. Intra- and intervillage feasts and displays are often planned much in advance, and far from being staged in order to use up a surplus of produce, they generally render a community exhausted and having to live "on short commons till the following harvest" (Firth 1959:333). Food to be displayed at a feast is grown, hunted, and raised specially: "Sometimes the event was planned on such a large scale that the initial labour was begun more than a year before the feast itself was timed to take place"; "New ground was planted with kumara, birds and rats were taken in the forest and preserved in gourds to serve as dainty morsels. . . . fish were caught in large quantities. . . . certain inland districts were famed for their special products. . . . efforts were always made to include large quantities of such a delicacy in the food supplies especially to delight the appreciative tastes of the visitors" (ibid.:318).

Firth goes on to note that one early observer recorded how Chief Te Wherowhero had about one thousand men planting kumara (sweet potato), which gives some indication of the organization of labor power involved. But the point is this: the chief does not derive his prestige and rank from simple redistribution of goods received. He derives it in exchange for the *added value* he puts on the goods received and returned. First he mobilizes the labor on a scale unique to such occasions and resulting in the production of huge quantities—in itself a demonstration of power. The massing and display of produce and artifacts is itself a product with the added value of a spectacle, which, in turn, impresses all those invited to see it. The sheer size of the display/feast and number of witnesses is also a display in itself, especially if, as is often the case on such occasions, people dress up (for the occasion). People do not just sit down and eat: whether they are in New Guinea or New Zealand they are shown the results of their hosts' labors, which are displayed in a visually impressive style and scale. And whoever masterminds these performances and displays is rewarded with prestige, esteem, honor, and rank. It is this masterminding ability that merits the prestige, and it is the successful and impressive demonstration or display of these abilities—the show, the meal, the monument—that provides the tangible, sensual product which the guests/visitors/followers can appreciate and to which they physically respond. Big men and chiefs are not honored for their role as regulators of distributive justice or prudent economic managers. They are admired and followed for their vision, their planning, and their organizing ability. Proof of these capacities is shown in the magnificence of the shows they organize and put on. The standards by which such displays are adjudged are, in many societies, not absolute but relative, because they are subject to competition. Firth describes how, in some cases, a chief and his people had to give land, their most prized possession, because they could not match their rival's display. It took Big Man Ongka of New Guinea ten years to prepare his moka to end all mokas, his "last big show" (Strathern 1979:119). As the highlight of his audacity and planning capability he proposed not only to give the customary things but things that had never been given before, "in order to make our name." Part of the strategy was to keep his plans secret, thereby arousing curiosity. Then he revealed his plan, which was to give a car. When it was brought back, "everyone exclaimed, and some famous big men came down to our place to see if it was true—I directed them all to check with Parua and see for themselves" (ibid.:123). Ongka sums up what makes him a really big Big Man, his masterminding ability to plan, organize, and execute, when he says: "So I finished my show after very many years of planning, after holding several small moka in preparation, after saying so many times I would do it. In the end I did bring it off. I wrapped all the strong things of men and women from the past and laid them in their graves with my last big moka" (ibid.:128).

So, displaying the ability to organize labor, to produce or obtain large quantities of special things, to create out of these products an exhibition impressive in all possible dimensions, to feast and accommodate large numbers of guests, and, finally, to overawe them with spectacle and organization: these are the main ingredients that are added to the value of the goods, produce, and labor which are donated to the finite center. These qualities and properties mark the difference between the center's input and outflow. And prestige is the measure of recognition accorded to this difference.

Why is it that in domesticated societies the principal way in which prestige is acquired and rank bolstered, confirmed, or demoted should be through elaborate displays and exhibitions that have an architectonic form and that center on, without exclusively involving, food?

Hospitality

Big men like Ongka and chiefs like Te Wherowhero did not own the land from which they produced the vast quantities of food used for displays. They organized their associates for a concerted production, they took responsibility for that production, and eventually the credit was theirs. In producing for their own daily needs they worked in field and garden in the same way as everybody else, participating in cooperative and reciprocal labor. There was no question of such big men and chiefs "owning" the materials or the means of production (that is, owning land or labor power). But they did organize the relations of production, which were instrumental in the construction of these focal displays. Chiefs and big men came by their positions and/or held them by virtue of their initiative, planning, and organizing abilities. Their prestige was an appreciation of those talents, the esteem and respect in which they were held a recognition of those abilities. But the events and activities through which these capacities were realized and given their opportunity differed only in degree and not in kind from the ordinary, everyday subsistence activities that everyone pursued. Feasts and displays were exaggerated or enlarged forms of household meals and presentations between neighbors. They were, in short, domestic events in which the hospitality called for whenever a householder receives a neighbor is extended toward community, regional and group bonds—that is, toward the point where such domestic activity becomes transformed into political activity. The salient status is that of host and guest; the practical qualification for being acknowledged as big man, or chief, in domesticated society is how good and able a host a man (and his followers) turn out to be. The context of conspicuous feasting and display is hospitality, and the model for this hospitality is structured in the conditions that determine the relationship between neighbors. And so, too, is the competitive aspect of feasting and display.

Following Mauss, most observers and commentators consider feasting and display as gift giving and competitive displays as reciprocal gift giving. This means, of course, that in the long run and taking everything into account (Mauss's total prestation), gift giving is nothing of the kind but is an ongoing series of transactions in which debt and credit are locked in a dynamic exchange. In Mauss's view, then, the people engaged in feasting and displaying to one another stand alternately as debtor and creditor—that is, in a quasi- or even proper economic relationship. Yet, as Mauss

92

himself notes, "These men have neither the notion of selling nor the notion of lending, and yet carry out the legal and economic activities corresponding to these words" (1967:31). If domesticated people lack economic and political notions like ours, they don't have them, and it is misleading to imply that, in spite of this, they carry out "economic" and "political" activities and to suggest that the discrepancy is due to "an incapacity to abstract and analyse concepts" (ibid.:30). Rather we might better understand what has been observed by attending to the ways in which such activities are viewed and spoken of within the culture. Trying to ascertain this, however, is difficult: ethnographies do not supply native terminology for participants in these events but tend to name the particular episodes and artifacts involved. However, ethnographers in their descriptive rather than analytical moments and synthesisers such as Firth do use status terms to denote the participants. Interestingly, the terms most frequently used are not debtor/creditor or borrower/lender but host/guest or donor/recipient, and the total activity is frequently (not always) referred to as hospitality. The following quotation from Firth's summation of his investigation and analysis of "the feast" clearly indicates the central (yet unofficial) notion of the host and guest:

> Feasts and gifts of this kind show the extent to which chiefs and their followers would go in order to emulate one another and maintain their name for generosity; and also the intensity of the obligation which was incurred by acceptance of hospitality at a feast. Not only the prospect of having to entertain guests but also the state of having been entertained as such was a matter of grave responsibility. By giving a feast one repaid one's obligations, by being fêted one saddled oneself with fresh ones. And the greater the entertainment provided by the one side the more did the other have to work to outdo this display. [1959:337]

The interesting implication of Firth's interchanging of terms is the way in which the political concept of hierarchy (chief/follower) is equated with the domestic, spatial concept of host/guest, which in turn is equated with the modal, directional concept of donor/recipient. Could this apparently unintended set of equations have general theoretical implications that have not been fully recognized up to now? Ethnographic evidence from a variety of societies, all of which could be said to fall within the broad category of domesticated society, suggests that a fundamental structural evaluation derives from a combination of the spatial and modal dimensions to produce the hierarchical dimension. In other words, whatever else the hierarchical differentiation between chief and follower may involve in specific cases, it is constituted by being an ongoing incorporation of the statuses of host/guest and donor/recipient. As long as one person (or a group) retains and sustains the position of host and donor vis-à-vis others who remain guest and recipient, then the former will be regarded as ascendant. A "chief" (one of regular, confirmed higher status) is one who serves consistently as host and donor. Correspondingly, whoever aspires to such ascendancy must continue to function successfully as a host and donor.

While I cannot profess to have examined every ethnography of domesticated societies and while a statistical tabulation of instances would be tedious, it seems to me a reasonable finding that the "development" of hierarchical political organization from "big man" to "monarch" is bound up with the development of hospitality from the reciprocal but competitive alternation of entertainment and display between neighbors as hosts and guests, donors and recipients, to the institution of an elaborate and permanent display of hospitality and donation enshrined in "court" society. The statuses of donor-recipient are in constant oscillation (reciprocation) in such open societies as the !Kung-San. And since individuals are constantly on the move, changing their places of residence and their companions, the status of host and guest has no stability or permanence. Political relations are egalitarian.

An example of going "up the ladder," so to speak, is the Para-Pirana, whose residential organization we have already observed. The Para-Pirana live in scattered longhouses, but they counteract this dispersal by frequent visiting, which varies from the brief and casual to the protracted and formal. How consistently and well a man and his longhouse (*maloca*) provide hospitality is, very explicitly, the measure and hallmark of "a man's social standing, and that of his maloca (longhouse) community" (S. Hugh-Jones 1979:42). The headman of a longhouse becomes so in the first place by building the longhouse. In order to accomplish this he has to attract helpers, who are recruited first as guests for a meal and entertainment and who are retained by being provided with food (that is, by being maintained as guests). In turn, the eminence of a longhouse among its neighbors is achieved and maintained by the standard, and frequency, of dances it hosts. The case of the Azande is particularly instructive. They, too, live in well-scattered homesteads and counteract this sociospatial dispersal by frequent visiting. However, Zande is a stratified society. Commoners are politically equal and rank below princes and nobles. Among commoners people constantly visit *one another's* homesteads, and quite explicit norms of hospitality are laid down: the hosts should, minimally, provide refreshments, especially beer for the guests, and guests should show a degree of restraint and politeness toward their hosts. Each visit, furthermore, should be returned, and the former guest should provide at least matching hospitality as host. In the event that real or supposed imbalances in reciprocal hospitality are perceived, suspicions and accusations of witchcraft surface (Evans-Pritchard 1937:110). I shall return to this point. Here I want to emphasize the contrast between commoners and aristocracy. Princes maintain a court at which the nobles from their princedoms are present as guests receiving the prince's hospitality. They also host commoners, and the competition between princes for a following is based on their generosity and accomplishments as hosts: "The more the wives the more the labour and the more the food; the more the food the greater the hospitality; the greater the hospitality the greater the following; and the greater the following the greater prestige and authority" (Evans-Pritchard 1971:223). The prince is enabled to provide hospitality not only through the products of his wives' labor but also by means of the tribute from his subjects, the commoners. But, as Evans-Pritchard notes, the prince places added value on this tribute, for his hospitality involves a transformation of the raw into the cooked, since the produce presented to the prince is returned to the commoners as a cooked meal (ibid.:215). Commoners, by contrast, never entertain princes, nor are there ever accusations of witchcraft between the two strata. Furthermore, among the Azande, as indeed among many people, the hierarchical distinction between neighbors as host and guest is marked and portrayed spatially. Zande commoners who come to court remain in the outer area of the prince's compound while the prince and the nobles eat in the inner court, and "a man lacking official status or badge who tried to follow the others into the inner court might be humiliated" (ibid.:192). Likewise, when Para-Pirana neighbors arrive as guests at their host's maloca they have a place just inside the main door, and the men remain in the center front of the house (C. Hugh-Jones 1979:48–49).

The native lords of Quito achieved and maintained their superior position in the same way, through "institutionalized generosity," which entailed dispensing food and maize beer: "The most respected man among the natives was the bravest chief or *principal* or the one who made the best plantings; for since he would use them up in giving the Indians food and

95

drink they would attend him with more good will and affection than they would those who failed to do so" (Salomon 1986:125 citing [Anonimo 1573 (1965)]). The actual house of the native lord was, ideally, the "symbolic center, not only of political activity, but of cosmic order" (ibid.:125). Then each principal in fact maintained a dual residence, one in the locale of his domain (*Parcialidad*) and the other at the chief's court (ibid.:124).

Finally, in Mediterranean and southwest Asian tribal societies the sustained demonstration of status is also principally through hospitality. According to Barth, among the Swat Pathans, "Gifts and hospitality . . . are of prime importance in the building up of a political following" (1965:77). He notes further, "The chief also establishes a reputation for lavishness, shows himself capable of profitable management of his estates, and in general gains prestige as a desirable leader. Followers flock to his men's house and his political influence increases" (ibid.:81). But, as Ahmed (1976:59) points out, chiefly hospitality with political intent is but a particular instance of the general cultural role of hospitality as a means of ensuring and maintaining respect. Generosity in hospitality is said to have always been accorded a supreme value among the Bedouin and hence to be the hallmark of status (Zeid 1966:250), while Black-Michaud (1975:183) claims this is more generally true of all circum-Mediterranean and Middle Eastern societies.

Looking at hospitality the other way round, when a chief and his community fail to live up to the norms of hospitality, his and their moral and political status are immediately destroyed in their own eyes and those of their neighbors. The following story from Maori ethnography illustrates the point:

> [Paoa] was visited one day by a group of his wife's kinsmen. Noticing that the ashes of the cooking fire were lying in ridges, one of the guests surmised aloud with gustatory anticipation that eels (a highly prized food) must be cooking under the ashes. In reality it was only fern fronds—an inferior food—and Paoa had no other provisions on hand to offer them. He was mortified, and eventually had to inform his guests that he had nothing to serve them. They lingered on for several hours before departing, unmistakably signalling both their hunger and indignation of Paoa's inability to feed them. So utterly shamed was Paoa by this episode that he left his village and family for ever. [Hanson and Hanson 1983:114]

Hospitality is a widespread if not universal moral and political activity. People who live equivalently as neighbors do not just visit each other in their dwellings and communities and take what is offered. They abide by a groundplan of minimum prescription, which, if not observed, results in hostility and/or denial of the relationship of neighbor. Being a permanent host is universally a central duty, hence qualification for superior political status. Hospitality is not usually reckoned by political theorists as being a central and defining activity of the political and the moral. In domesticated society political position is more usually defined via prowess. What then are the grounds for arguing that hospitality is an elementary dimension of the moral and political life, and not just an expressive activity?

First, it is worth observing that whereas hospitality is invariably mentioned in the ethnography of domesticated societies, it is, to my knowledge at any rate, never described among hunter/gatherer societies. Among the latter, people from one company certainly visit those of another, but when they do they are absorbed into the company rather than separately identified and treated as guests. Provisions in a company are shared on principle rather than consumed by separate consumption units like hearth-holds, and visitors not only join in but also help in the provisioning. Then again, companies are usually temporary, forming and disbanding, losing and receiving members. The sense of identity and proprietorship in regard to place implicit in the term *host* can have no grounds in open society. Hospitality, and the concomitant relationship of host/guest, is possible only with the advent of domesticated society.

The idea of settlement in dwellings locates people in a clearly demarcated domain (the household) separate from but identical with other domains. Whereas hunter/gatherer bands consist of a small company of people constantly exposed to one another's attention, domesticated settlements are divided into household units (neighbors) at least partially shielded from one another's attention and pursuing at least some (or part) of their necessary activities independently. Domestication creates certain elementary and minimum conditions of empirical "unit" independence or privacy in the sense that the household is physically, economically (cf. Sahlins 1974:94–95), and to some extent sensorily separated from other households. Whatever other ties people may claim to connect themselves to each other, such as kinship, descent, or generation, the contiguity of neighbors who are divided and united by common physical boundaries (namely walls) is the first tangible, sensible bond. Members of the same household and the same village always exist, and can *see* themselves as existing, as a unitary and exclusive entity. Kinship groups, descent groups,

97

and the like are primarily ideological and achieve a practical, political existence only occasionally—usually at rituals. Thus through domestication people achieve unification in composite, practical, everyday, ongoing social units (the household) divided from similar units. This in turn creates the grounds for a distinctive and necessary relation between households and between communities. Whereas the relationships and activities within a household may be considered private, those occurring between households (or communities) may be considered public, hence political. In most domesticated societies there are well-defined and recognized rules of etiquette prescribed between neighbors, especially when entering one another's houses, rules that are political in essence since they ask and receive permission for entry, which in turn implies identity and ownership status. The request to enter a house is a request to enter the domain of privacy of the household. The host, then, is one who is being requested to expose or reveal something of that private domain to neighbors. The generosity a host then displays is not only the mark of his respect for his guests but is also a revelation or exposure of his privacy to outsiders. Hospitality is that form of activity specifically contrived to display the private domain in public. It is what is implied in this display that is central to the understanding of hospitality as elementary political activity.

Privacy

Writing of the Sakalava of Madagascar, Gillian Feeley-Harnik describes the formalities attached to visiting another household as follows:

Permission to enter the house (beginning with the fence, if there is one) is always requested first with the cry *Hôdy?!* [Anyone at] home?!, to which the proper response, *regardless of inclination* must be *Karibo!* or *Karibo An-traño!* "Enter!","Enter into the house!". No one would refuse another entrance into his house *unless he were hoarding or hiding something* (it is curious that the word *mody* of which *hody* is the future tense, in addition to meaning "at home" or "heading home", also means "to pretend what one is not"). These greetings are further distinguished by their guarded treatment of *vaovao* ("news", reduplicative of *vao* "new"), which is essentially any information of the status of family members. [1980:580]

The occupier of the house *must* give permission to enter, just as the visitor *must* announce his or her presence and request permission—that is, must not barge in. What is the force of this imperative? The answer is, I think,

98

provided by Feeley-Harnik's parenthetical observation about the other meaning of *hody*, which is not at all curious. Privacy, made universally possible with dwellings, provides both protection and concealment for people, their actions, attitudes, intentions, and property. In so doing it provides a foundation for ambivalence and suspicion among neighbors. With the aid of privacy neighbors have the opportunity to evade the attention of one another, attention that serves to keep people fully informed about one another. One is obliged to bid a visitor enter so as to reassure him or her that the privacy of the home is not being used for purposes of concealment, conspiracy, or surprise. And the guarded exchange of news about the family suggests the visitor's curiosity (or perhaps even suspicion) and the host's defensiveness. Even within the closest knit community neighbors divided from each other by walls and inward-looking household independence (such as suggested by Sahlins 1974:94–95) can often find reason to be suspicious or curious about goings on. There is, for example, Reo Fortune's (1963:47) anecdote about his assistants: They overheard their next-door neighbors plotting to bewitch someone of the same name as Fortune's assistant. The man was terrified until Fortune himself cleared up the misunderstanding. But the fact remained that within the privacy of their dwelling the Dobuans were plotting. Or there is Monica Wilson's observation about the Nyakyusa of Tanganyika, folk who consider they live together in good company, that the chief grounds for accusations of witchcraft is the envy aroused from smelling meat cooking in a neighbor's kitchen (Wilson 1951:165). The Mehinaku of the Brazilian Amazon employ a network of secret paths leading to hideaways where people can meet in private because, among other things, conversations can be heard through walls up to one hundred feet away (Gregor 1977: chap. 6). They, like the Trobriand Islanders, live in circular villages, and while the center of the village comprises the sacred and public part because it consists of the facing fronts of dwellings, the outer rim, called the trash yard by the Mehinaku, is semiprivate because it cannot be seen by most neighbors. In the center/front of the village behavior is public, formal, and geared for the attention it is given, while in the rear, trash yards are the scene of informal, private behavior that passersby might notice but not watch (ibid.; Malinowski 1929:98–100).

It is frequently noted by anthropologists (for example, Forge 1972; Sahlins 1974:98) that villages in what I am calling domesticated society seem to reach an optimum size and then break up, one faction (one set of households) leaving. The explanations given tend to be in terms of ultimate causes—that the carrying capacity of the land has been reached, that the number which can constitute a unitary population has been surpassed, that the day's journey to work has become too long. One immediate cause of such fission is, I suggest, the strain between neighbors unable to trust one anothers' privacy or countenance one anothers' surveillance. Under cover of household independence and privacy neighbors can plan to, for example, steal from one anothers' gardens and then hide the spoils: too diligent a scrutiny of the comings, goings, and doings of neighbors can quickly build to resentment, evasion, and the eruption of hostility. No matter how "open" the walls of a community's households are, I suggest that there is a built-in contradiction between the economically self-sufficient household, "a group with an interest and destiny apart from those outside and a prior claim on the sentiments and resources of those within" (Sahlins 1974:94), and its spatial coexistence with other such households in village and territory. In other words, however blurred the dividing line between the private household and the private household and between the private and the public domains, the very existence of such differentiation engenders a dynamic and unstable relation between neighbors.

The more difficult it is to sustain domestic privacy the more pronounced are likely to be the efforts of individuals and households to evade the constant scrutiny of neighbors. In Dobu, where the attitudes of people toward one another are hostile in the extreme, is it because of some collective psychobiological deficiency or quirk? Or is it because, as we have seen, domestic privacy is difficult? The Dobuan reaction to neighbors is: "a constant and silent war, a small circle of close kindred alone placing trust in one another. The whole life of people is strongly coloured by a thorough absence of trust in neighbours and in the practice of treachery beneath a show of friendliness" (Fortune 1963:137). "Dwelling houses are all close together like tents pitched as a camping party, and, like tents close-pitched, hold secrets badly" (ibid.:278). What is more, so close in the separations are the Dobu and so great their mutual distrust of one another that the "fear of being poisoned dominates native life" and "food or tobacco is not accepted except within a small circle. The woman of the house when cooking does not leave the pot and go away for as long as half a minute even" (ibid.:170).

In other words, the Dobuans do not offer each other hospitality for fear of exposure. But neither do they barricade themselves against all comers or live a sealed up life. Children are used as informers to report on the sexual misdeeds of their parents (ibid.:7), and all members of a village can come to suspect one another of witchcraft (ibid.:8).

In the Trobriands village domestic arrangements seem to leave more leeway for domestic privacy, and the prevailing atmosphere does not seem to be as disturbing as that of Dobu. But people keep a "suspicious watchful gaze" on one another so that "privacy is almost impossible to maintain" (Wiener 1976:191). To evade the furthest range of this surveillance Trobrianders say of themselves: "we hide who we are" (ibid.:89). From this Annette Wiener concluded that a degree of fear underlay all Trobriand social relationships which stemmed as well from the lack of knowledge of what was in other people's minds (ibid.:217). Trobriand magic, beauty magic, for example, is a formal, albeit private, attempt to get to other people's minds, to influence them in spite of their public indifference; Trobriand witchcraft is the technique above all others by which the social mask is pierced.

Another way in which the lack of spatial privacy in particular is countered is by the development of a formal etiquette of respect in public. Samoans live in houses without walls and this openness to the view of neighbors is enough to keep everyone in line during the hours of daylight. But at night law and chiefly authority come into their own with a curfew and *matai* (chiefs) patrols (Shore 1982:148, 164). This exposure to surveillance leads to the donning of social masks, as it does in the Trobriands: "Samoans, whatever may be their real feelings about a social situation, soon become adept at assuming an outward demeanour pleasing to those in authority. By the time they are adult males in particular have acquired the ability to hide their true feelings behind, as Wendt puts it, "an impregnable mask of controlled aloofness". In both men and women this aloofness is commonly joined, as is socially appropriate, with an elaborate politeness and engaging affability" (Freeman 1983: 216–17). Controlled, formal, respectable behavior (*aga*) is distinguished from private personal desires and drives (*amio*). Amio, if it must express itself, should do so in private, not in public. It is one of the big problems of Samoan life to preserve this separation.

Contrary to the generalizations sometimes made by anthropologists based on their personal reaction to their fieldwork situation (such as Srinivas 1976), domesticated societies recognize privacy and counter it with varieties of surveillance from the direct surveillance of Samoa to the indirect witchcraft of Dobu and the Trobriands. The demands and norms of living as neighbors conflict with the establishment of privacy as a by-product of living in house and household. How is this inherently dynamic and often unstable condition managed and kept under reasonable control? In a society such as Dobu (and there are probably few societies like the Dobu described by Reo Fortune) the answer to this question is, "very badly." Dobuans live in a state of perpetual mistrust, suspicion, and antagonism. Privacy and surveillance seem virtually to cancel each other out. In Samoa and in the Trobriands, our exemplary societies, privacy is acknowledged (formally in the Samoan concept of amio) but it is relegated below the public (exemplified in the concept of aga.) In both Samoa and the Trobriands people confess that they appear to others behind a social mask (Albert Wendt, cited above by Freeman, is Samoan). So we have a situation in which much of people's interaction, specifically where they are in public view, is interaction "between social masks." It is behavior less spontaneous than formal and impassive, according to known rules, predictable and objectively judged or appraised. In such societies as these the public dominates the private, and people's behavior tends to be formalized, to concentrate on etiquette and manners, and to insist on respect. Even within the confines of domestic space people are more likely to act toward one another in a formal and respectful manner, as if they were being watched by some sort of "audience."

Clifford Geertz (cited in Westin 1967) makes a similar observation about the demeanor of Javanese people who live in houses open to public view and access: "The Javanese have literally almost no defence against the outside world of a physical sort," and thus their "defences are mostly psychological" (Westin 1967: 14). Elsewhere Geertz describes the Javanese in much the same way that Shore describes Samoan demeanor. Dissimulation is approved as "proper lying," and there is a "nearly absolute requirement never to show one's real feelings directly, especially to a guest" (1960:246). This is especially interesting because the guests likely to be present in anyone's house, whether formally invited to *slametans* (celebrations) or informally dropping in, are above all *neighbors:* "In the slametan ritual the two fields of relationship (kin, neighbour) are most distinct. The ritual itself stresses the power of location—that is of the locus of the ritual—for drawing together the mystical forces of the spiritual universe and of human society to ensure the well-being of the host, his family, and his

102

enterprise. . . . The guests . . . are the host's closest neighbours" (Jay 1969:236). Javanese peasants "behave more or less in private as they do in public"—that is, in more general terms, the public domain dominates and takes priority over the private domain, and this precedence is continually confirmed by the proferring of hospitality (in Java as the slametan feast) among neighbors. In the slametan the house features prominently as the mystical and physical connector of the family to the land (ibid.:209), and after presenting the guests with food the host "thanks them for coming and asks their blessing on the occasion" (ibid.:208). At the slametan a neighbor is keeping his neighbors informed as to his doings and in a way preempting any interference from them as well as forestalling misunderstanding. Significantly, all guests are presented with identical offerings of food, thereby affirming the equality of neighbors.

The thinness of domestic privacy in such societies as Samoa or Java is by no means comparable to the absence of domestic privacy in open hunter/gatherer societies. There personal attention is unobstructed, and there is no sense of a dualism in behavior or character such as the difference between aga and amio, no development of a sense of distinction between the public and the private. In domestic societies the existence of a dwelling situates a household distinct from other households; hence it imposes some sense of the private and exclusive. Where domestic walls are thin I suggest we will find a prevailing dominance and priority of the public toward the private, behavior will tend to be formal and respectful, and, consequently, spontaneity will tend to be repressed or shunted into covert outlets. Among the most prevalent and repeated ways of reaffirming the priority of the public is through formalized and conforming hospitality of a reciprocal nature in which the equality of neighbors is reaffirmed through their displays of openness and alternation of status between host and guest. People in these societies, which I could call "public" societies, are always putting on a show and acting as if they are being watched (which much of the time is true). Furthermore, a strong sense of social place or an order of precedence between peoples organizes etiquette and respect.

Such societies as Samoa and Java represent an extreme development of public cultures. One such as the Trobriands is less extreme in that it manages to retain some autonomy of the private. This however, may result in personal relations being marked by a degree of mistrust and suspicion, the

103

extreme of which is found among the Dobuans. Where there is a distinction between the domestic, private realms but the former is dominated by the latter, surveillance is direct and more or less continuous. Accordingly, when there is room for private evasion of public scrutiny, as in Dobu or the Trobriands, there is a greater tendency for indirect surveillance and intrusion on privacy. In particular, wherever the private manages to resist public intrusion, witchcraft is likely: people may believe their sense of privacy to be at risk from the covert interference of those who are close to them but are excluded by that privacy, especially neighbors. Moreover, witchcraft as belief and practice can only operate in a society with a reasonably developed sense of privacy.

Although it is not my intention or wish to construct typologies, by setting up a loose category of "public" societies in which the dominance of the public over the private is the key point I have unwittingly moved toward a classification. The next obvious move is to consider the possibility of the reversal of priorities between public and private—that is, where the private dominates the public. In concrete terms, and in the context of the investigation into domesticated societies, this would ideally refer to societies in which the household is not only an independent production/consumption social unit but also where it is effectively sealed off from the attention of neighbors. Examples of such societies are found in many areas of the world studied by anthropologists, but I shall cite Mediterranean societies as representative.

Compared, say, to the Samoan house without walls, the house of a Greek mountain villager is "impregnable" (Du Boulay 1979:13), "surrounded by its own little oasis of semi-privacy" (p. 12), is a total unit whose "four walls . . . housed an exclusive group in which everything, down to the last chicken, was a full member" (p. 16), is "the chief stronghold of those values which are basic to that society" (p. 17), and is "solidly constructed [of] stone walls about 1 ft 6 in. thick" (p. 15). Though often not as solid and opaque, the Sarakatsani of the Zagori mountains in Greece live in a

> hut or house [that] is inviolable. No stranger may invade it without an invitation. Similarly, whatever takes place within the sanctuary of its walls is private and sacred to the members of the family. This understanding makes possible the warmth affection and easy intercourse of family life secluded from the public gaze. It is a sin, and a source of the greatest shame, if a man is

104

caught with his ear to the wall of his neighbour's house or hut. It is nevertheless true that people are insatiably curious about the details of domestic life
and relations in other families. [Campbell 1964:292–93]

Though the Spanish village is compact, the houses are solid and substantial. Those of Andalusia resemble a "fortified bunker," "a defensive
redoubt," and "each house turns inward.... Each ... contains an inner
sanctum, a charming patio decorated with fragrant flowers.... Here the
family enjoys nature in splendid seclusion and privacy. The façade of the
house, on the other hand, presents a blank, featureless anonymity to
the street." (Gilmore 1987:38). Elsewhere, in Ramosierra, for example, the
new houses are built of red brick, whereas the older ones serve as "dwelling, stable and barn combined" (Kenny 1966:11). And the same pattern
applies in Alcala (Pitt-Rivers 1961: esp. illustrations).

In circum-Mediterranean societies, both Islamic and Christian, the
house and the household are strongly identified with the female. In Spain
"women play a predominant part in the home, and on that account, in the
structure of neighbourly relations" (Pitt-Rivers 1961:112; Kenny 1966:
81). The relation is even stronger than this, for in many ways the male is
excluded from the house, although he is its head and its integrity is crucial
to his standing and reputation among neighbors. Thus Bourdieu writes of
the Kabyle of North Africa "that the house being the domain of women,
the men are to some degree excluded from it. The place of the man is out
of doors in the fields or in the assembly of other men. Men who remain
too much in the house during the daytime are suspect" (1966:222). Exactly the same sentiments are reported of the Greek villagers of Ambeli
(Du Boulay 1974: 124), of the urban poor in Cairo (Wikan 1980), of the
Sohari (Wikan 1982), and of numerous other Islamic societies (for example, Pathans [Barth 1965], Bedouin [Peters 1978: 322]).

This does not mean to say women are prisoners in the house: they leave
to work in the fields, to draw water from the village well, to shop. But the
house and its interior form a female preserve, and women are the significant *content* of the household, its most valuable feature. In these societies
the private domestic domain is physically as well as socially clearly
demarcated from the public domain, and this demarcation also segre-
gates the sexes. But while males frequent public places (cafes, bars, village
squares, and places of work), the hub of their public demeanor and interaction, its *subject matter*, is the privacy and integrity of the house and its

females. When out in public, among his public, a man must behave and act as a man; he must respond unflinchingly to insults: "It is highly significant that the more serious insults which can be directed at a man refer not to him at all but to a female member of his elementary family and in particular to his mother" (Pitt-Rivers 1961:115). That is to say, a man's public image, his manliness and honor, ultimately refer back and focus on *his private domain* and his readiness to uphold and defend the integrity of that privacy, to counter any attempt to invade it or cast doubt on it, to ensure that his household in its privacy conceals weakness, dissension, conflict, and infidelity. As Bourdieu writes of the Kabyle: "The principal aim is to conceal the whole domain of privacy. Internal dissensions failures and insufficiencies must on no account be displayed before a stranger to the group. The house is the first small world of secrecy" (1966:223).

Not only must the house never be displayed imperfectly, but it is the male's responsibility, the content of his honor, to ensure neither suspicion nor imputation is allowed to take hold, particularly among neighbors. The house and its inhabitants are, as Kenny remarks, held in sacred regard, and strangers, at least in Spain, are offered hospitality not in the home but in public. The private is dominant; it is what public concern is all about. If the house and its occupants are to be displayed, then it must be shown in its perfect state, as conforming to public ideals. Women must give every appearance of fidelity and chastity, and "whether or not they are so is another matter" (Du Boulay 1979:112). If ever neighbors and guests are invited to the house it must appear as "a cornucopia which is filled not just with fruits but with fruits of the family land" (ibid.:38). Du Boulay provides a brief anecdote which illustrates the embarrassment that can be caused when strangers come by surprise and the private household is caught unprepared. One old Greek villager could find no food to offer his guests: "He was distressed about this but when his wife came in and produced bread, cheese, olives, and wine, set out on a table with clean napkins, he said, 'Look, when the woman is here the house is a garden'" (ibid.:132).

This also brings out the complementary nature of the relations between the sexes where the male is proprietor of the house. Often he has built the house before marriage. But the woman is responsible for its integrity and for ensuring that if and when the veil is ever lifted on its privacy (as is the case with life-cycle rituals, for example) it appears in public as it pretends to be. Thus, as some writers have suggested, the woman in effect controls the private domestic domain and thereby exercises considerable, if not total, power over the male. It is *her* fidelity or chastity that must be preserved inviolate, so that she holds her man's honor in hand by the ever present possibility that she might decide to be unfaithful. By performing her domestic duties imperfectly, or even withholding her services, the woman has the power to reveal her husband's home to be other than what it should be. Thus are public values, actions, and performances concerned with protecting, undermining, and in general exploring the private domain. The private dominates the public, and the private is chiefly expressed, as well as defined, by the house and the activities particularly associated with the house. A person's honor is constituted by his or her ability to establish and defend a private domain of unquestioned integrity. And the most persistent threat to this honor and integrity comes from neighbors because they are in the best position to know or to speculate about what goes on next door, behind the front that faces the public world: "A neighbour who refuses to help without good reason, or who goes to a house to help and then gossips about what she sees there, is not acting properly. The fact that the latter is frequently done, and that a woman's closest neighbour is her closest observer and frequently abuses the fact does not weaken the value ideally placed on this relationship" (Du Boulay 1979: 216–17). It may not weaken the ideal of the neighborly relation, but it reveals the dynamic and stressful ambivalence, the tension that makes the relationship of the neighbor so central to domestic life. David Gilmore provides a vivid description of the relationship of neighbors in Andalusia that captures my point:

> Neighbors in a town play a surreptitious game of hide and seek. A game, but a deadly one. The world is divided between the street and the house. The street is public; there everyone knows your business. That is the point and the value of the street. And the house is private, a sealed world of dark secrets and mysteries, a woman's private sanctuary. Women must guard this secret realm from the prying eyes of a hostile and predatory world. . . . No one is safe from exposure. "The worst of all," [Nati] hissed, "are your neighbors." A secret battle is in progress in the streets and alleys, a wary warfare of words and looks. In this battle, neighbors are spies, traitors, Judases. [1987:7]

Wherever people live in communities of dwellings, ambiguous conditions of boundaries and walls must be met. At one extreme a culture insists that the separating and obscuring function of walls be minimized, that the public domain dominate and take precedence over the private domain. At the other extreme the privacy of the domestic domain is given priority over the public realm, and the integrity of the household is reinforced culturally. The house is more a social and moral bastion, a world within a (larger) world.

In what I have called public societies hospitality is a key activity to display the public unity of neighbors—the meals offered by a household to outsiders are to everyone in the community or, as in Java, to anyone passing by. But hospitality in private societies is more selective and serves to admit outsiders to a carefully planned glimpse of a household's privacy and resources, a display of its prowess and integrity, an exhibition of its success as an independent unit, and a source of pride for its members, particularly its head.

The honor of a man in so-called private societies depends on how well he can support the fidelity of his wife and mother and the chastity of his sister and daughter against the real and insinuated seductions of other men. But this sexual factor is only the pivotal one among many, all of which entail the house and the household. As we have seen, in the Greek village a man depends on his wife to provide hospitality at any time, to keep the house presentable, and so forth.

A wife's reputation and standing among her neighbors depends first on how well she keeps up the appearances of a well-managed household, for from such appearances may be deduced such less ascertainable factors as her sexual fidelity: "Thus evidence of infidelity is direct proof of a woman's worthlessness in all other fields, and, conversely, careless behaviour about the house and neglect of household duties are referred back to the basis of a woman's honour and cause aspersions to be cast on her chastity" (Du Boulay 1979:130–31). One would predict, then, that the most disgraceful thing that could happen to a woman would be to be caught committing adultery in her own home—this would be the worst insult to her husband's honor. And the most insulting thing a husband could do to shame his wife would be to have sexual relations with another woman in her (and his) home. In Spain, for example, "a husband's infidelity is only legally adultery *if it takes place in the home* or scandalously outside it" (Pitt-Rivers 1961:116, my emphasis). An even more interesting confirmation of this possibility is provided by Wikan's study of Sohari, in which she questions whether honor and shame are complementary and suggests that a man's reputation is made or broken among the large public of strangers whom he mingles with in the workplace and public cafes, while a woman's reputation is reflected by a small audience of intimates, her neighborhood friends (Wikan 1984). Wikan suggests also that "in the male world, females are interesting mainly in terms of their sexual trustworthiness, because this is where they so strongly affect the lives of men," but in the female world, "hospitality and a number of other qualities are highly relevant and have priority" (ibid.:645).

In the man's case it by no means follows that hospitality is irrelevant, because at some point the domestic world of the female and the public world of the male have to intersect. How else could a wife's sexual trustworthiness or otherwise ever have any factual foundation? Nor is female sexuality entirely marginal to the mutual concerns of women if questions of sexuality are brought close to home—that is, if neighbors might be affected by, perhaps, witnessing an act of infidelity or by being contaminated through eating in a house stained by irregular sexual liaisons. Although I agree with much of what Wikan has to say about the difference in the level of conceptualization of honor and shame, her test case shows the separation between male and female standards to be less complete than she suggests and indicates that sexuality, privacy, and the house are indissolubly linked. This case concerns a twenty-five-year-old Sohari woman, Sheikha, who was married and had two children but became a flagrant prostitute who "pursued her activities so blatantly that no one, except possibly her husband, could be in any doubt" (Wikan 1982:149). Extraordinarily, Sheikha was not censured in any way by her female neighbors, and the men, too, "treated Sheikha with politeness and respect" (Wikan 1984:643). Wikan gives as the reason for this the priority of hospitality over sexuality in the value systems of women, and it was true that with her earnings from prostitution Sheikha extended extremely lavish hospitality to her female neighbors. Before taking up her career in prostitution Sheikha's hospitality had been restrained, and this was blamed on her husband, "who was known to be stingy" (ibid.:644). The contrast between before and after was marked and furthered Sheikha's reputation. But since her previous reputation was low because of her husband's stinginess, it is likely that he had a poor standing with the other neighborhood women and possibly their husbands. We do not know whether this was so, but since men respected Sheikha, there was clearly a crossover of regard between men and women.

Wikan gives a brief account of Sheikha's behavior: "When her activities had reached an all time peak, she would take off most mornings at nine o'clock sharp, come back at noon, go out again at three o'clock and return around five. In defiance of public morality, she let herself be picked up and dropped off by car at the gate of her house, for everyone, save her husband, to see. Her times were carefully set to harmonise with his" (1982:143). I do not know what the normal practice of prostitutes is in Sohari and how far Sheikha conforms to or departs from the norm. I cannot say, then, whether prostitutes entertain their customers in their own rooms, visit their customers' quarters, or rent a "neutral" place. But it seems to me from Wikan's account that Sheikha went out of her way to convey to her neighbors that, whatever she was doing, she was not doing it *at home* or at her husband's home. Whatever the neighbors might suppose, they would not be able to see, and hence confirm for themselves. Although Sheikha's infidelities are a sad reflection on the marital bond, they cannot be said or shown to have violated the integrity of the house and the household (which included two children, whose whereabouts when their mother was off on business is not specified by Wikan). I doubt if even Sheikha's lavish hospitality paid for with her immoral earnings would have impressed her neighbors if she had engaged in prostitution in the home. In fact I doubt that they would have accepted an invitation from her to enter a house that would have been considered polluted and contaminating. After all, had they done so they could have been seen or thought of as prostitutes as well. I am sure their husbands would not then have been so polite or uninterfering. Sexual infidelity by itself does not undermine the honor of men and the respectability of women. Even in Spain a "girl's morals are not what they used to be," and throughout the Mediterranean men *away from home* are expected to have extramarital sexual relations (whereas women are not expected to be away from home). The context of infidelity and unchastity is what matters; specifically, the inviolability of the household is most seriously ruptured, for infidelity means that the very privacy of the home has been disturbed and thus that the household members' and especially the head's control of their own affairs and relations, has been eroded. Conversely, the effective maintenance of privacy is an ever-present measure of a household's authority and autonomy. Such a control is the means toward sustaining the productive and reproductive independence and integrity of private societies.

Marcel Mauss's *Essai sur le don: Forme archaïque de l'échange* was first published in 1925. One of its central and most influential points was that "social phenomena are not discrete; each phenomenon contains all the threads of which the social fabric is composed. In these *total* phenomena

. . . all kinds of institutions find simultaneous expression: religious, legal, moral and economic" (Mauss 1967:1). This is the root both of Polanyi's position that economic relations are submerged in social relations and of the revisionist Marxist position in anthropology that denies economics its orthodox infrastructural standing and claims instead that in precapitalist societies kinship relations are dominant. But if this is the case for archaic or traditional societies why begin from a position that conceptually isolates economics and then seeks to locate its submerged position? What Mauss and others after him are saying is that in primitive societies there is no such thing as economics (no economic institutions, no economic relationships, and so on). If we as Western scholars begin to speak of primitive economics, archaic forms of exchange, precapitalism, and domestic mode of production we are not, in fact, talking about anything substantive. Rather we are speaking metaphorically, we are speaking first of our own society, then about activities and pursuits that seem to be on a par or are analogous in other societies. The terms of the discussion are those of our own social system, not those of the societies under study. To avoid this situation we must first accept Mauss's finding not only as an observation about others but also as a premise from which any account and understanding of these other societies must start. We must ask first whether the totality of phenomena in archaic societies is a totality of the *same* phenomena as are found in our own society. There are no grounds for thinking this must be so a priori. Next we must ask whether the totality is a fact in which all phenomena have equal or different weighting.

Mauss's total phenomena in theory assigns no priority to any field of relations or activities; no infrastructure supports an ideological superstructure. Neo-Marxist thinking, by contrast, tends to substitute kinship relations (relations of reproduction) for economic relations (relations of production) as the infrastructure of precapitalist societies. But in so doing these neo-Marxists are pulling out the existential foundation of Marx's entire philosophy (not just his study of capital). For Marx, scholars daydreaming in their ivory towers can identify the human and separate it from the nonhuman by the presence of consciousness, religion, "or anything else you like." But real men in their real lives "begin to distinguish themselves from animals as soon as they begin to *produce* their means of subsistence" (1970:42). Reproduction, by contrast, is something all species undertake, so that kinship as a mode of reproduction will hardly do as a structure unique to human society.

I do not want to get mired in the demarcation dispute, so this is as far

111

as I will go. But the relevance of these arguments to the present chapter (indeed to the whole book) can easily be spelled out. At some point in actual time humans produced a built environment, and at the present time many people exist for whom architecture is the dominant as well as universal feature of their material and technical environment. That being so, and for no other reason, the living space occupied by people has imposed on them a general structure of public and private, and this structure interferes with the free flow of attention between people. Now attention may not be unique to human beings, but architectural interference with it is, so by living in a built environment people create for themselves, quite unknowingly, problems that affect functions of the senses vital and essential to the conduct of all other activities instrumental in survival, subsistence, and well-being. Whether kinship or economic relations are fundamental, once people become domesticated they must confront and are confronted with a structure arising, as Durkheim would say, sui generis, out of those conditions—the structure of relations between people as neighbors and as host and guest.

These statuses, or this structure, is put into motion, or realized, in the visiting between neighbors, and this visiting, the activation of the structure, is formalized in the development of hospitality. Hospitality makes demands on the material resources produced by people, and to the extent that it does so it could be argued that "hospitality and neighboring are economics" as much as "kinship is economics." Being a neighbor is an inevitable and significant feature of the lives of all people living in domesticated societies. How it is dovetailed into other features of existence no doubt varies in specific cases, and all I have attempted to do in this chapter is exemplify the argument with particular, somewhat extreme (though not necessarily atypical) examples.

I address a second, general theoretical issue in this chapter. At the risk of overgeneralizing, let me follow up Max Weber's contention that there is an "ethos" or a "spirit" of capitalism with the contention that there might be an "ethos" or a "spirit" of domesticated society. Or, rather, since I have drawn attention to only one facet of domesticated society, can it be shown that that aspect contributes salient characteristics to such an ethos?

Weber argued that what differentiated Western capitalism from other forms of capitalism was that it provided an ethos which in turn held up to its subscribers a preeminent motive for action. It was a moral duty, a calling to make an honest profit from one's labors: "One's duty in a calling is what

112

is most characteristic of the social ethic of capitalist culture, and is in a sense the fundamental basis of it" (Weber 1958:54). The spirit of archaic exchange societies, by contrast, is the moral duty to give, receive, and repay gifts. If there is a "calling" in such societies it is to become a renowned giver, a more than generous repayer and a gracious receiver. If under capitalism "acquisition is the ultimate purpose of [an individual's] life" (ibid.:53), then for the precapitalist, according to Mauss, disposal is the ultimate purpose. Capitalism was powered by economic rationalism (*zweckrational*) whereby profit could be realized by producing more at less cost. The problem for Mauss, investigating archaic societies, was to identify "the principle whereby the gift received has to be repaid. What force is there in the thing given which compels the recipient to make a return?" (1967:1). Mauss's answer closely resembles Locke's labor theory of value or, even more closely, Hegel's theory of property. Basing his argument on Maori ethnography, in which the gift is said to have a spirit, or *hau*, Mauss argues that in these archaic societies "to give something is to give a part of oneself. . . . one gives away what is in reality a part of one's nature and substance, while to receive something is to receive a part of someone's spiritual essence. To keep this thing is dangerous. . . . The thing given is not inert. It is alive and often personified, and strives to bring to its original clan and homeland some equivalent to take its place" (ibid.:10). The key ethnographic instance used by Mauss to portray and substantiate his general hypothesis was the Maori concept of hau. But Marshall Sahlins has argued that in Maori thought the hau does not denote the presence of a person in the gift he profers. Rather, argues Sahlins, the hau is best understood as the natural fecundity or fertility of anything, so that the moving spirit behind the gift, the source of the moral obligation to return it, is that "the benefits taken by man ought to be returned to their source, that it may be maintained as a source" (1974:168). However, the "real" or deeper compulsion is to be found in the argument that the "gift" is a rationalization of the threat of war: "The compulsion to reciprocate built into the *hau* responds to the repulsion of groups built into the society" (ibid.:174).

Part of the difficulty with swallowing either or both of these hypotheses is that many of the gifts are simply eaten (most gifts are food), are often destroyed, or are exchanged with apparently identical items, and the "natural increase or fecundity" is not evident. The exchange of goods as gifts is as often the cause of friction and fighting as it is a substitute for it. However, I do not wish to argue with the fundamental importance of organized gift exchanges or with their undoubted relation to war. I want to extrapolate from the present chapter an argument for expanding the Maussian thesis and shifting its emphasis.

The gifts that concern Mauss were rarely given impetuously, on the spur of the moment, but were handed over at a planned time, in a determined place, amid certain other activities such as the feeding and boarding of recipients. In other words, gift giving occurs chiefly (though not necessarily always) in the context of hospitality. Hospitality, as well as victualing, is the controlled exposure of the private in public. A controlled exposure is a display or exhibition. It is an indispensable feature of hospitality (and hence of gift giving) that the materials used are transformed so as to create and provide a display. Food offered in hospitality is not offered in its natural state but cooked and fittingly presented (food contributed as a levy is not so treated). Items presented as goods are not simply handed over with nonchalance; they are specially prepared as individual items and often pooled to form a composite spectacle: the *vay'gua* shells used in the kula are set out in arrangements, the pigs and pearl shells of the moka are not thrown together in a heap, nor are guests at a Maori or a Greek peasant meal given any old food presented in any old everyday way. For that matter, people do not present themselves to each other in their ordinary guise when they are offering gifts: they spruce themselves up and make themselves objects for exhibition and display.

It seems to me that what is being dramatized and expressed on these occasions of gift giving and hospitality is not only the obligation to give or to restore to its source the natural fecundity of produce and artifacts or to return a part of a person to himself but the calling to create and display something of beauty which can be admired (and for which one receives prestige in return). To varying degrees I think that domesticated societies are "governed" and domesticated people are "motivated" by a sense of "aesthetic duty." Beauty, especially but not only visual beauty, is the "added value" put into gifts, feasts, and displays. Sometimes the beauty is imparted simply as a calm patina of age, as in the kula valuables, or by the history of ownership enjoyed by an item. But mostly it is the artistic skill and loving care lavished on kula canoes, Samoan mats, New Guinea shells, and body decoration, on pots and ornaments of Neolithic cultures, and on the monumental structures erected by many domesticated societies.

While the aesthetics of primitive peoples may often be mentioned, the possibility that an aesthetic motive may pervade their lives and institutions has not been seriously entertained. One reason for this is because a frequent starting point for investigation has been the economic. We have always viewed other people's productive activities as being aimed in the same way as our own: to provide first and foremost for material needs, mainly eating. Hence, it is typical of the domestic mode of production that it is underproductive, meaning that "labor power is underused, technological means are not fully engaged, natural resources are left untapped" (Sahlins 1974:41).

Perhaps this is irrelevant. Perhaps different measures of proficiency count for far more. Malinowski writes of the Trobriander, for example, that "half the native's working life is spend in the garden" (1961:58). In fact, he goes on to say that they *overproduce*, growing about twice as much as they require and allowing the rest to rot. However, "Much time and labour is given up to aesthetic purposes, to making the gardens tidy, clean, cleared of all debris; to building fine solid fences. . . . There can be no doubt that the natives push their conscientiousness far beyond the limit of the purely necessary" (ibid.:58–59). What is more, most of the produce that rots does so because it has been left on display. Yams, the staple crop, are displayed in the gardens when they are dug up, in specially constructed galleries (Malinowski's storehouses) in the village, and whenever they are used for urigibu payments.

Who then may say that what Malinowski thinks is "purely necessary" is determined by the same criteria as the Trobriander thinks is the purely necessary? What may be necessary may be the aesthetic value of yams and gardens rather than, or in addition to, their subsistence value. Similarly, one might ask whether New Guinea Highlanders raise pigs for their productive value alone or for their aesthetic value. If the sole consideration in the giving of gifts was the redistribution of pork protein, why bother with all the fancy stuff? If Maori people were concerned only about the big feed they were going to get at the hakari, why bother to expend all that extra energy and resources on building gigantic structures on which to arrange and display the food? Or, to shift to the narrow domesticated setting of the Sohari prostitute Sheikha, the lavish hospitality she was able to extend to her neighbors had little or no utilitarian purpose or function. They were not going to improve their nutrition at her expense. Rather were they given an admirable show and the chance to put themselves on a show: Guests would arrive "cloaked in the all enveloping black *abba*," which after the greeting they shed to emerge as "gold-bespangled birds of paradise wearing colorful prints and gold jewelry, often to the value of $4000" (Wikan 1982:121).

5

The Surrealities of Power

Previously, the art of building corresponded to
the need to make power, divinity and might
manifest. . . . Architecture manifested might, the
Sovreign, God.

—Michel Foucault, *Power/Knowledge*

Bertrand Russell defined power as
"the production of intended effects" (in Lukes 1986:19). Steven Lukes,
discussing Russell's definition, as well as the definitions offered by many
other scholars, questions whether power lies in the actual *production* of
effects or in the *capacity* to produce them. He queries, then, whether power
is a fact or a potential. Lukes also questions whether intention is necessary
to the notion of power; presumably, bearing in mind the social philosophy
of Hayek and Popper, power may be produced unintentionally. For all the
criticism it draws forth, Russell's idea of power is provocative. It is not
meant to be, but it is ambiguous—or at least the notion of producing effects is ambiguous. Russell clearly means by effect a "result" or a "consequence" of material, measurable, observable or quantitative nature, and I
suspect that in the back of his mind his paradigm is mechanical or chemical power. But when used with regard to people, the term *effect* has a wider
range of application and reference. When people engage with one another,
"producing an intended effect" can mean, in addition to a noticeable physical effect, something less tangible but no less real: an impression. One
person can produce an effect on another person by acting in such a way as
to make an impression without necessarily accomplishing anything else.
To make an impression, or to have an effect on someone, insinuates that
power can reside in something less than the material and measurable. If
power is the production of (intended) effect by some persons on other
people, then producing an effect can be an end in itself, and we are carried

117

straight to possibilities of illusion, superficiality, insincerity, and deception. Furthermore, producing something intentionally for effect implies acting with a degree of exaggeration, acting flamboyantly, doing more than is necessary to achieve a designated purpose. Producing an intended effect, when applied to interpersonal engagement, can mean showing off. Russell did not mean showing off, but the ambiguity of his definition opens up a novel and appropriate line of inquiry that is particularly suited to an examination of power in domesticated society.

Showing off is a way of trying to convey to spectators one's capacity to produce a state of affairs without actually producing it, or of indicating a fact without revealing it, or of concealing a fact or state of affairs. Power as production of an intended effect, when given the meaning "to make an impression," can be extended to the successful fulfillment of deception, to the successful creation of an illusion, and, most important of all, to the conviction that one sort of effect (the impression) may be taken to be a reliable confirmation of another sort of an effect. In short, by producing something that makes a great impression it is possible to confirm the possession of the capacity to produce other, more material effects without actually having to do so. To reconcile Russell and Lukes, one would affirm that making a certain sort of impression identifies a capacity to produce as itself a product of power, without that capacity ever being put to the test. In this way, for example, a candidate, by making an impression, establishes a claim to power without ever demonstrating the power to lead. Lukes's separation of production and capacity is misguided because attainment of power may be made by producing evidence for a capacity. One can thereby show a capacity before it must be manifested. A threat could be sufficiently impressive that the resistance of others may be overcome, yet the threatening party need never demonstrate possession of the physical force implied in the threat. Much nonhuman primate aggression is like this. The threat "works," or power is gained through effect, because it persuades the spectator into a belief in the real, albeit unseen, existence of the power or force claimed: the production of surreal effects may be taken as evidence of the existence of real effects. The surrealities of power produce, or reinforce, *beliefs* in the realities of power without those realities having ever to be materialized. This process of power is, I suggest, particularly accurate and essential to understanding the operation and preoccupations of domesticated society.

But acknowledging power as an effect is not sufficient to understand power in domesticated society. A further suggestion comes from Hannah Arendt, who proposes that "power corresponds to the human ability not just to act but to act in concert" (in Lukes 1986:64). Whereas Russell's suggestion was concerned with power in general, Arendt means specifically the power of people vis-à-vis one another. Power is joint or group action; it is not a function, as it is for Russell, but a state of being—the unity of the group. Habermas criticizes Arendt for retreating to "the contract theory of natural law," which in turn reflects her reliance on the Greek world, especially the world of the polis, as the universal background for her thinking. Her approach, argues Habermas, cleanses politics of socioeconomic issues, relieves the state of administering social problems, and in general "leads to a conception of politics which, when applied to modern societies, leads to absurdities" (in ibid.:83). But Arendt's ideas about power may not be so absurd when applied to premodern or domesticated societies simply because in the thinking and practical way of life of domesticated people, what we moderns consider to be "economic issues" may simply not have existed or may have been entirely subordinate in policy and philosophy. Later I shall try to show how this might be so. The value of Arendt's notion is that it points to the grouping and unison of otherwise individual humans as a source of power, or to the organization of the many into the one. Before I explore the implications of this I do want to question another feature of Arendt's understanding of power. She writes: "When we say of somebody that he is 'in power' we actually refer to his being empowered by a certain number of people to act in their name. The moment the group, from which the power originated to begin with (*potestas in populo*, without a people there is no power), disappears, 'his power' also vanishes" (in ibid.:84). A prior, or at least a coeval, question to the act of empowering is: How does the group decide whom to empower? Some features of this decision must rest on acknowledging the qualifications of a candidate, and any such individual with qualifications has an effect on "the group" and in this sense has power. A candidate, whether he puts himself forward or is noticed from among the many is one whose capacity is viewed as a product, which in turn is indicative of a power, which, at the moment of election, can only be believed in. To some extent a person is "in power" or has power before being empowered by the group.

A second question concerns Arendt's assumption that a group or a number of people will come together spontaneously, that individuals will join with others of their own accord and then they will empower. This certainly does happen (and Arendt gives as an example French radical students). But individuals also form groups because they are brought together and organized. Once mobilized and organized it is true that a group may authorize and empower a leader, who may or may not be the founder, ancestor, or convener of the group. Be that as it may, the fact remains that the original convener of a group does, by that very attribute, possess power or, in the case of ancestors, is posthumously accredited with power. Rather than the group empowering the ancestor, the group attests the power of the ancestor, and this power is in turn frequently invoked to sanctify and authenticate the group. Arendt herself makes this point (in ibid.:68), but what she does not point out is that this ancestral or founding power resides initially in the past, which is no more, and so, ultimately, on belief and a metaphysical sense of power.

The acknowledgment by the group of the founder or ancestor is an act of faith practiced, in the present, as loyalty. This loyalty may often become so strong and total that it turns into adoration and worship. From this point of view the individual whose power is most complete and total is the individual whose candidacy for leadership is marked by the claim to be the founder—that is, the direct descendant of the ancestor. Hence the emphasis, in domestic societies, on a principle of leadership by descent. Even successful usurpers frequently try to establish their power by claiming descent from a founder or by proclaiming themselves founders.

This surreal sense of power is allied with realistic power as the control of force (with which I am not concerned), and with the observable, hence realistic, recognition of surreal power in the loyalty (and often sycophancy) paid by followers or group members to leaders or group representatives. The maintenance of loyalty is achieved through the leader's noticing of individuals, publishing that notice by bestowing titles, marks, emblems, and badges, and, in a more material sense, conferring rewards.

> The Emperor supervised even the lowest assignment, because the source of power was not the state or any institution, but most personally His Benevolent Highness. How important a rule that was! A special human bond, constrained by the rules of hierarchy, but a bond nevertheless, was born from this moment spent with the Emperor, when he announced the assignment and gave his

blessing, from which bond came the single principle by which His Majesty guided himself when raising people or casting them down: *The principle of loyalty.* [Kapuscinski 1984:31, emphasis added]

The successful candidate has an effect on the many that influences them to come together as one, if only initially to make a unified choice. The successful founder or ancestor has the effect on others of mobilizing them as a group, a unit. Loyalty of the many to the one is the minimal activity necessary for the continuity of the many as one (though individuals can, of course, vie with one another as to who is most loyal). Russell's idea of the central aspect of power and Arendt's notion of acting in concert are interwoven, and the resultant whole cloth provides a useful means by which to approach the understanding of ambitions and achievements exemplary of domesticated society.

In this chapter I want to argue that the domestic conception of power is realized and expressed principally in the development and elaboration of graves into monumental tombs and of houses into vast, grand palaces. In conceiving, initiating, and organizing the building of monuments, individuals employed the most effective means available for making an impression. At the same time, by mobilizing and organizing the vast number of individuals necessary for building such monuments, individuals created the largest group of the many acting as one. And in the product itself this process of unification, of creating unity out of many, was most dramatically exemplified. A temple, tomb, or palace is a singular, massive entity constructed out of a mass of minute, individual items. Ideologically, the tomb created the visible place where the power of the ancestor could reside and thence be appropriated by the claims of the candidate and, vice versa, where a present leader could simultaneously establish himself as an ancestor and thereby attain total power. In domesticated societies, tombs are not symbolic, or not only symbolic, standing for something else, they are a real and inseparable part of actuality. In a sense, monumental building was the principal means available to domesticated people for having and demonstrating power, and it was not until the intensive use of steam, dynamite, electricity, and atomic energy that people had access to greater sources and demonstrations of power.

On the basis of what has been said so far it is possible to argue that, at a critical point in its life cycle, power may correspond to the human ability to act in concert. At an earlier point in the life cycle power lies in the

121

agency by which that plurality of abilities is mobilized and organized, and at a subsequent point, power manifests itself in the individual empowered by the group. At the former, power becomes evident as an effect in the sense that the capacity or potential betrays its presence without showing itself as a production: the candidate who is selected (who represents the group, who speaks for the many) shows off. At the latter, the individual originally empowered by the group holds the group in his power by empowering individuals in return for their loyalty. But the demand for this loyalty is based on an appeal to the past, which is the initial condition of the founding, mobilizing, and organization of the group. This is the logic of power developed furthest in domestic societies; it is the logic of ancestors and divine kings. It is also the logic of a society in which the principal, and often only, way in which humankind could approximate the natural creative powers of the universe (or at least of nature), whether by imitation or for defense, and thereby consider itself to have power, was to mobilize the strength of individuals into construction gangs and organize them into a labor force. This possibility arose only when people settled in one place for a length of time; where the plurality of houses fused into the unity of the larger settlement; where the transcience of nomadic hunter/gatherers with their foreshortened view of existence was transformed into a settlement that persisted and was accompanied by the stretching of time so that life and death extend each to other as the house and the grave are the revolving points that form the circumference of material existence.

In the second part of this chapter I shall discuss a notable example of deconstructive power typical of domestic societies, namely witchcraft. Witchcraft is consistently associated with illness, bad luck, misfortune, or, in general, with the mysterious collapse of things, enterprises, and people. The mystery of these pervasive collapses is accounted for by the construction of a set of surreal beliefs or, rather, a set of beliefs about surrealities and a consequent set of practices that follow from those beliefs. The surrealities of power are, for the most part, operative on the underside of daily life, where they are the concern of ordinary people in their day-to-day efforts to achieve a balance of power among themselves.

Powerhouses

The construction of graves and the likely performance of burial rites did not originate with domestication; Neanderthal people interred their dead at Skhul in a flexed position along with the jaw of a wild boar as a burial object, and at Shanidar the corpse was buried in a grave that had been strewn with flowers (Shackley 1980; Solecki 1971). But the development of grave construction and mortuary rites and their universalization as a generally human practice did not occur until the Neolithic era—that is, as part of domestication.

Recent thinking about the Megalithic monuments of Atlantic Europe has recognized the close connection between tombs and houses. Ian Hodder argues that the long burial mounds "evoke symbolically the earlier and contemporary long-houses of Central Europe" (1984:59). Hodder claims an even more direct analogy between the tombs and houses for the Neolithic period at Skara Brae (ibid.).

It is characteristic, though not universal among them, that contemporary hunter/gatherers dispose of their dead in a relatively peremptory fashion. In his study of the death practices of four African hunter/gatherer societies, James Woodburn notes that beliefs tend to be "simple, unstructured and straightforward" (Hazda); "when you're dead, you're dead and that's the end of you" (Baka). "Grave sites are neither marked nor visited," and the Baka left their dead to be eaten by wild animals until the Bantu villagers taught them to inter corpses (Woodburn 1982:195). In general, among all four societies (Hadza, Baka, Mbuti, and !Kung), "the actual procedures for treatment of and disposal of the body are relatively simple and mundane. They go beyond, but not very far beyond, the directly practical requirements for getting rid of a rotting corpse" (ibid.:202). But even in those hunter/gatherer societies with a developed conception of an afterlife and where disposal of the dead is attended by ritual (societies such as the !Kung, the Australian aborigines, or the Andaman Islanders), grave or mortuary architecture has not developed. Compared with this absence of a mortuary architecture among open societies is its focal presence and elaboration in domesticated societies, where in different ways the grave and death are made the center and focus of life itself. However it is expressed, this relationship is conceived as a transition from temporary to permanent residence, and the grave or tomb is the eternal house. In Dobu the village is a union of house and grave:

> The ideal village of Dobu is a circle of huts facing inward to a central, often elevated mound, which is the village graveyard. . . . In the centre of the village a clear space lies open with only scattered brilliant leaved croton shrubs upon it. Here below the sod within their stone set circular enclosure lie the mothers

and mothers' brothers, the grandmothers on the distaff side and their brothers, and so, for many generations back, the ancestors of the village on the distaff side. [Fortune 1963:1]

Bloch and Parry point out how this organization of the village may be related to the nature of the dominant relations among Dobuans, the instability and hostility between affines: "All this however is only a problem of life, for at death one attains a permanent haven in the village mound where one is at last free from untrustworthy outsiders" (1982:29). In the rituals that follow a death, the conception of the grave as a permanent dwelling in contrast to the house as a temporary dwelling is emphasized by the destruction of the house. This also dramatizes the resolution of the instability between kin and affines, for the house is the "key symbol of the conjugal unit," whereas burial in the mound is the key symbol of the *susu*, the matrilineage. But the burial mound or tomb is not thought of as something other than a dwelling; it is the house rendered as near to permanence and perfection as is within Dobuan technical capabilities. The house, the architecture of domestication, is the key form and means through which domesticated societies can strive to evolve, the means toward the development and growth of power.

Not all domesticated societies have as elaborate an ancestor cult or funerary architecture as the Merina of Madagascar, but the Merina do represent an extreme expression of a widespread tendency among such societies. Tombs among the Merina are the most solid and best-built structures they undertake. Some are more elaborate than others, but all are costly: "The expenses involved in building a tomb are far and away the greatest enterprise a Merina ever undertakes" (Bloch 1971:113). The permanence and solidity of Merina tombs contrasts with the relatively temporary nature of their houses and villages, and the same logic justifies the expense involved: "Informants often told me it was normal to spend more money on a tomb than a house since they would stay very much longer in the tomb" (ibid.). The solidity and permanence of the tomb, like the monumentality and permanence of the Dobuan burial mound, represents the ultimate cohesion and permanence of the descent group in contrast to the "fluidity of Merina society and indeed of all the societies of the living" (ibid.:114). Bloch also suggests that the expense and ornamentation associated with the tomb is a form of conspicuous consumption associated with the competition for prestige. All tombs pretend to permanence, and a solid tomb is a minimum and universal requirement. Differences between tombs are most apparent in style, decoration, and workmanship, and these aesthetic differences—of good taste and of expense—provide Merina groups and their leaders the opportunity to gain prestige. The people who construct and maintain the tomb are the tomb group; the expression of their solidarity is the tomb, which at the same time represents the group. The fact of the tomb group as a group which actually assembles within confines and which has common interest in common property contrasts with the hypothetical ideal of the kinship group, which in fact is "a bilateral web of relatives which is not a group at all since it does nothing and owns nothing in common" (ibid.:121). The tomb, then, is the focus and purpose for the mobilization and organization of individuals as a labor force. This practical activity establishes or leads to the permanence that contrasts with the temporary nature of life and the fluidity of Merina society.

This same theme is expressed in a more directly political fashion through the building of mausoleums among the Berawan of Borneo. The traditional "great man" heads a longhouse community, and his position is signified in the chiefly apartment (Huntington and Metcalf 1979:134). A difficulty of traditional Berawan society was the tendency for individual households to go their own way, perhaps with one or two others, and thereby compromise the unity of the longhouse. In the past this unity was critical because warfare was endemic and survival was achieved by living in fortified longhouses whose unity relied on the effectiveness of the leader, or "great man" (ibid.:137). Longhouses often took some time to build because each household was responsible for its own apartment, so "what the new leader requires to cement his position is a demonstration of community solidarity behind him personally" (ibid.:138). This he accomplished by organizing people and materials to build mausoleums:

> Berawan mausoleums vary considerably in style. Some are single massive posts up to forty feet tall and four in diameter, with a small niche in the top to accommodate one small jar. Others have chambers varying in capacity from one to forty coffins or jars, supported six to thirty feet above the ground on one, two, four, five, six or nine posts, or sitting on the ground, or even underground. The aboveground styles are frequently elaborately decorated with fine incised carving in floral, abstract, and anthropomorphic designs, filigree buttresses and ridgepoles, all highlighted in red, white and black. Often they are decorated with expensive brassware or pottery. Invariably they are carved out

of dense hardwoods. Their construction requires *a considerable effort on the part of a community* with a simple, shifting agricultural system and little specialisation. [Ibid.:135–37, emphasis added]

The hopeful or incumbent leader mobilizes the considerable effort required and then organizes and rewards the labor. By this means he welds together the group, which in turn empowers him to be the "great man" by remaining under his wing in his longhouse. The mausoleum holds not the corpse of the leader but whichever relative of the leader happened to die at the right moment. By organizing the construction of a mausoleum, then, an individual is able to demonstrate the *capacity* for power without making it a production. An inert structure—the tomb in all its finery and a house of the dead—realizes and embodies that capacity. It is not a symbol but rather a sign, an index of the power that could otherwise be only supposed as a capacity. It is an earnest of success, an effect of power achieved by showing off and making an impression.

The contrast between the stable and the shifting, between the permanent and the temporary, is realized as tomb and house and seems to have been as characteristic of ancient Egypt as of these exemplary contemporary domestic societies. Edwards writes of the ancient Egyptian that "his house was built to last for only a limited number of years and could be renewed or replaced whenever necessary, but his tomb, which he called his "castle of eternity" was designed to last forever" (1947:36). To prevent spoliation of the grave and its destruction by the elements, a superstructure was built over it. These *mastabas* "were almost certainly close copies of the contemporary houses" (ibid.:38). With time these became stylized houses, retaining the outward form but being filled with solid rubble, while the substructure, the tomb proper, was expanded with halls, underground apartments, and storage rooms. Early mastabas were built of brick, but by the third and fourth dynasties stone was also in use. By the fifth dynasty, statues, carving, relief work, and painted decoration became standard. Mastabas were the tombs of officials as well as early kings.

Zoser's step pyramid seems to have evolved as a series of additions and modifications of what began as a mastaba. It was at the center of a complex of stone buildings and courtyards to service the afterlife of the king. It ended up a massive structure 204 feet high, with base measurements of 411 feet by 358 feet (ibid.:46). It was also equipped and decorated on an unprecedented scale (ibid.:64). Pyramids and funerary palaces proliferated, and some, such as the pyramid of Khufu, attained a volume of 95 million cubic feet. To sheer bulk must be added the artistic perfection and high standards of workmanship and craftsmanship achieved. To construct the Great Pyramid, which took twenty years, Edwards estimates that 100,000 men were levied annually just for the purpose of transporting the blocks of stone from quarry to site. About 4,000 permanent workers— skilled masons and laborers—lived in barracks on site and worked year round (ibid.:230). The building and equipping of funerary monuments probably represented the single largest industry throughout both the Old Kingdom, and, to a lesser extent, the Middle Kingdom. Kemp (1983:86) suggests that such construction work was the source of inspiration for technological innovation, improvements in craft and artistic skills, and the development of the organization and management of labor. And this administrative apparatus was aimed first and foremost at building a structure that was identified with "the pinnacle of the country's power structure: the king" (ibid.:87). It must be emphasized that no other motor power was employed in the transport of stone and in the construction of these gigantic structures than human muscle. Not even the pulley was available to the Egyptians. Such purely mechanical aids as ramps and sleds were used, but these do not generate power.

Such feats of organization and mobilization were not unique to Egypt. They were echoed throughout the premodern domesticated world wherever civilization evolved. Thus the Anu *ziggurat* at Warga, Mesopotamia, "could not have been achieved by less than 1,500 men working ten hours a day for five years" (Wheatley 1971:258); the two *dagobas* at Anuradhapura, Ceylon, each contained more than 20 million cubic feet of solid brickwork; the pyramid of the Sun at Teotihuacan, Mexico, is estimated to have absorbed the labor of 10,000 workmen over twenty years. It was not just that these men had to work and apply their skills—they had to be fed and looked after as well. The building of the great shrine of Ta Prohm in 1186 in what is now Cambodia required the enfeoffment of 79,365 people from 3,140 settlements. The provisioning of the shrine known as Pra Khan required contributions from 97,840 persons living in 5,324 settlements (Wheatley 1971:265). These enormous undertakings represent the zenith of achievement of domesticated societies, but remembering that all was focused on the tomb and the shrine, which were forms of the house, the only difference between the civilizations of Egypt, Java, Angkor, Mexico, India, Bali, and the local societies of Dobu, the Merina, and the Berawan is one of scale or degree, not kind. And the fundamental task and achievement of these societies was the mustering of labor in ever larger cohorts, together with its organization to produce an effect. To the extent that this was indeed the central concern, the main aim of warfare was to increase the population, especially its manpower, rather than to increase territorial domains. "The king who was a successful conqueror not only demonstrated that he was a true representative of the gods on earth but also gained sway over a large enough labour force to be able to translate his power into architectural symbolism of monumental proportions" (Keyes 1977:70).

Karl Wittfogel (1957:39) has argued that the construction of monumental palaces, shrines, and tombs was a consequence of and secondary to the mobilization and organization of labor for building the massive, utilitarian, and nonaesthetic hydraulic works characteristic of Oriental despotism. His materialist/realist approach leads him to assign priority and motive to the practicalities of irrigation and to relegate belief to a backup role:

> The position, fate and prestige of the secular masters of hydraulic society were closely interlinked with that of their divine protectors. Without exception, the political rulers were eager to confirm and bulwark their own legitimacy and majesty by underlining the greatness of their supernatural supporters. [Ibid:40]

While much labor in these ancient civilizations was undoubtedly coerced in the form of slavery, corvée, and capture, many regimes enjoyed long periods of stability during which it is fair to conclude the various emperors, pharaohs, divine kings, and monarchs were empowered by the people— that is, they were granted their position, and their claims and demands were considered legitimate. If, as Wittfogel says, hydraulic works tend to be unimpressive and purely functional, they are unlikely to appeal to the populace in the same way as the spectacular and beautiful monuments. In which case they will not present to their builders a sense of accomplishment and wonder that the erection of a splendid monument or tomb would. Their efforts on canals, ditches, and the like will seem pointless drudgery compared to the concentrated monumentality and aesthetic appeal of the temple that will emerge at the end of their labors. Such workers have something to see for their efforts, something beyond their capacity as individuals and which not only the organizing ability of their superiors has made possible, but also the vision of such grandeur from which such an enterprise was conceived by he to whom it is dedicated. In other words, the greater the monument, the richer and more beautiful it is, the easier it is for all involved in its construction to see something worthwhile for their efforts and to be suitably impressed by the vision it presents.

"But what distinguishes the worst architect from the best of bees is this, that the architect raises his structure in imagination before he erects it in reality" (Marx 1967:178). Marx himself notes the "colossal effects of simple cooperation are to be seen in the gigantic structures of the Ancient Asiatics, Egyptians, Etruscans etc." (ibid.:333) but considers this to be simply residual from the supplying of the expenses of civil and military establishments (ibid.). He also considers this cooperation a form of power developed gratuitously by capital. The capitalist, he argues, employs a number of laborers *as individuals*. He pays for individual labor powers, but having done this he can set them all to work together and thereby get the benefits of their *combined labor power*, which is something new and for which he does not pay. And it is precisely this combined labor power that makes possible such colossal productivity, the profit from which goes to the capitalist: "Because this power costs capital nothing, and because, on the other hand, the labourer himself does not develop it before his labour belongs to capital, it appears as a power with which capital is endowed by Nature—a productive power that is immanent in capital" (ibid.:333). Marx then makes an odd comment: "This power of Asiatic and Egyptian kings, Etruscan theocrats etc., has in modern society been *transferred* to the capitalist, whether he be an isolated, or as in joint stock companies, a collective capitalist" (ibid.:334). The cooperative power of labor, then, is *not* the unique preserve and product of capital, because it was created in pre-capital times. If the emperor did not have and use capital to bring labor together, what did he have? Referring literally to such leaders, the immediate answer is, as Wittfogel argues, organizational ability. But how could such application of ability be justified and made legitimate? To answer this takes us beyond emperors.

As soon as domestication becomes the condition for living of the human species, burial becomes a condition of death. And whereas houses shelter the living, graves and tombs shelter the dead. In contemporary domestic societies such as the Dobu, Berawan, Merina—any that have been mentioned in the preceding pages—housing the dead is analogous to but distinct from housing the living. Tombs may be more permanent, of larger proportions, or more elaborate than houses. The individual and/or the group achieves legitimacy and substance from its (or his/her) relation to the tomb by way of investment (of labor, direction, supply, and so forth). Those actions entailed in the construction of the tomb have a purpose that reaches beyond material construction. They aim to produce *the effect of permanence*. At the deepest metaphysical, spiritual level, tombs overcome death. If this is so, then the greater, more solid and monumental the tomb or mausoleum, the greater the effect of overcoming death, the more convincing and successful the effort would seem to be, the more probable it would appear to onlookers as well as perpetrators that death has been conquered. To appear to have achieved immortality is to appear to have overcome that which is unconquerable for human beings: death. It is the ultimate realization of *relational* power, the power of any "one" over an "other."

Tombs and shrines in prehistory and in ethnography are not only monumental; they often represent the peak of a culture's artistic and craft achievements. They are the impressive and visible evidence of the creative or *intentional* power to which human beings aspire. The monumental tomb, then, is the point at which the relational and intentional aspects of power fuse (see Ng 1980:50). The ultimate aim of relational power must be *permanence*—to be able to achieve a permanent, once and for all, utterly stable position of dominance over the greatest opposition. And the ultimate goal of intentional power, the power to create and produce, must be *perfection*. If the idea of power may be so divided, it follows that the total or unitary form of power is the perfection of permanence and the permanence of perfection. In domesticated society the idiom in which this quest could be expressed, or rather *performed* as a realistic task, was above all architecture. People in such societies visualized ultimates, transcendants, and metaphysicals as architecture. The walled garden was Paradise; the ideal city of Jerusalem was "symbolically represented by the Temple [of Solomon]" and became the source of the idea of a heavenly city (Manuel and Manuel 1979:38). The sheer ingenuity and skill of builders enabled them to construct edifices that were beyond the imagination, even the credulity, of the ordinary person, the laborer, and this "magic" served to confirm the supernatural ability, if not divinity, of the sponsor. If Angkor or the pyramids, Knossos or Borobadur, impress twentieth-century denizens of skyscrapers and proprietors of atomic energy, then how much more daunting their effect on the primitive and the peasant.

> [The dome of the Hagia Sophia] seems not to rest on solid construction but to hang by a golden chord from heaven to cover space . . . and this those who

have studied every part, and bent their brows over them all, fail to understand the art, but go away struck by what to sight is incomprehensible. . . . one understands that it is not by human power or art but by the influence of God that this work is fashioned. [Procopius, in Havelock 1978:96]

In return for their labor the people were provided with a spectacle, a sight, a creation that rivaled, if it did not outdo, natural landmarks. Monuments, quite simply, are designed to have an effect on the spectator, on generations of spectators, and their intent is usually successful. Such vast, substantial, and beautiful productions are beyond the capacity of the individual, and it might be claimed that the bonus of combined labor to which Marx refers is reciprocated by the bonus of inspiration, vision, and energy revealed or unleashed by the great man in his monumental tomb. If the combined power of labor appears endowed by nature, something beyond the simply human, then, too, the vast products, the monuments, of that power will appear as superhuman productions that point not to their builders but to some hidden power of the totality. The finished temple stands total and complete, drowning completely the millions of individual efforts and labors that constructed it, dissolving the infinite number of separate bricks and stones into a vast singularity. The pyramid or temple as single object is a visible, tangible existence, evidence that the sum is not only greater than, but different from, the parts. Like combined labor it represents an immanent power without visible, tangible origin. It may be claimed by or attributed to God, the emperor, the divine king, whose monument it is so often said to be.

Marx's surplus labor power arises as if from nothing, from the simple mechanical act of adding and mixing the labor power of individuals: mixing inert chemicals may produce an explosion; growth of natural things, of plants and animals occurs as a power without a source; movement, eruptions, and explosions are all features of the natural world whose cause is not apparent; and phenomena appear sometimes to be activated from a distance; unanticipated things like accidents happen. These seeming mysteries may exist to be explained, but they exist also to be appropriated. Marx's explanation of capital was his revelation that the mysterious value of surplus labor power and combined labor power had been appropriated by the capitalist. The forerunner of the capitalist was the builder of ancient monuments who also appropriated the power hinted at by the mysterious emergence of the monumental whole from its insignificant parts.

Once established, the monument exerts an effect on those associated with it, as builders, officiants, congregation, or plain onlookers. In this way the "power" embodied in the monument is felt as a living force within the individual. This same process is expressed and captured in the spectacular rituals and dramatizations of everyday behavior which are notable features of those pinnacles of domesticated society, the divine kingdoms and court societies that gave life to the corridors and courtyards of their monumental palaces and shrines.

Life within the confines of the palace in particular was a continuous show in which every act, word, and movement had effect as its primary object. In nineteenth-century Balinese kingdoms the king and his court were the "still point of the turning world," the "exemplary center" whose immobility was the embodiment of a living permanence on view to all. The king "sat for long hours at a stretch in a strictly formal pose, his face blank, eyes blanker, stirring when he had to with a slow formality of balletic grace. . . . the King was the Great Imperturbable . . . an icon . . . [depicting] the equanimous beauty of divinity" (Geertz 1980:130). For Geertz the nineteenth-century Balinese polity was a "theatre state," and the greatest performances were the mortuary rituals. These "stupendous cremations, tooth filings, temple dedications, pilgrimages and blood sacrifices, mobilising hundreds, even thousands of people and great quantities of wealth, were not means to political ends: they were ends themselves, they were what the state was for" (ibid.:13). Balinese peasants, says Geertz, were stagehands in an endless pageant. But is Geertz accurate in describing such displays as theater? Did the participants think they were acting, or did they think that what they were doing was for real and believed in it? Huntington and Metcalf suggest, following Geertz, that the "ceremony is also assessed in terms of its impact as drama" (1979:131). What all this was for was to achieve an effect, to move people by exposing them to *the real thing* (that is, the Balinese conception of the real thing). The Balinese mortuary ritual, the ancient Egyptian burial, the mass human sacrifices of the Aztecs were the real thing: *power made visible,* the mystery solved, people moved to awe and wonder, not by a distant and impersonal nature but by the abilities and efforts of their human masters.

It is not simply the performance of the spectacle that counts, it is also that the spectacle as a thing in itself, in addition to whatever it is supposed to represent, *moves* people. It is a nonrational (but not irrational) method of influencing, changing, or moving people, of arousing their emotions, feelings, and thoughts. Such displays, performances, and monuments *have*

132

power, they do not just represent or portray it. They are signs, not symbols, and they do things to people like astonish them, fire them up, make them sad, or make them feel good. The medieval pageants of the French monarch and of the Elizabethan English court, like the Oriental mortuary rituals, aimed to move people and by so exercising *surreal* power to signpost the real power required to run a state, to rule people with legitimacy (that is, with their consent).

> Bayonne was designed to project the French monarchy internationally as rich and splendid not only in financial but also in cultural terms. The four great fêtes were not given this time by private individuals, but were the result of prodigal government spending to ensure a series of events which would astonish the onlookers, as each eclipsed the other in a mounting crescendo of invention and ostentation. [Strong 1984:106]

"Magnificence thus became a princely virtue. A prince must be seen to live magnificently, to dress splendidly, to furnish his palaces richly, to build sumptuously" (ibid.:22). Strong suggests that the authenticity and effectiveness of the Renaissance court festival "stemmed from a philosophy which believed that truth could be apprehended in images. . . . Fêtes speak to the visual sense in a lost vocabulary of strange attributes which we can no longer easily read" (ibid.).

Interestingly, this appraisal reverses an increasingly influential explanation of the efficacy of otherwise mysterious processes. Strong here likens acts and images to words and language: Renaissance people would have understood what they *saw* in much the same way that we understand what we *hear*. Philosophers of language, notably Charles L. Stevenson (1944) and J. L. Austin (1962), have pointed out that words may serve as acts and deeds. Stevenson noted that some words, or some uses of words, are emotive and have a certain force, particularly of persuasion; the use of such words adds nothing to the meaning of a sentence but does convey feeling and emotion. Primitive examples are such interjections as "alas," "ouch," "hurrah," or "wow"—these words vent emotions (Stevenson 1944:38). More subtle and complex is the use of words to persuade. Stevenson gives the following example:

> A. It is morally wrong for you to disobey him.
> B. That is precisely what I have been denying.
> C. But it is your simple *duty* to obey. You ought to obey him in the sheer interest of moral obligation.

Here there is a reiteration of ethical terms. "Duty," "ought," and "moral obligation" do not provide any additional information beyond that given by the initial "wrong" (so long as the first pattern is presupposed), but with proper emphasis they may have a strong cumulative effect on B's attitudes. [Ibid.:141]

Austin's "performative utterances" or "illocutionary acts" (1962) are words that perform deeds. Simple examples are when a priest "pronounces" a couple husband and wife; when the monarch "dubs" a knight; when a dignitary "names" this ship the *Mary Jane*. As distinct from Stevenson's persuasives, these speech acts declare something to have been accomplished by the utterance of the words. Strong is saying that acts "speak"; Stevenson and Austin claim that words "act." Words and deeds can be, or are believed by some to be, other than what they are at the same time as they are what they seem. Acts can convey meaning, they can point to a hidden inner essence or source; words can create, can conjure something of nothing. Acts, icons, and words, when presented in a certain way, provide, as it were, the circumstantial evidence for the existence of an invisible potency.

Roy Rappaport, in a brilliant paper, "The Obvious Aspects of Ritual," has developed Austin's notions along with ideas of his own to provide a most useful and convincing explication of ritual. Among the necessary conditions of ritual that enable it to bring envisaged states of affairs and entities into existence are formality, invariance, repetition, permanence, conformity to an established order, and unison. These are not themselves the substance of ritual, what people do; rather they are properties that constitute the method or the receipt for doing something with the substance; for example, specific words or acts that gain their ritual status and efficacy by being *repeated*, by being repeated in a *formal* manner, and in *unison*, and so forth. These conditions of ritual in particular signify that "ritual performance is not in itself merely, nor even necessarily, factitive. It is not always performative in a simple way, bringing into being conventional states of affairs through conventional actions. It is, rather, *meta*-performative and *meta*-factitive, for it *establishes*, that is, it stipulates and accepts, the conventions in respect to which conventional states of affairs are defined and realized" (Rappaport 1979:194). By applying the same metaphysical procedures of repetition, formality, unison, precision, invariance, and conformity, the architecture of the house, and the house of the dead in particular, postulates the power beyond it but which brought it into existence, while the solidity and material permanence embodies that sense of power so as to convince the spectator of its actuality. In a sense, architecture, especially funerary architecture, is ritual materialized and petrified. The tomb is that shaded area that marks the overlap of surreal and real power.

So, massive, expensive tombs and monuments, superfluous to the business of daily living, so bizarre from a utilitarian point of view as to appear surreal, are as near as mortals can get to incarnating absolute real power. Their building and existence testifies to and legitimizes the right of some people to be empowered by others so that they may assume all power, divine power. But what of the power, not of the people, but among the people?

Of Powers That Be

Although the difference may not be absolute, it is notable that most hunter/gatherer societies do not seem to attach much importance or significance to witchcraft and sorcery, whereas among domesticated societies it is fair to say that beliefs in magic, sorcery, and witchcraft are often central to epistemology and ontology. Such beliefs are universally important in the theory of illness and in the practice of medicine. Hunters and gatherers fall ill as often as sedentarists, so this apparent difference in beliefs is hardly owing to the relative presence or absence of illness! May the development of the complex of beliefs and practices subsumed as witchcraft (that is, including magic and sorcery) be correlatively, if not causally, associated with the adoption of sedentism and the domestic life? I admit that putting such a proposition forward as having historical validity—as being a feature of social evolution—falls afoul of the pitfalls of the ethnographic analogy, but I believe the questions it opens up are too interesting to shy away from.

Writing of the Hadza, James Woodburn says that traditionally they "believe in witchcraft and sorcery but they do not believe that other Hadza (except those who are very closely associated with members of neighbouring pastoral and agricultural tribes) are capable of practising them" (1982:192–93). The parenthetical phrase is important because it suggests that Hadza beliefs and practices in these matters were influenced by their domesticated neighbors. A similar situation is suggested by Turnbull (1962: 45, 89) in his account of Mbuti beliefs and practices concerning witchcraft. Service (1966) in a textbook on hunters, now out of date in many respects, has no entry under witchcraft but refers the reader to shamanism. However, shamanism and witchcraft represent radically different approaches to

135

problems and cannot be considered equivalents or as interchangeable, as Service implies.

In a footnote to his remarks on Hadza witchcraft, Woodburn has this to say:

> In the government settlement schemes of today, witchcraft fears are rampant and people fear both non-Hadza and now, increasingly, other *Hadza*, who are said to have learnt witchcraft from non-Hadza and to be using it against their fellow Hadza. This change in belief has happened during a period in which there has been a great deal of genuine ill health and many deaths in the settlements and in which it has become more difficult for Hadza to move away from those with whom they are in conflict without sacrificing vital interests. [1982:208–9]

Whatever other factors might be involved, a connection between sedentism and witchcraft is clearly implied, with the suggestion that this happened because illness and death increase with settlement. Hygiene, poor sanitation, property and stealing, unequal and unsatisfactory work opportunities, and incomes and alcohol are usually the realistic features of settlement singled out to blame for illness, hostility, and witchcraft. But this does not explain why witchcraft beliefs (and practices), which have epistemological implications of a particular nature, become so apparently appropriate whenever people become domesticated. Witchcraft, though it is believed in and considered efficacious, is nevertheless a surreal phenomenon. The illnesses it may cause may well be physical and real, but witchcraft operates metaphysically and magically. The distribution of witchcraft, witches, and witchfinders is a reflection or refraction of the locus, distribution, and balance of powers in a community, because it is a prime changer of states, a significant instrument in causation. People and events are altered (usually for the worse) by witchcraft. Magic, regarded by some as the accomplice of witchcraft, by others as the same thing, can be the means by which changes (or effects) may be made for good and advantage as well as for worse and disadvantage. Witchcraft, sorcery, and magic are absent or underplayed in hunter/gatherer societies. Such people are not devoid of belief or of practice that goes beyond the immediate and real. Shamanism, or trance possession, is widespread among the such people, and it retains its presence and influence among domesticated people as well.

The critical difference between shamanism and witchcraft, both of which have dealings with the supernatural, is that the shaman, or the patient whose illness originates in possession, is the agent (or the victim) of a spirit—of the dead, of nature, of the above or the below. But witchcraft is something that operates *between people*. It may enlist the aid of supernatural entities like spirits through the agency of magic, but these spirits act not on their own but only at the bidding of the witch or magician. One who is possessed is "taken over" by another, by the spirit, but one who has been bewitched is *invaded by another person* who has withdrawn after the successful invasion. The witch may have enlisted spirits and magical agents to act on his or her behalf, and diviners often profess to "find" and "extract" the witchcraft substance from the victim, but the ultimate cause is always not the spirit or substance but another person, the witch.

Witchcraft can be said to be, or to say something about, the relations between people: accuser and accused are in a state of witchcraft relationship. Whatever the relation between two people, if they come to stand as accused and accuser of witchcraft that relation takes on a new and more complicated complexion. Shamanism, by contrast, implies a deflection of relations from the person to the suprapersonal. An illness brought on by, or attributed to, possession by spirits is a problem, or a change of state, the cause of which is shunted from other people. As a diagnostician, the shaman is one who stands above and beyond others and whose insight enables him or her to "see" the world and other people more clearly. Shamanism is not intrinsic to or constitutive of the relations among people, whereas witchcraft is.

It is possible to insert a category between shamanism and witchcraft as sources of powers that have an effect, especially on people. Ancestral spirits, or spirits of the dead, are widely believed in by domesticated people. They, like the spirits of place, may act of their own accord, but usually for a reason: they have been upset or offended by a failure on the part of their descendants, the living, to respect them, fulfill obligations toward them and to observe *taboos*. To redress the upset balance an expiatory ritual is carried out; to ensure the continued exercise of ancestral spiritual power on people's behalf propitiatory rituals are performed. Although individual members of a community are implicated directly in illnesses and misfortunes attributed to ancestral spirits, particularly by their failure to observe taboos, the state of relations between people is not involved; a new component to interpersonal relations is not added.

Illness, misfortunes, mishaps, good luck, surprises, and so forth are among the most frequent and prevalent manifestations of the presence of a power that has an observable, tangible effect on people. When these are

137

attributed to witchcraft then the distribution of power among people is at issue, and we are concerned not so much with the sovereignty of power as with the tactics of domination; with power as "something which circulates, or rather as something which only functions in the form of a chain." Individuals "are always in the position of simultaneously undergoing and exercising this power. They are not only its inert or consenting target; they are always also the elements of its articulation. In other words individuals are the vehicles of power, not its point of application" (Foucault 1980:98).

The classic description and analysis of witchcraft is Evans-Pritchard's account of witchcraft, oracles, and magic among the Azande. As Mary Douglas observes, this was "first and foremost . . . a book about the sociology of knowledge" (1970:xiv). It has become the inspiration for many philosophical discussions of rationality (see Winch 1958; Wilson 1971), but I want here to take up and develop an aspect of witchcraft implied by Evans-Pritchard but left undeveloped. In chapter 4, Evans-Pritchard illustrates Zande thinking about witchcraft through a number of examples. The most famous of these is the example of the granary collapsing on people, but I wish to cite another:

> One of my chief informants, Kisanga, was a skilled wood-carver, one of the finest carvers in the whole kingdom of Gbudwe. Occasionally bowls and stools which he carved split during the work, as one may well imagine in such a climate. Though the hardest woods be selected they sometimes split in process of carving or on completion of the utensil even if the craftsman is careful and well acquainted with the technical rules of his craft. When this happened to the bowls and stools of this particular craftsman *he attributed the misfortune to witchcraft and used to harangue me about the spite and jealousy of his neighbours.* When I used to reply that I thought he was mistaken and that people were well disposed towards him he used to hold the split bowl or stool towards me as concrete evidence of his assertions. If people were not bewitching his work, how would I account for that? [1937:66–67, my emphasis]

Kisanga's superior skill and success are exceptional and therefore mark him from others. He could be said to have either a special power or an extra ration of power, or he could be thought to have access to powers that others do not have. In any case, he believes that his success makes *his neighbours* jealous and that they bewitch him or his pots, an action that has the effect of neutralizing his superiority or good luck.

In fact, all accusations of witchcraft among the Azande take place between neighbors and not between kin, strangers, or people of different rank. It should be noted, though, that there is some evidence that kin may

sometimes be neighbors, for another student of the Azande, Conrad Reining, writes, "My informants told me that there had been no rules as to
where a man would settle but that usually some of the sons of the household would make their homes nearby" (1966:99).

Neighbors among the Azande like to live in well-separated homesteads
(Evans-Pritchard 1937:37), but they also like to spend a lot of time in one
anothers' company, and there is considerable visiting between homesteads. Furthermore, there is considerable borrowing and lending, as well
as mutual assistance in gardening and the like (ibid.:109–11). Correspondingly, there are well-articulated and understood rules of hospitality
and reciprocity between neighbors (ibid.:116–17). Economic reciprocity
"was of paramount importance in the political and jural organisation of
Azande society" (Singer and Street 1972:9), and both within and between
households a precise account was kept of who owed what to whom
(ibid.:102).

The principal context of witchcraft accusations was precisely this field of
relations between neighbors, a field that encompasses hospitality above all
but includes cooperation in building, gardening, borrowing, and lending
and mutual sensitivity to privacy and to feelings. Witchcraft accusations
came when people perceived their neighbors to be in some way remiss and
delinquent toward their obligations to entertain, to loan, to respect; and
accusations occurred when people seemed to be taking advantage, to be
borrowing more than they loaned, to visit more than they were visited.
Such importunity causes strain because it is hard to refuse a request for a
loan, and an inveterate borrower or visitor puts the pressure on and seems
to be exerting a power over the other person, forcing him or her either to
break the code of reciprocity or to conform to it feeling hard done by,
seeing the situation as unjust. In a social climate of equality, such as pre-
vails among Azande commoners, imbalance between people, exceptional
talents and achievements, appear contrary to the ideal. Kisanga, the tal-
ented carver, felt that his neighbors were jealous of him; how else could
they perceive his success? Given that all Azande commoners were equal
and were supposed to share equal access to resources, the exceptional success of individuals, even if based on a natural endowment, is likely to be
seen as the result of that person's access to hidden powers, which, in turn,
have to be countered by the controlled and directed operation of equally
covert powers, such as witchcraft.

Explanations of witchcraft locate its occurrence in situations of stress and hostility where the identification of the enemy is uncertain or un-known and where the exact reason for the stress is unrecognized. The in-spiration for accusations of witchcraft is said to be envy, jealousy, suspi-cion. Both Evans-Pritchard (1937) and Clyde Kluckhohn (1944), whose analysis of Navajo witchcraft has been equally influential on subsequent studies, agree on the role of such emotions. But such emotions, though they may be objectively irrational, do not spring forth without their own reason: emotions are set going by a trigger, and, being intentional, they take an object. Whatever sets emotions going has, ipso facto, some sort of power, and I want to suggest that whenever witchcraft is suspected of op-erating it is in response to the supposition that cognate powers have been harnessed covertly to secure an apparent advantage. Witchcraft as a social phenomenon is a pivotal feature of noninstitutionalized justice whose area of reference is the domesticated community. It is not simply that people living as neighbors, thence as community equals, appear at certain times or occasions to enjoy privileges, benefits, and successes but that given the ideal equality of everyone, the only way this could have happened is that these people must have come by their success through secret or covert means, and that is *unfair* and *unjust*. The only way to combat such "cheat-ing" is to deploy equally powerful and covert counters. Or, if someone appears to be failing and falling by the wayside when they live in a context of idealized equality such as an ethic of neighborliness, they are the victims of malignant but covert powers that can only be countered by exposure and equally potent powers.

Whereas it was claimed that accusations of witchcraft among the Azande take place between neighbors, and not between kin, Kluckhohn says that accusations of witchcraft among the Navaho take place among kin and not between neighbors. However, just as there is some reason to suppose that Zande neighbors may sometimes be kin, so among the Na-vaho it turns out that kin are also neighbors. The basic unit of living is the "consumption group," which comprises between two and six households and is composed of "a group of Navahos related by blood and marriage, who live most of the time within easy walking distance of one another and who habitually cooperate in many economic activities" (Kluckhohn 1944:238, n. 24). Consumption groups, which sound more like hamlets, are likely to be from one to ten miles apart (ibid.:93), and Kluckhohn maintains that people are thrown in upon one another, especially in win-ter. They get too close, get on one anothers' nerves, and lack the chance to let off steam about grudges, suspicions, and jealousies to outsiders (ibid.). In short, neighbors, just by being themselves, seem to have an effect on one another, and when the effect is felt, when someone's emotions are triggered into suspicion, envy, or frustration, they feel as if a hidden power is at work on them and in them. Among the Navaho a woman moves to live with her husband's kin, and especially in the winter she cannot get away, so "under these conditions her antagonisms against her in-laws mount, and one way in which she can discharge them in a socially approved manner is by murmuring to her own folk that her father-in-law seems to be a witch" (ibid.:100). A woman residing among her in-laws lives under constant and critical scrutiny, a situation that is not only difficult but, from the daughter-in-law's point of view, manifestly unfair and unjust. Accusations of witchcraft help to redress the balance and to restore justice.

Remember that witchcraft is said to be one of the principal causes of illness in those societies where it is recognized. This means, then, that the responsibility for causing illness is imputed to other people, specifically one's neighbors. And so, too, the cure for such illness begins with diagnosis and identification, through divination, of witchcraft and the witch, and ends in treatment and/or punishment. The control of illness (and health) in domesticated societies is vested in and distributed among members of the community. There is nothing new, then, in Foucault's identification of medicine as politics and power, and neither is such control unique to our own capitalist society of experts. The main difference between domesticated societies and industrial societies is that control over illness and health becomes organized in the latter, whereas in the former it remains diffused and unself-conscious. It remains at the level of "subjects in their mutual relations . . . [as one of] the multiple forms of subjugation that have a place and function within the social organism" (Foucault, in Lukes 1986:232).

In the exemplary societies of the Azande and the Navaho, people of the same rank live together as neighbors. Zande princes live apart in their courts, and under such conditions they do not employ witchcraft against their low-ranking subjects, although they may use it among themselves. However, in societies where the chief lives as a neighbor among subjects and followers, he may claim and flaunt a power of magic and an ability as a sorcerer. As Anthony Forge says of New Guinea, "a reputation for being concerned in sorcery marks a man as one to be treated with caution, even respect" (1970:258). In the Trobriands, "the chief has the best sorcerers of the district always at his beck and call. . . . He can do this openly, so that everybody, and the victim himself knows that a sorcerer is after him" (Malinowski 1922:64). In fact, when someone dies the chief may strut about the village claiming responsibility for the death by sorcery, thereby strengthening his claims to power over his subjects. Moving from Melanesia to those societies of Africa where the chief lives as neighbor, a vital aid to his power and position is his publicly avowed and acknowledged claim to exercise magic as witchcraft. The function of mystical power is to maintain dominance, and a "chief must, above all, guard the reputation of his mystical powers" (Goody 1970:233).

A similar, though more complex, situation appears to have existed among the Cewa of central Africa. Sorcery occurs within the village, which consists of a number of separate matrilineal kinship units, which may or may not be connected by kinship ties. Each village has a headman, as does each matrilineal section. Accusations of sorcery may occur between matrilineal segment leaders as a means of discrediting rivals or as part of their bid for overall headmanship of the matrilineage (and the village), or they may occur between segment leaders as part of the process of lineage disintegration (Marwick 1963, in Middleton 1967:113). Sorcery does not seem to be a factor in the power relations between the chief and his subjects—that is, between those of unequal ranks who do not live as neighbors.

Among the Cewa, as in other societies, accusations of sorcery arise in response to the discovery or manifestation of an illness, a misfortune, or a death, usually because there is no other obvious explanation. To imply sorcery or witchcraft, then, is to imply that another person—a neighbor—has managed to perform an activity prejudicial to a fellow neighbor without ever being observed—that is, in the privacy of the home and/or under cover of darkness. Illness and misfortune are, among other things, proof of the occurrence of conspiratorial, deceitful, and malicious behavior perpetrated by people to whom one is close but from whom one is partially shut off by the privacy of the household. Since illness and misfortune are likely to strike anyone at any time, they are pointers to a constant, and often unpredictable, erratic circulation of power—namely, of the power to have a drastic effect on the well-being and survival of people. It is often in the interest of a neighbor to become known as a successful witch because this will cause fellow neighbors to treat him or her with awe. They are afraid of not only the ability to cause illness or misfortune but the ability to do so *without being observed, without giving warning.* Even more frightening is the witch's ability to penetrate the privacy of his or her neighbors. To cause another person to fall ill is evidence of an ability to get inside the other person, to invade not just the privacy of another's house but also the privacy of the body itself. In a similar way, the individual who seems to be extra successful, to be better than neighbors in performing certain skills or in achieving better results, is someone who seems unnaturally advantaged.

One explanation for the occurrence of witchcraft under the conditions in which it is found is provided by Max Gluckman, whose position is closely akin to that argued by George Foster in attempting to explain the evil eye. Witchcraft and the evil eye are thought by many to be the same thing, and it does not come amiss to lump the two arguments together. Foster suggests that peasant communities live in a finite world and they know it. Anyone who looks to be getting ahead can only be doing so at the expense of fellow villagers, so they react because they share an "image of limited good." Accusations of witchcraft or the evil eye serve as a leveling device in such a situation (Foster 1965, 1972). Gluckman observes that in small, face-to-face communities of tribal society, the *locus classicus* for witchcraft, subsistence is stationary, and everyone enjoys pretty much the same living standards. It follows then that "exceptional achievement is bought at the cost of one's fellows. The man who is too successful is suspected of being a witch and himself is suspicious of the witchcraft of his envious fellows" (Gluckman 1955:96). But if the community is that small and face-to-face, and if everyone knows resources are finite, the puzzle is not just that one has appeared to get ahead at the expense of the others but that he or she has done so *in spite of there being face-to-face relations—* that is in spite of everyone being able to keep an eye on everyone else. The *means* used to secure such an advantage are perhaps even more upsetting than the end achieved, because they indicate *unfairness* and *secrecy.*

In as much as witchcraft employs medicines and magic, and in as much as it is successful, witches (and sorcerers) have control over the instruments of power. These instruments are, it turns out, specific: their modus operandi is to penetrate surreptitiously, to infiltrate the barriers of the house and the body, and to assume control of the interior. Witchcraft magic is often borne on smoke or along a magical beam that emanates from an implement pointed at the victim; medicines are smuggled into the victim by mixing them with the victim's inner substances—mucus, hair, sweat, urine, feces; piercing implements, such as claws, roots, pointed sticks, and

143

blades, are the vehicles that bear witchcraft into the victim. A witch, says Mary Douglas (1973:139), is someone whose inside is corrupt; he or she works harm on victims by attacking their pure, innocent insides. Witches use or disguise themselves as animals that sidle and sneak unnoticed in and out: "There were those which saw a weavil runne from her [the witch's] houseward into his yard even a little before he felle sicke" (Mac-farlane 1970:91, of witchcraft in medieval Essex). Witches are those who see through and behind where ordinary vision is blocked; they attempt to experience the "numinous world of non-ordinary reality" (Baroja 1964: 13). Witches are imagined, variously, as involving reversal, inversion, interiors, backsides, opposites, contrariety, and as Needham (1978) suggests, witchcraft is everywhere to some extent predicated on the existence of a hidden, occult side of all forms and appearances.

Witchcraft certainly arises where there is strain and conflict in interpersonal relations, in situations that engender envy, jealousy and suspicion. Individuals are likely to find themselves under such strains in several conditions, and being placed in rival kinship positions in relation to office and property is undoubtedly common. Whatever else may generate witchcraft, its particular form and intention, endeavoring by occult means to get behind and inside people, is consonant with the elementary form of domesticated life: the creation of the household as a private space separate from but bordering on similar households. The unity of a settlement as a physical entity implies a social harmony, but the separation of households implies a separation of interests and some degree of independence of those who would be as one community. To some extent witchcraft is a response to the intensification of mystery, particularly of another person's will and intention, which is brought on by domestication. The stereotypical witch is often the person who feels left out and who gives the appearance of trying to break back in. The Zande who comes too often as guest and welcomes too seldom as host; the medieval widow or old man who borrows incessantly and who has little to lend in return; the caller who stands at the door looking over the occupant's shoulder; and, in cases of the evil eye, the culprit who is guilty of the too intense stare, the penetrating gaze, the too admiring glance (see Maloney 1976). Witchcraft, then, is not just a reaction to and an expression of hostility and jealousy. It is a particular sort of reaction that occurs under particular sorts of living conditions. The structure of the reaction is, it seems to me, at one with the structure of the living conditions. Whereas the house and the village are viewed not just as dwelling spaces but as microcosmic representations of the macrocosm, so witchcraft formulates itself as an epistemological discipline shaped by the house and the settlement: for every outer structure of the cosmos, there is an inside and a reverse; for every helpful and benevolent spirit, there is a malign one; for every public side there is a private one; where there is Heaven there must be Hell; and God is opposed by Satan. The known forces of the world are multiplied twofold by witchcraft, which specifies the occult forces and harnesses them to people, especially to those who live together. They use these as mechanisms, instruments, and aids in their continual struggles for power, in their protests against domination and the achievement of domination by unfair means.

Witchcraft is not all there is to domesticated village society. But it is a typical institution in the sense that it is common to such societies while it is hardly to be found at all in either hunter/gatherer groups or urban industrial societies. It is, however, a practice and a set of beliefs that has fascinated urbane anthropologists, scholars, and lay people living in a society dominated by science and psychiatry. And this for good reasons not always apparent: witchcraft addresses the problems and difficulties that arise from living in a state of what Kant called "unsocial sociability," which is brought about by the simultaneous working of neighborliness and separation that comes with domestication. Particularly in some of the rural areas of industrialized Europe, witchcraft as the means of working out problems of power between individuals is still viable and effective. In the Bocage region of France, deadly witchcraft was part of everyday life where "silence and secrecy were fundamental values" and where there was "an inordinate taste . . . for enclosures—in the literal and figurative sense" (Favret-Saada 1980:106).

Witchcraft is important and pervasive in domestic society not only because it springs directly from the spontaneous structuring of domestic space into public and private but because it is a system of thought, belief, and practice that confronts, with success, the major problems of power as they arise at an immediate, personal level. Like architecture at the level of political power, witchcraft secularizes and objectifies the mysterious and transcendental nature of power by joining the real to the surreal. Speaking of political power Edmund Burke pinpointed the problem, the contradiction of power: "The use of force," he wrote, "is but temporary. It may subdue for a moment, but it does not remove the necessity of subduing again." And so, too, with the clash of individual wills in intimate behavior.

145

Force and physical aggression may easily and quickly become self-defeating. But by appropriating illness and misfortune, natural but random (or inexplicable) effects on the human person, through supernatural control, witchcraft allows power to circulate and to maintain an eternal but shifting presence throughout a community on both a practical and an ideological level. Settlement compresses people together more intensively and for longer periods than living in a temporary open camp. Frictions between people that might otherwise be defused by a simple parting may smolder to ignition in the domestic situation. The development of property in goods and land provides a new and major source of contention and wariness between people. The presence of privacy barriers to full attention and total communication leads directly to an increase in suspicion, uncertainty, half perceptions, muffled tones, improperly taken hints, half-glimpsed shadows, distorted eccentricities, circumstantial evidences, furtive glances, impolitic stares, uninvited intrusions, neuroses, and paranoias. From these and from quirks, accidents, good and bad luck, coincidences, and discrepancies in talent, accentuated by proximity there arise frustrations, envy, jealousy, learned helplessness, cunning, deceit, and cheating and the uncontrollable desire to attack or the unavoidable feeling of being attacked.

Such sources of discomfort, unease, dis-ease are not apparent, visible, or tangible. Someone with a grudge who comes charging in with a big stick is obviously contesting for control and can be countered with a bigger stick. But is someone's "dirty look" as sure a sign of aggression? Is a certain tone of voice a definite indication of evil intent? Is a failure to return something borrowed on time innocent negligence or calculated insult? One may never know until it is too late, until, that is, illness and bad luck have struck and in retrospect the signs of impending and intended disaster become apparent.

Witchcraft especially welds these elusive and diffuse effects people have on one another with the dramatic and tangible effects the natural world has on them in the form of illness, death, and misfortune. This link between the natural and the human through the supernatural allows power to be ever circulating and ever present. But its surreal form ensures that it will not self-destruct, as would "real" power exercised through force and coercion. Suffice it to say, however, that the realities of power from warfare to judicial punishment, from property to class, are a salient, developing feature of domesticated society throughout its evolution and in all its local manifestations. Village chiefs claim rank through descent and hand down judgments from authority; they may have many wives, receive much trib- ute, and redistribute food among their followers as signs and instruments of their power. But to make their position as near irrefutable as possible, to put it beyond the question that its vulnerability subjects it to, chiefs claim, and are awarded, supernatural and surreal "powers." In some cases they assume divinity. Ordinary people, too, engage in real power—they fight, they work hard and competitively, they are proven right or wrong, they get their own way by force of personality and persuasion. But they, too, find the hidden subtleties of the engagement of personalities demands transcendant, surreal approaches.

Writing as one whose childhood was deafened by the explosions of World War II and whose adulthood is being lived in the fear of atomic holocaust, it is difficult to conceive of power as anything other than control over instruments of destructive force. Everything else seems metaphor: the "power" of the media, the "power" of big business, the "power" of the church, the "power" of knowledge, even the "power" of the people seem to be phrases that require power in quotation marks. Even the once "awe- some" powers of nature, the eruptions, earthquakes, and floods, no longer maintain their absolute distance from humanity because their effects may now be measured in terms of equivalents to so many megaton blasts—that is, to manmade power. Before atomic power, human power, however high it aspired, whatever it claimed, however much force it mastered, remained dwarfed by the powers of nature and their collective summation as God.

The realities of power are now overwhelming, but before this conquest by reality, power was more complicated, elusive, indirect, and chimerical. Total destruction was conceivable but hardly practicable unless through divine intervention. Now we can do it all by ourselves. Then power was, for all people knew, as surreal as real. Without the means and instruments of total destructive force available, human power had to rely on claiming some influence with nature, on entering into partnership. And then the human partners had to advertise the partnership and, from time to time, demonstrate it.

Until the modern industrial age, the age first of steam, then electricity, and now atomic energy, the most moving and dramatic advertisement for and demonstration of the human attainment of power was monumental architecture, especially the expanding architecture of the house. In its real form the house expanded to the palace; in its surreal form the house as tomb expanded to the mausoleum. The temple was the architectural expression and embodiment of the two. The act of construction was, through the mobilization and organization involved, an act of real power, while the end product, as something greater than the sum of its parts and more moving in its magnificence than anything within the capabilities of an individual, was both testament and realization of power beyond the real. The ancient monument brought the gods to earth or assembled together in one place the scattered powers of nature.

Overawed by the real power of our energized machines to change the face of the world as a matter of fact and on such a scale, we tend to be skeptical or dismissive of archaic ideas of power. The divinity of kings is just not sustainable, so how could anyone have believed in it? The idea that magic can have real effects seems mere superstition. The rationality of the people of domesticated society is here in question. The functional theory in anthropology sought to reinstate the rationality of non-Western societies by proposing that no matter what they did, it could be shown that such deeds and beliefs performed a rational function—that is, desirable in terms of our own way of thinking. Totemism was a way of ensuring the solidarity of the group, witchcraft vented hostility. But one must ask in such cases why on earth people did not pursue their aims more directly? In this chapter I have offered a refined functionalist argument. I have suggested that amid all the things the house as temple, palace, and tomb "did," it made power visible, it turned potentiality into ever-present act. The monumental architecture of the domestic age presented permanence as a reality, and the aesthetic treatment and elaboration bestowed on these monuments, on their fittings, furnishings, and personnel, presented perfection. As the fusion of permanence and perfection such architecture was power, not a symbol of it. It was by and through their association with these monuments that men in the office of king, and their agents, had access to power, and their "realistic" job was to direct, aim, and beam that power.

My understanding of power here differs a little from that of modern political theory, which relies in some way or other on the Weberian idea of establishing one's will over the resistance of that of another. This, to me, seems a special case of the more general notion of power as "having an effect," "making an impact" on a person. This goes far beyond the physical, and it is my contention that in domesticated society ultimate power was conceived as an aesthetic and mystical "force" rather than as a violent physical force. Domesticated society contains within it numerous peaks, the civilizations which, though long dead and gone, still move us greatly by their artistic and architectural achievements. One might object that simple circumstance determines that only such artifacts could survive the years and that, when those civilizations were alive there was far more to them. But it could also be that their makers *intended* their aesthetic achievements to last, and if we can still be moved at such a distance, then how much more moved were those in whose presence they lived. In short, the millions of people whose sweat and labor constructed the civilizations of the past may have found reward for their efforts in the aesthetic and spiritual pleasure and assurance the constructions gave them. And for the vision, initiative, conceptualization, and organizing ability that made such monuments possible, the relative few may well have been willingly empowered by the many.

The house in its extensions was a means for power as sovereignty and divinity. The house in its contractions, as the structural conditions of everyday life, is the context for the fractioning of power, for its dispersal among the members of a community. Settlement concentrates people and thereby compresses their emotions as well as providing those emotions with more objects to take. The conditions of privacy in particular conceal people from one another and complicate the relations between them. Privacy emphasizes autonomy, but autonomy threatens the security of social relations and necessities. In which case autonomy seeks to strengthen its protective power against intrusion while social interdependence demands powers of surveillance. The symptomatic institution of this condition, which is special to domestic society, is witchcraft. Though certainly not the only way by which relations between people is expressed and governed, nor the only practice through which illness and misfortune are accounted for and dealt with in such society, witchcraft belongs to it in a way in which it does not belong to either the open society of hunter/gatherers or the urban/industrial societies of the present.

The most frequent and obvious way in which people are affected by what we would consider natural forces is illness and death, and only slightly less so when human enterprises are dogged by accident and "bad luck." By developing and believing in witchcraft people appropriate natural forces, which they can then direct and aim in their attempts to affect

149

one another. Since in a given community the probability of anyone being capable of witchcraft is as great, unknown, and random as the probability of anyone falling ill, dying, or having bad luck, the power contained in witchcraft/illness, and thence the power between people (because witchcraft is a relation between people), is constantly shifting and dispersing.

6

The Domestic Influence

In *The Savage Mind* Claude Lévi-
Strauss identifies what he calls the "neolithic paradox" (1966:13). Some
of the great arts of civilization—pottery, weaving, agriculture, and the domestication of animals—were all accomplished in Neolithic times and
could only have been so if Neolithic man inherited a long scientific tradition. But if this was the case, how could "several thousand years of stag-
nation have intervened between the neolithic revolution and modern science"? His solution proposes "two distinct modes of scientific thought"
(ibid.:15). One is modern scientific thought of recent origin, and the other
is what he calls *Bricolage* (improvisation), and this latter served mankind
very well, both in practice and in theory. Jack Goody (1977) has criticized
Lévi-Strauss for introducing here what is a thinly disguised "we"-"they"
dichotomy, and he implies that the dichotomy of bricolage and technical
knowledge by no means covers all the forms of thought and intellectual
capabilities of the Neolithic. Many inventions between the Neolithic and
the modern period were significant for intellectual development: the urban
revolution of the Bronze Age, developments in Classical Greece and Rome,
and the advances made in twelfth-century Europe or early China, for example.

Note that neither Lévi-Strauss's list of Neolithic accomplishments nor
Goody's examples of interstitial invention makes any explicit reference to
architecture, yet the Bronze Age urban revolution and the developments
in Classical Greece and Rome, as well as in twelfth-century Europe and

151

early China, all featured architecture at their center. Goody quite rightly emphasizes writing and its contribution to the growth of knowledge, especially scientific knowledge, but in so doing he fails to note that between oral and written traditions there exists architecture as both a mode of information communication and storage and a tool of thought. Lévi-Strauss's bricolage and mythical thought are concerned especially with classifications—notably, those of the sensible world in sensible terms (1966:16), a science of the concrete. These classifications are the foundation of structures of thought and activity, edifices of knowledge and interpretation. "Mythical thought builds ideological castles out of the debris of what was once a social discourse"—the very metaphor of this observation indicates, albeit incidentally and unconsciously, that bricolage and mythical thought may themselves rest, at least in part, on a more visible, substantial, literal, and material foundation: buildings and their metaphorical possibilities. In turn, architecture itself is founded on the discipline and imperatives of geometry. Not that the abstract "science" of geometry had to come before the practical activity of building, but the science of geometry is implicit in architecture and both together were at the heart of the ancient Greek accomplishment. Neither Lévi-Strauss nor Goody gives Neolithic people any credit for geometrical prowess and advance. Goody observes that oral cultures seem to cope well with problems of addition but need to be literate to become skilled at multiplication. Maybe so, but arithmetic is not all there is to mathematical knowledge and logical skill, and it seems evident that even without writing many Neolithic cultures advanced geometry and the arts based on it: this was their "scientific" accomplishment, and it is in perfect accord with modern scientific thought. We are the direct heirs of Neolithic geometry and the arts and sciences that derive from it: tonal music, perspective painting, architecture, mechanics, ballistics, formal gardens, town planning, and theater, to mention but a few.

In earlier chapters I have sketched the cosmological significance of the house and the village, which derives of course from their geometric properties. The cosmological symbolism of the house, the palace, the temple, the tomb, and the city not only has its own development within cultures and civilizations; it is solid evidence of the communication and information storage functions of buildings as well as their political functions. Not only were the early literate philosophers of ancient Greece concerned with putting into words the geometry of their Neolithic world, but their political theories were also architectural in origin. Aristotle's polis was not a system of living so much as a place for living that exercised control spatially (Arendt [1959] provides some interesting insights on this question). Architecture's capacity to speak, guide, signify, and move people is nicely illustrated in a quotation taken from the Chinese and used by Goody to introduce the topic of literacy: "When they reached the Dragon Gate the guild head pointed to it and said, 'This is the gate for scholars'. They went into a corridor with examination cells on both sides, and the guild head told them, 'This is Number One. You can go in and have a look'. Chou Chin went in and when he saw the desk set there so neatly, tears started to his eyes" (1977:19). An intending mandarin is shown not only the place that writing occupies but also his place: his hopes and fears are signified by architectural features. The building is a diagram of the system. This diagrammatic quality is what seems to me most distinctive about the role of the structure of place in domesticated life. In the examples discussed in earlier chapters the house structure, the ground plan, the settlement plan, and their cosmological meaning portray to people their relation to one another as well as to important features of their environment. People coming into the society, whether as strangers or particularly as children, have in their built surroundings a diagram of how the system works—their place in the household, their place in the village, their place in the territory. At the same time, they can perceive, graphically, how the individual, the various orders of groups, and the cosmos are linked and related. This is neither the only information available nor the only mode by which principles are represented; myths, rituals, and precedent present the same information and ideals in different forms. But in architecture and settlement plans a person's and a people's visual and material diagram of themselves is presented most systematically and, perhaps, invariantly.

This, I claim, is a primary reason why Neolithic domestic societies strike ethnographic observers as living their lives as if with some sort of reference to a structure, whereas observers trained in the same tradition but studying hunter/gatherers, have great difficulty in overlaying their thought and practice onto a structure. Domesticated society is founded on and dominated by the elementary and original structure, the building, which serves not just as shelter but as diagram and, more generally, as the source for metaphors of structure that make possible the social construction and reconstruction of reality. Hunter/gatherers, or people who organize social life by focus, might be described as using maps rather than diagrams, by modes of thought that concentrate on locating people and relocating them—in the environment and vis-à-vis each other. Maps show where things and people are, and it is of the essence of nomadic hunter/gatherer life that the location of plants, animals, water, and people is made known, is mapped. But in domestic life location tends to be fixed, and the increasingly important fact is to know how things *ought* to be if they are going to work properly, as expected. How, what, and when to plant, and where; how, where, and when to herd; who should (has to, has the right) to be where and to have what; how to maintain a working arrangement in one place over the changes of time. Diagrams have this specific technical function of depicting, in principle, how things ought to be if they are to work properly because they model working relationships. Diagrams—the reconstruction of maps by geometry—are the principal, though not exclusive, images of domesticated society.

This does not mean, however, that domestic society is necessarily immobile, static, and tyrannized by its own representations, though even anthropologists have in the past asserted that in tribal society, custom is king. Bourdieu (1977) and Holy and Stuchlik (1983) have questioned the existence of ideational structures that blueprint social activity. Rather, they suggest that norms are being continually revised and hence reestablished to suit present purposes and changing conditions and that the "structure" is in many ways little more than an ex post facto rationalization of a present situation. But diagrams are always of something, and they show how that something has to be if you want it to work. No diagram or structure imposes the necessity of the structure itself: people choose what they want to do and whether to do it, and the subsequent diagram depicts how they need to act and what they need to do to realize the structure they want. You can change the diagram. Or existing structures may be retained to diagram different functions. The architectural structures that diagrammed the Merina circumcision ceremony, especially the palace, the house, and the tomb, for example, had different functions superimposed on them as historical conditions changed in the nineteenth century. But their solidity and geometry served to preserve the illusion of an unchanging reality (Bloch 1985).

Another dimension of this objectification through architecture that characterizes domesticated societies is the emergence among them of history as a supplement to myth. Predomestic societies rely almost entirely on myth; certainly they do not seem to have any history. Conventionally, history is accorded to those societies with writing, but this is misleading and does oral societies a disservice. In the architecture and settlement plans of Neolithic society the past is incorporated as a living, influential part of the present, principally through monuments, buildings, and, especially, tombs and mausoleums. One of the most distinctive developments of the Neolithic from the Paleolithic is that constructed graves become increasingly common and their occupants are ever more decorated and ornamented. It is a most prominent feature of the development of the Neolithic and beyond that these graves evolve into monumental funerary architecture, of which the Egyptian pyramids or the newly found Chinese emperors' tombs with their terracotta armies are but spectacular examples of a worldwide phenomenon. Tombs dominate the domestic landscape through the centuries, but so do imposing palaces and temples, preserving the past in the present and embodying this history of the place and its inhabitants. Their permanence and perfection are the incarnation and articulation of power and the means of its perpetuation.

This engendering of history and power, though by no means exclusive of myth, strikes me as a major development of Neolithic domesticated society and, consequently, as a critical difference between it and predomestic hunter/gatherer society. In the latter the past is undifferentiated into a "dreamtime," which is as general and universal as the unchanging landscape with which the mythical personages and events are associated. Mythical ancestors have no monuments built to them by their descendants; only historical ancestors are so commemorated.

The elements I have so far mentioned as being characteristic of domesticated society—geometry, diagrams, and history, and their foundations in architecture—have, as I have noted, a connection with power in that they strive toward permanence and perfection. Collectively, these functions of architecture are sufficient to provide people with the impetus, inspiration, and ambition to concentrate on the development of this human, cultural endeavor. So, considered objectively, one could argue that the evolution of domesticated society is typified by the striving toward the perfection of architecture, the geometry that is its abstract counterpart and foundation, the arts and sciences which spin off from that geometry—music, sculpture, painting, mechanics—and the technologies that combine geometry and architecture, such as artillery, siege works, ballistics, plowing, formal gardening, and the theater. Feeding into this cultural development is display and the desire for power (which no doubt is partly induced through feedback from these developments).

Neolithic domestic society may well be characterized by considerable

155

cultural, technological, and intellectual development, though it has not been my purpose in this essay to detail such an evolution. I have sketched in some features here only because at least two influential chroniclers of intellectual history have somehow missed the vital features of this phase of human history and have in effect reduced its significance. Lévi-Strauss in particular has diminished the continuity between the past and the present by overlooking geometry and architecture as Neolithic accomplishments and asserting that Neolithic thinkers were only bricoleurs; Goody, his gaze fixed firmly on writing, has not seen how architecture and geometry served as powerful cognitive tools for people with an oral tradition.

It is not just anthropologists of the mind who have overlooked some of the key features of domestic society—features that in many ways are missing links in theory and empirical reconstruction. In this book I provide, I think, some insight into problems of political theory and into the interpretation of archaeological data and its bearing on political evolution. In a work that has exercised considerable, and well-deserved, influence on political theory, and especially on interpretations of archaeologists, Morton Fried feels more or less nonplussed when it comes to the question of the origins of the pristine state—origins, that is, in the sense of how it was possible, not just the place and time of its emergence. Speculating that there were once stratified societies in which the institutions of social control eventually specialized and coalesced, then

> Through time . . . there emerges a power, held and manipulated perhaps by a priest, a warrior, a manager, or a charismatic madman who just happens to be the genealogical leader of the largest kin group in the now heterogeneous social fabric. The power itself represents a quantum leap over anything previously wielded, but it is a long time before the wielders of the new power realize its full extent and possibilities. Far from being a conscious creation of naturally power hungry psychological types, it is at least as probable that the power develops more rapidly than the abilities of its handlers. It takes time for a king to become a god. [1967:231]

According to Fried, the power of individuals may be obtained by happenstance (power wielded *perhaps* by a priest, and so on) and may develop of its own accord. In this work I indicate that political power in domesticated societies (which, in time, began their emergence in the Neolithic era) may well have been charismatic in many cases but was far from contingent and was well under control. To understand how this might be so we must go back to Weber's original discussion of charismatic authority.

Charisma for Weber is a certain quality of an individual's personality "by virtue of which he is set apart from ordinary men and treated as endowed with supernatural, superhuman, or at least specifically exceptional powers or qualities" (1964:358). A charismatic authority can only dominate so long as he or she receives recognition from followers (p. 362), and charismatic authority is strictly temporary. In fact, says Weber, charismatic authority may be said to "exist only in the process of originating," for as soon as an attempt to stabilize it occurs, it becomes "either traditionalized or rationalized, or a combination of both" (p. 364). Charisma changes as efforts are made to routinize it chiefly because when the charismatic assumes political authority, the economic and judicial affairs of everyday life, the routines, have to be managed, and this requires rules, order, and calculability. And these charismatic authority does not provide, for it is against rule, it is revolutionary. But is this in fact so? Without denying that extraordinary individuals have achieved power by virtue of their personal gifts, it is also true that many societies recognize certain *positions* as part of their routine political culture, positions thought to be endowed with supernatural, superhuman, and specifically exceptional powers and qualities. The position of the divine king or the Dalai Lama is such, and the individual who fills such a position becomes at once endowed with these qualities. In the case of the Dalai Lama, as Weber himself points out, a child who is thought to have the requisite qualities is selected after a long search. The result of this, says Weber, is a process of traditionalization.

But what of the situation where the charismatic position exists (the divine kingship) but can only be filled by a successful candidate who has outdone all other rivals—that is, who has demonstrated that he has charisma? And what of the situation where rival charismatics try to outdo one another so as to attract followers and thereby lay claim to the traditional title? Competition between charismatics and the pressure to keep it up allows for the continuance of the charismatic state beyond its moment of origination. Likewise, when the succession to a charismatic position is open to competition between individuals who must demonstrate their superpowers to potential followers, charisma need not face the problem of routinization inherent in sucession. The charismatic state may not be permanent in any significant measure of generations, but it may continue over time as a type. The *mandala* of pre- and protohistoric Southeast Asia were continually forming around individuals who were perhaps something like the "big men" or "men of prowess" of New Guinea (Wolters 1984:5–6).

These princes demonstrated their superiority and dominance through their achievements, and these achievements were most often and most impressively manifested in their building enterprises, as well as in their warlike abilities. Mandala were not fixed, bounded states so much as they were vaguely defined circles that revolved around a fixed "center," the ever more grandiose palace-temple-shrine-tomb complex. People who attended the center could be presumed to do so only for as long as they received attention from the center. So loyalties, particularly at the periphery, were always negotiable, and mandala tended to overlap (ibid.:17–18). Charismatic authority was wielded through its embodiment in the architectural center, and the greater the center the more it could command. As each charismatic leader succeeded his predecessor he sought not only to demonstrate his own powers, and not only to demonstrate his superiority over his rivals, but also to outdo the charisma of his predecessors. In the early historic "states" of Southeast Asia we find that former complexes were extended or were built over or were even completely abandoned while the successor built his own capital. In this sense the specific tradition of particular royal "houses" was denied even while the more general "tradition" that power is manifest in architecture was continued. These vast, sumptuous complexes were in essence worlds in themselves; each one was an *axis mundi* where the ruler was personally and totally supreme, a world creator and ruler completely independent of all else and wholly absolute—all essential properties of charisma. This was an absoluteness in time as well as space, so that there grew a seeming contradiction in terms, a tradition of charismatic authority.

It must be remembered, however, that these palace-temples were also households, the dwelling place of the king, his court, and their servants. The domestic functions were one and the same as the political functions, and the charismatic authority showed his charisma as head of a household, a great father as well as a great or divine king.

As well as succession, the problems of charismatic authority arise because the business of managing everyday life must be attended to, and this demands organization, some form of accounting, a system of delegation, and so forth, all of which are noncharismatic. Weber argues that some administration can be achieved charismatically when disciples are assigned duties, but sooner or later this must be systematized, particularly when the personal loyalty of disciples ends and their enchantment wears off. Although Weber's generalizations are essentially accurate, they rest on a supposition that economic and rational ends are necessarily dominant and therefore that the otherworldly, nonrational ends of charismatic authorities must be subordinate, if not sooner then certainly later. Providing we do not insist on lengthy time scales this is not necessarily a sound assumption, particularly when considering domesticated societies.

The Weberian assumption about the necessity for the management of everyday affairs, economic affairs in particular, is anchored firmly in the materialist philosophy that dominates the society of which Weber was a member. For this form of culture, economic necessity is paramount and, because it is a necessity, is to be considered objective. But it is perfectly possible for alternative forms of thinking to elevate other values above the economic and to assign to them the necessity we reserve to material existence. Given another framework of beliefs, another culture may well see as necessary and prior the fulfillment of aesthetic purposes and ambitions for immortality, in which case economic management need be given little specific or rational attention and costs may count for little. I have tried to show that this is true to some extent for domesticated society as a whole. It was specifically true of certain historic Southeast Asian societies.

Clifford Geertz calls these societies "theatre states" because they conceived of themselves as being one huge show. I think, however, that comparison with the theater suggests a degree of insincerity (acting) that was lacking in those states. What they did they did for real. Geertz invokes Walter Bagehot's distinction between the "dignified" and the "efficient" parts of political life and suggests that political theorists have supposed, quite mistakenly, that the dignified parts exist everywhere to serve the efficient parts. In fact, in the case of Bali—the subject of Geertz's study—as well as in numerous other societies elsewhere, the efficient parts served the dignified parts as the means whereby power could be made apparent, visible and real. Geertz describes it for Bali:

> The whole of the *negara* court life, the traditions that organized it, the extractions that supported it, the privileges that accompanied it—was essentially directed toward defining what power was; and what power was was what kings were. Particular kings came and went, "poor passing facts" anonymized in titles, immobilized in ritual, and annihilated in bonfires. But what they represented, the model-and-copy conception of order, remained unaltered, at least over the period we know much about. The driving aim of higher politics was to construct a state by constructing a king. The more consummate the king, the more exemplary the center, the more actual the realm. [1980:124]

The "theatre" state is a "charismatic" state and, in Fried's terms, a "pristine" state, and this state is the embodiment and realization of a transcendental purpose, the creation of an everlasting kingdom of perfection here on earth, surely the epitome of the charismatic promise and ambition. It follows that the "efficient" parts of the state, the day-to-day running of it, the raising of funds and supplies to support the numerous builders, could be conceived of only as being subservient to the dignified parts. Bagehot saw echoes of this were present even in the more modern, Weberian form of the rational state. The dignified parts of government, he argued, are "those which bring it force—which attract its motive power. The efficient parts only employ that power" (1974:206–7). Such was generally the case in earlier societies and remains the case in modern stratified societies where the common people are more interested in the theatricalities of power than in the "plain, palpable ends of government." This is because those theatricalities "appeal to the senses . . . claim to be the embodiments of the greatest human ideas . . . are mystic in their claims . . . brilliant to the eye" (ibid.:209). The mass of followers, who can be assumed to be quite sane but who yet follow the (mad) charismatic leader, or who subscribe without protest to a charismatic position that seems to exploit them economically, is that the leader, be he king or divinity, is an attraction which transcends reality, which aspires to elevate men by some interest higher, deeper, and wider than that of the ordinary life (Himmelfarb 1968:230–31).

The charismatic state is not confined to past times and exotic places. The Ethiopia of Haile Selassie, whose last days of power have been vividly chronicled by Ryszard Kapuscinski (1984), was a state concentrated in the person of the emperor and his court. The court and the bureaucracy were one and the same, a heap of irrational titles of great significance and meaning to their holders and their rivals, all of whom buzzed around the emperor and one another within the palace confines. The Lion of Judah and his court dominated the people in large part through the dominance of his many palaces over the landscape. As in Bali or the Versailles of Louis XIV, the life of the palace was the life of the state, and the government of the state was at one with the government of the palace household, of which the emperor was master, host, ruler, and patriarch. Courtiers existed as their titles, and their titles were bestowed only through the grace of the king. Grace could be elicited most effectively by coming to the king's favorable notice, and in return came their loyalty, their recognition of his divinity, and, incidentally, their material contributions. Notice was earned at the palace in the performance of domestic duties that were simultaneously political. Ranked by their titles, the Master of the Bedchamber or the Master of the Third Door were officials at court and thereby officials of the state.

The "charismatic" state maintained a continuity of power and authority between the household and the territory and not the discontinuity that Weber (1948:257) suggested between the state and the patriarchal power of the household. Weber could not appreciate how the house could be extended in other people's sense of reality to become the heaven on earth promised by the charismatic, nor did he realize that because the house (palace) can be built or rebuilt repeatedly, the charismatic can compete with rivals trying to outdo each other to show that he can fill the charismatic position. Such societies as the Bali described by Geertz and, more extensively, the bygone states enshrined in such monuments as Angkor Wat and Isanapura were extreme domesticated societies in which the dignified dominated the efficient so completely that people could act accordingly. In other words, it was expected that individuals would constantly emerge to lay claim to supernatural and superhuman powers and furthermore that they would prove their claims by their efforts in mounting spectacles. In the traditional and the rational society the charismatic is the exception, achieving legitimacy (that is, recognition) usually only when the society is unstable or in crisis. Hence social and political theory, as exemplified by Weber, has tended to construct a universal and objective typology, in Weber's case of ideal types, built on rationalist assumptions. Weber is thus blind to the possibility that charismatic authority may extend further than its period of origination even though it may depend on what we might consider a destructive logic.

The mandala centered on Angkor Wat or Isanapura, or a brilliant court society such as that of the Sun King at Versailles, differ more in degree than in kind from the simple domestic structure of the Para-Pirana longhouse. Both are dwellings and both are representations of the cosmos, the axis mundi. The scale, the priorities, the emphases, the grandeur differ enormously. Versailles is to the longhouse as Chartres is to Stonehenge, the culmination of a long progress of achievement in a single tradition: domestication. The break came when the politics of the household separated from the politics of the kingdom and each gained its own chambers.

The scale and elaborateness of an Angkor Wat should not blind us to the fact that it is a building (or many buildings) in which people lived—it was a glorified home. The kingdom it encapsulated and concentrated was a domestic one where to be king of the state was to be master of the household and vice versa. This class of domestic states, which is the limit of the political possibilities of the household, is missing from the classifications of political theorists, as is the strategy by which they were both administered and controlled (in the sense that followers acknowledged the power of kings and title holders). How such a state worked is the subject of a marvelous analysis by Norbert Elias, who discusses what he calls the "court society" of the Sun King, Louis XIV of France, who ruled the kingdom as an extension of the Palace of Versailles. I cannot quote Elias's entire book, but I will cite some particularly relevant passages that convey how a relatively modern kingdom can be ruled as a domestic society, how such modern and rational institutions as a bureaucracy and an army can serve as ends for the displays which, with the monarch at their center, constitute the surreality of power, the presence of absolute, divine power here on earth:

> What we refer to as the "court" of the *ancien régime* is, to begin with, nothing other than the vastly extended house and household of the French Kings and their dependents, with all the people belonging to them. . . . The court of *ancien régime* is a highly differentiated descendant of the patriarchal form of rule whose "embryo" is to be sought in the authority of the master of the house within a domestic community. . . . The king's rule over the country was nothing other than an extension of and addition to the prince's rule over this household. What Louis XIV, who marked both the culmination and the turning point of this development, attempted, was to organize his country as his personal property, as an enlargement of the household. . . . the court and court life were the place of origin of the whole experience the whole understanding of men and the world, of the absolute monarchs of the *ancien régime*. . . . The necessity that existed for the king at the end of this development to rule the whole country from his house and through his household understandably transformed this household the *Maison du Roi*. The conspicuous product of this interaction between the size of the country and the size of the royal household is the château, the court of Versailles, within which the most personal actions of the King always had the ceremonial character of state actions, just as outside it each state action took on the character of a personal action of the King. Not all the social units or integrating forms of men are at the same time units of accommodation. But they can all be characterised by certain types of spatial arrangement. . . . And so the precipitate of a social unit in terms of space and indeed, more narrowly, in terms of rooms is a tangible and—in the literal sense—visible representation of its special nature. In this sense the kind of accommodation of court people gives sure and very graphic access to an

understanding of certain social relationships characteristic of court society. [1983:41–44]

Elias goes on to describe how the townhouses of the ancien regime, the *palais* or *hôtels*, were transplanted, though modified, country manors— rural or domestic structures in which the layout, the furnishings, and the structure itself reflected and diagramed etiquette, social relations, and activities. For example, "The position of man and wife in this society could scarcely be more succinctly or clearly characterized than by this equal but wholly separate disposition of their private apartments" (ibid.:49). The great house was also the expression of rank and status rather than it being a measure of wealth so that the physical appearance of the house in space symbolizes for the grand seigneur and the whole of his society, the rank and importance of his 'house' in time, that is, the significance of his family over generations and therefore himself as its living representative. High rank entails the duty to own and display an appropriate house" (ibid.:53).

The court society of the Sun King was likely the last as well as the grandest of European court societies. But the shadow of the court society, and of its domestic nature, lingered on into the parliamentary state of the eighteenth century, and the symbolic idea of the great house has passed on into the industrial, bureaucratic age. Writing of country houses in England in the eighteenth century, Raymond Williams observed:

> They were chosen, you now see, for the other effect, from the outside looking in: in a visible stamping ground of power, of displayed wealth and command, a social disproportion which was meant to impress and overawe. Much of the real profit of a more modern agriculture went not into productive investment but into that explicit social declaration: a mutually competitive but still uniform exposition, at every turn, of an established and commanding class power. [1975:133]

Even in our modern bureaucratic democracies we still cherish a domestic image of government, personified in its houses of parliament or representatives, in its white house, and in its numerous chambers and palaces. However, what I have here tried to illustrate and analyze are the beginnings of this development of power from the adoption of the house and from the realization that, in creating permanent, monumental displays which at the same time bear witness to the human quest for perfection, a widespread but underestimated mode of political activity has evolved.

163

I do not want to give the impression that I think Angkor Wat, Boroba-dur, Knossos, Chichen Itza, Cuzco, Versailles, and other architectural won-ders of the world are typical of domesticated society. I am arguing that these magnificent monuments of departed civilizations are the pinnacles of Neolithic aspiration. They represent what other, humbler domesticated societies would like to have become; they are the successes of domestic society, the extremes to which the countless petty chiefdoms and feudal kingdoms that make up the bulk of Neolithic society (and the bulk of eth-nography) aspire. By the same token, the pharaohs, Louis XIV, and the divine kings that Sir James Frazer recognized as being so important in the record of human political and religious endeavor are not so much typical as exemplary of the aims of the Neolithic domesticated state. Many an obscure chief or feudal lord might have dreamt of being recognized as di-vine, and these absolute exemplars come the closest any human beings have come to being taken for the philosopher kings who, as Plato thought, would be the ideal rulers. The ideal philosopher kings are those who "see the absolute and eternal and immutable," for they guard the essential and beautiful unity of the ideal community, the Republic (*Republic* 6.479–80). In fact the Balinese king, the pharaoh, the Tongan monarch, and the Af-rican divine kings went one step better than the philosopher kings. In their stillness and immobilization they *were* the unity, the absolute beauty that the philosophers could only perceive. In the highly stylized court behavior, protocol, and etiquette, in the conventionalized masques, allegories, and dramas that the court played out the ideals of permanence and perfection were given shape and form here on earth, before people's very eyes. As I say, not all Neolithic domesticated societies reached this peak, but in the formality, the rituals, and the conventions that are observed in the count-less recorded and probably unrecorded tribal and village societies there is an aspiration toward such grandeur.

Domestic society made many technological achievements, and archae-ologists have given them much attention. But they and subsequent histor-ians have underestimated the significance of architecture and the rise of permanent settlements. Of course the practical, utilitarian consequences of settlement have received due notice—changes in food production, distri-bution and consumption, alterations in population density and pressure, a growth of the division of labor—but what to my mind is among the far-thest reaching consequences for the conduct of human affairs, be they util-itarian or leisure, technical or theoretical, political or social, has been almost completely overlooked. This is the creation in space of a distinction between the private and the public, accompanied by ideological and behavioral analogues and developments built on this structural division. The oversight can be traced right back to the original theorists of domesticated Neolithic society, Plato and Aristotle. Not that they were unaware of the distinction; in many respects it was crucial to their respective, though opposed, theories. Rather, they both missed the crucial point, and because they did so every subsequent social theorist seems to have done so as well.

Both Plato and Aristotle drew a distinction between the household and the larger community. For Plato the existence of the household was a threat, in fact a critical danger, to the ideal of the state and to its wellbeing. The fact that people lived and supported themselves within the household meant that they had the chance to serve their own interests, especially in the accumulation of private property. This would mean that within the city there would be diversity rather than unity of interest:

> Both the community of property and the community of families . . . tend to make them more truly guardians: they will not tear the city in pieces by differing about "mine" and "not mine"; each man dragging any acquisitions which he has made into a separate house of his own, where he has a separate wife and children and private pleasures and pains; but all will be affected as far as may be by the same pleasures and pains because they are all of one opinion about what is near and dear to them, and therefore they all tend towards a common end. [*Republic* 5.464]

The solution, at least as far as the intended guardians was concerned, was to abolish the household and hence to do away with the possibility of privacy.

Aristotle disagreed with Plato but, like him, recognized in the household a fundamental feature of domesticated life. The household was both natural and necessary because it was within the household that the necessities of reproduction and nurture were carried out. Because the household was the domain of necessity, Hannah Arendt (1959:35) has suggested that the Greeks saw it as the domain of unfreedom: one was cut off from life with others, the public life of the polis. The household for Aristotle was the living context for women, children, and slaves; the master ruled over it, and it was a good training ground and a natural place for its members to give one another the benefits of necessary affection and to provide them with the pleasures of ownership (*Politics* 2.3.30–35). The real importance of the household, however, is to Aristotle's political theory, which centers on the polis. Being a natural unit, the household offers Aristotle the grounds for demonstrating that the polis is also a natural unit, because the polis is a natural outgrowth of the household, emerging from it via the village (ibid. 1.2.15). If the essence of the polis is germinated from the household, the latter can hardly be prejudicial to the success and functioning of the polis. The purpose, or *telos*, of the household was the polis. Such an abstract argument completely blocks out the real relations (1) between individual households and (2) between the household and the larger community, and to the extent that this is so it is fair to say that Plato's admittedly idealistic account was more realistic in its appraisal of the significance of domestication than Aristotle's more empirical discussion.

Both Plato and Aristotle, though, pay attention only to the counterpoise between the household and the larger community—the polis or the city. Plato argues for an opposition between individual interest and good and the common interest and good, between the individual and the unity that is the group. Aristotle saw no conflict of interests but rather a separation of interests between the privacy of the household and the public life of the polis, which conferred on men (but not women and slaves) all the rewards in life that were worth having. The idea of a common good, a *conscience collective*, a public well-being as being the right and proper domain of political thought and the purpose of political action, has preoccupied political thought ever since, reaching its heyday, perhaps, in the work of those who subscribed to a doctrine of the social contract. But what consistently gets overlooked, or at least underplayed, is that, common good or no, in the course of the everyday business of living in a domesticated environment people living in separate households can, under the cloak of privacy, pursue courses of action that may undermine the life and programs of people living in nearby households, their neighbors.

This may be intentional or not, people may deliberately set out to sabotage a neighbor, or they may simply devise a course of their own that will advance them in comparison with their neighbors. Nor are these courses of action to which I am referring necessarily economic. It is not inevitable that Neolithic neighbors will subvert one another, but the conditions of privacy inherent in varying degrees to domestication make this an ever present possibility. There is, therefore, an intrinsic undercurrent in settled Neolithic life that may, according to circumstances, become more or less explicit: an undercurrent of curiosity that may become suspicion, an undercurrent of caution that may become paranoia, an undercurrent of in-

166

quiry that may become surveillance. Where walls exclude some and confine others, the possibility of intrusion, and hence of interference, is present. When these undercurrents flow they inspire their particular responses: in order to allay suspicion or to divert curiosity one may employ deception and pretense, and privacy may present to its neighbor a false front. Or, as we have seen, convention may insist on conformity in the public presentation of the private domain and its periodic opening to inspection. The rules and etiquette of hospitality are crucial here. Depending on the particular interests of the household and its members we find particular responses to the problem of privacy: as the political position of the domesticated authority moves from tenuous power to supposed divinity, so the inaccessibility of the claimant becomes greater. Chiefs and kings all live in households among neighbors whom they may suspect of seeking to subvert, undermine, or conspire against them, and it is as much for such reasons as any that political surveillance becomes specialized. What I have tried to show in this book, however, is that surveillance (and evasion) are among the universal and significant activities of all who live in domesticated societies. They are part of the *routine* of daily life.

The regulation and adjudication of problems that arise from these privacy conditions form much of the task of the political, legal, and religious apparatus of the Neolithic community. It is not simply the legitimation and sanctioning of the inequalities and the maintaining of equalities that concerns people; it is, far more, the ways by which inequalities are achieved—specifically, how, under natural conditions of approximate equality, some people are able to do better than others. Is their success come by through fair or unfair means—that is, through overt or covert means? Justice, in domesticated societies, is not merely whether an individual's desserts are met appropriately but whether an individual or group achieves what they do, gets where they are, gains what they gain, by open means, in a fair contest, or by covert, unfair means such as cheating, witchcraft, deception, conspiracy, and the like. All such means are founded or strongly aided, abetted, and facilitated by privacy.

This intrinsic, structural fact of domesticated life—the division between the public and the private—is not, of course, as clear-cut in emphasis in every Neolithic society. It is, I suggest, a permanent theme developed more in some than in others. But it suggests an inherent weakness in such societies that could be self-defeating. Houses and settlements are by nature more permanent than camps and hearth sites. They offer their inhabitants the chance to live with each other in more stable and cooperative groups, and domestication presents the opportunity of a greater and more reliable food supply. But the separateness and privacy of the household is a source of aggravation, stress, and divisiveness. Can this inherent "contradiction" in domesticated society be countered?

Two features of ethnographic observation and social theorizing prompt a suggestion. Although virtually every study of a tribal, or Neolithic, people ever made has been of a village or some such similar community, the reality that these villagers live as neighbors has received little if any conceptual recognition. Instead the ethnography of domesticated people has been conceptualized as revolving around kinship structures. Coresidence is subordinated in ethnographic analysis to kinship and descent connections, and only in regard to marriage is residence given any primary significance, as when rules of postmarital residence are formulated for a society. Neolithic societies, as distinct from Paleolithic hunter/gatherers or urban industrial societies, are specified as being "kinship and descent" based societies. But the *household* and the *settlement* are the physical basis for whatever unity exists and for the performance of routines. While people may choose to live together and be neighbors because they are kin, the fact remains that kinship only serves as the means to the end. What is more, not all those who acknowledge themselves to be kin or members of the same descent group live together as a real, functioning group of cooperating people, let alone regard themselves as forming a collective with a common will. Rather, the real on-the-ground-cohabiting-group is defined first and foremost residentially. But it is an uncertain alliance, an unstable collectivity that contradicts or at least goes against the image of unity imposed by the boundaries of settlement itself. It might be said that the development of kinship and descent as the bases for socially uniting individuals into groups is an ideological development that counters the brittleness of households and settlements. So, kinship, rather than being the primordial basis by which people organize their relations and govern their affairs, is, even among the exemplars of "kinship" societies, but a dialetic response to the problems of a domestication, especially to problems deriving from privacy. Of course, the fact that hunter/gatherer societies cannot be said to be kinship based but rather friendship based has already undermined the claims of theorists for the primacy of kinship in social evolution. Kinship and descent play their biggest part in Neolithic societies as the mechanics and agents for creating an ideological basis for political and social unity;

they are, to put it bluntly, not the empirical but the fictional structures of an ideal or hoped for unity. Saying this does not mean that in some, indeed many, cases a kinship structure might not exist as the basis of a real organization of people into active and cooperating groups. That is always possible and must surely have been accomplished by some Neolithic societies. But in general terms we have to say that kinship is more fiction than fact as a structural element in human society, a claim that aligns itself partially with the arguments of Schneider (1984) that there is no such thing as kinship—that it is a fiction—and with Needham (1971) that the term *kinship* represents something of a category mistake, implying that there is a something in reality when in fact there is a variety of phenomena which between them do not possess the unity implied by the term *kinship*. For Needham, too, kinship is a fiction. Fictions, though, have their place in human affairs, and I would argue simply that kinship has a different sort of reality, a conceptual, if not an empirical, reality in Neolithic society. It has a strong ideological function to play as both a reinforcement for the weaknesses of domestication and a counterweight to the inherent individualism of such a life. In effect, kinship and especially descent, by virtue of their emphasis on generation, genealogy, and ancestors, contribute in a most important way to the creation of a sense of permanence, one of the primary aspirations of Neolithic life. The pivotal juncture of domestication, architecture, and kinship comes in the tomb, which is architecturally (as the mausoleum) and ideologically the focus, the center point, of many domesticated societies (but not, be it noted, of predomestic or postdomestic societies).

Maurice Bloch's analysis of the Merina of Madagascar provides an interesting example of this situation. The realities of life, the everyday business of getting a living from the land, compel the Merina to move around, to live in villages often far from their ancestral lands (*tanindrazana*). But this goes against everything the Merina holds to be right, proper, and traditional. It is customary and typical of being a Merina to live in unitary communities that have a permanent existence because the living simply continue the life of the ancestors. The focus of this ongoing unity is the tomb. Identification with the tanindrazana, however, means a separation from the place where one actually lives, hence a diversion of loyalties from real people and real obligations—neighbors, in fact. At the same time one cannot upgrade the place where one actually lives to the status of tanindrazana, because that would undermine the actual tanindrazana and its

169

focal tomb. The paradox is resolved by "pretending" that the fictive tomb group of ancestors is "real," although it has no sociological substance at all, while the "real" group of unrelated neighbors is denied as a dimension of social ideology: "The concept held by the Merina of their kinship system is one of segmentary, corporate groups. The illusion of corporateness and locality is maintained by its demonstrability for the society of the dead. . . . In contrast the actual structure of the kinship system is no longer one of localized corporate groups" (Bloch 1971:17). Bloch actually contrasts the modern Merina with other, particularly African, societies usually described as being entirely or purely kinship/descent based. But is even the most paradigmatic of segmentary lineage societies, one such as the Nuer, based entirely on kinship?

Among the Nuer the context of everyday living is "small local groups," which are linked together by kinship ties (Evans-Pritchard 1940:17). But these kinship ties are "brought about by the operation of exogamous rules" (ibid.), which means that the people who actually live together, in particular the women, are not all kin. Furthermore, like the Merina, the Nuer must move around, though in their case they look for better pastures rather than rice fields. So the composition of any real community does not necessarily remain the same from one season to the next (ibid.:93). In other words, even among the Nuer *the structure of the everyday routines rests on being neighbors,* and kinship serves as a backup, not as the set up. Kinship ties disentangle spatial or neighborly entanglements or give an ideological complexion to the often fortuitous proximity of being neighbors. Sometimes, it is true, people choose to be neighbors because they are kin, but as often it can be shown that they *avoid* being neighbors because they are kin.

Does all this mean that we have to agree with David Schneider that there is no such thing as kinship? I do not want to go so far, but I do want to suggest that the everyday routines of life in domesticated societies are carried on by people in a social manner on the basis of their recognition of neighborliness. This is a fragile "bond," extremely susceptible to outbursts, to spur-of-the-moment happenings, to personal likes and dislikes. But at the same time, living as neighbors is not without its rules, etiquette, and "structure." Kinship, by contrast, along with descent, is invoked as a principle that structures people's cooperation and exclusiveness—these are periodic rather than everyday and routine. They are ideological affairs, which call upon and express the beliefs of the people concerned about moral and metaphysical concerns: the inheritance of property; the right (preferred, prescribed) person to marry; the appropriate person to perform burial rites, or, in general, ritual tasks; the right or the wrong person with whom to have sexual relations; the identity and nature of the unseen forces of the world that from time to time affect the equanimity of life; the right person(s) to assume responsibility for upbringing and nurturance; the people one can (or cannot) trust. Many of these dilemmas arise from the conditions of neighborliness to which I have drawn attention (for example, because of the conditions of privacy or the dangers of trespass, people who are to be neighbors might prefer to be, or feel safer with, kin.) The point is which way round it goes, which is basic, and I am saying that practicalities and the necessities of daily routines make the placement of neighbors in proximity to one another the fundamental structural determinant in settled domestic societies, while conceptualizations such as kinship (or age sets and the like) are built and function on this foundation—they crosscut, they provide a sense of unity and solidarity that is a sort of haven from the tensions and unsettling stresses of daily living in neighboring houses. Above all, kinship crosscuts settlement, so that people separated by place may be joined by kinship and marriage. Kinship structures the ideological stability and cohesion of people that is realized in the more occasional occurrence of rituals and in resolving such problems of social disfunction as marriage and inheritance.

From this point of view kinship (and descent) are used to organize and group people into units only from time to time and on ideological or ritual occasions. Rituals are ideological performances to analyze and synthesize ideals, beliefs, eternal truths, and wished for conditions, and this is precisely matched by the nature and reality of kinship. Kinship does not function on an everyday basis, even in that hallowed but false institution of kinship, the nuclear family. The nuclear family is simply not a kinship unit, for husband and wife are not kin. However many societies certainly do try to convert the family into such a unit where spouses may be kin, in which case the moral and social problems of coresidence are being tackled in a certain way.

The central structural feature of life in domesticated society is, I have argued, the house, and the chief structural personae, the major role players, are "neighbors." These are the most important elements in carrying out daily routines. But in the anthropological and, for that matter, sociological literature, the house and neighbors are rarely elevated to a concep-

171

tual level. They are invariably buried beneath conceptualizations of kinship. Can the concepts (rather than the actualities) of the house and the neighbor bear the load of placing a structure on them? I have already discussed the concept of privacy as a physical feature of domestic life and the way in which it spurs such social activities as surveillance, inspection, inquiry, evasion, and demonstration. Before passing on to other aspects I want to say a little more about the implications of the present argument for the philosophical dimensions of privacy and for the senses in which the domestic, spatial formation of privacy underlies and supports key aspects of the behavior of neighbors living in their houses.

Judith Jarvis Thomson argues that nobody seems to have a clear idea of what a right to privacy is. She suggests that there seems to be a cluster of rights, each of which may be part of another cluster, and that "it is possible to explain in the case of each right in the cluster, how come we have it, without ever once mentioning the right to privacy" ([1975] 1984:287). The "right to privacy" may in fact be reduced to such rights as the right to liberty, the right not to be tortured, the right to ownership of property, the right to be left alone, and so forth. This makes privacy a sort of portmanteau word with no meaning of its own. On the other hand, many scholars adopt a more existential stance to claim that privacy is irreducible and unique. Privacy, it is claimed, is a state of human existence that makes possible the establishment, maintenance, and protection of certain necessary features of life. Privacy is said to be an aspect of human dignity without which a person would be impaired and lack a moral personality (Bloustein [1964] 1984). In their pioneering statement about privacy, Warren and Brandeis claimed that privacy sustained an inviolate personality ([1890] 1984). Such suggestions implicitly recruit biology to their cause by claiming that privacy denotes a "natural," hence necessary, element in the human constitution. In fact, in all the extant discussions of privacy it emerges not as a state of the person, like hunger or the sexual drive, but as an environmental condition within which the person and his/her necessary functions can operate. There is nothing necessary or absolute about environmental conditions; conceivably, and in fact, as we have seen, something like human dignity can be achieved and sustained in quite different environments, even in public. Nothing was more dignified than the public behavior of Martin Luther King, Jr., and Aristotle argued that dignity came with citizenship, which in turn came with membership in, and participation in, the polis. The same can be said of arguments that seek to justify privacy as an essential means to ensuring human intimacy, which in turn is seen as necessary for the creation and fulfillment of human relationships. Privacy is the external condition within which intimacy is possible; it is not a state of the person or being. Indeed, as Hannah Arendt (1959) pointed out, intimacy as we understand it is a modern practice that, I suggest, stems from the development of interior domestic architecture. Intimacy in the modern sense is still quite alien to many domestic people described by ethnographers.

Spatial privacy is an invention of domestication. More accurately perhaps, it is a byproduct, an unforeseen consequence. It certainly does not emerge as a well-defined, formal aspect of daily life before or outside domestication. It is a state of living that clearly bestows advantages, but it also raises problems, and this dual nature suggests that if we want to understand the significance of privacy for the human condition we should not try to establish a biological pedigree for it, trying to locate it in genes via needs; rather we should ask what necessary features of human existence are both positively and negatively affected by the development of privacy into spatial form with the coming of domestication. Is there a criterion of the private (Schoeman 1984:6)?

Arguments that seek to find the basis for a right to privacy are invariably functional. They claim that privacy is a right because it serves to permit intimacy, self-knowledge, and self-discovery, because it enables people to separate their different roles, thereby allowing relationships to function efficiently. These may all be true, but privacy is not necessary to any of them, as the numerous examples of predomestic societies make evident. What is more, privacy can equally be said to "function" so as to allow for deception, conspiracy, and other antisocial activities. The "functions" of privacy in these examples seem to be more or less coincidental or at least cannot be considered strong enough to count as a raison d'être for the continued existence of privacy or for a right for it to exist. If privacy, in its spatial form in particular, is, as I have suggested, a technical by-product of domestication, then clearly it is not natural to human existence, in the loose sense of that term. But, like other technological achievements, it might be seen to extend, enhance, or impede and hinder human capabilities. Tools are not natural, for example, but the invention and adoption of tools certainly enhances the power and ability of the human hand, while as weapons tools can also be said to be detrimental to human existence. What already existing, permanent aspect of the human constitution might be similarly enhanced, improved, or extended at the same time as, from other points of view, it might be shackled and hampered by that by-product of domestication, privacy?

In chapter 1 I argued that attention, especially visual attention, becomes increasingly important among the primates, particularly hominids, as one examines the mechanisms of adaptation. Attention is necessary not only for the effective performance of tasks and for navigation of the environment; it is crucial for the engagement of individuals in all forms of their relationships. It is especially vital in the performance of necessary tasks carried out in the context of necessary relationships: food procurement, defense against danger, selection of mates, reproduction, and nurturance. In the human case, it is a necessary, though not a sufficient, condition for learning, which in turn is vital for survival and well-being. Human physiology includes an apparatus of attention, and human activity consists largely of attending to oneself, to others, to what one is doing, to what others are doing, and to the environment in general. To be successful in undertakings, relations, tasks, and actions a human being must pay and receive attention. To accomplish what one sets out to do it is often not enough to simply pay attention; one must concentrate. Attention in general, and concentration in particular, necessarily implies an exclusion of peripheral, tangential, marginal, and irrelevant factors, including objects, activities, and persons. Attending and concentration are natural—that is, "uncultured"—forms or modes or privacy, because any individual who is concentrating on any other person or task excludes others from the relationship or activity just as, at the same time, the attending individual is cut off from involvement with others who are not immediately involved. The example of the G/wi individual whose taut neck muscles betrayed his concentration to others so that they knew to leave him alone and simultaneously could accept his failure to attend to them shows how attention operates as an "inchoate privacy," one that has not been formalized by and through space. This example clearly shows the dual nature of attention as exclusion: (1) a person excludes everything considered to be extraneous, and this includes people; a person relieves himself of having to attend to persons and things when paying attention or when in private; (2) other people's attention to oneself is excluded by rendering oneself more or less immune to intrusion and interruption.

In predomestic societies attending and concentrating are carried on unaided by much technology. Whoever wishes to concentrate on something by physically excluding others usually must leave their company—as

174

when intending shamans retreat to the bush or desert or when individuals simply go walkabout or seek new company to live with. Otherwise people allow one another to concentrate by not attending. Remember, however, that the individual who appears too withdrawn or introspective is quickly jollied out of it, and though people may not appear to notice all that goes on, the enforced intimacy in which they live ensures that they do know more or less everything.

With the adoption of architecture as the living environment, by contrast, attending and exclusion are given technology: a screened place facilitates concentration and blocking out distractions, and in this way the chances of success and of doing something more efficiently, more perfectly, are furthered. Privacy, as it were, comes into being as the "mechanization" of attention. What that attention is given to, whether it is good or bad, is irrelevant; simply, privacy is the improvement of attention by the application to it of technology, and what is done with that attention as privacy—that is, its function—is another question. Privacy is "fertilized" or "mechanized" attention, and therein lies the foundation for a right to privacy.

That this is so has long been intuited but for some reason has never properly been made explicit. In his survey of the literature Ferdinand Schoeman (1984) quotes a passage written by Leslie Stephen in 1873. I would like to reproduce much of that quotation and Schoeman's commentary:

> All the more intimate and delicate relations of life are of such a nature that to submit them to unsympathetic *observation* or to observation which is sympathetic in the wrong way, inflicts great pain, and may inflict lasting moral injury. Privacy may be violated not only by the intrusion of a stranger but by compelling or persuading a person to *direct too much attention* to his own feelings and to attach too much importance to their analysis. . . . That any one human creature should ever really *strip his soul stark naked for the inspection* of any other, and be able to hold his head up afterwards, is not, I suppose, impossible, because so many people profess to do it; but to *lookers-on from the outside it is inconceivable.*
>
> The inference which I draw from this illustration is that there is a sphere, nonetheless real because it is impossible to define its limits, within which the law and public opinion are intruders likely to do more harm than good. [Stephen 1873:160, 162, quoted by Schoeman 1984:11. Italics added]

Schoeman cites these remarks approvingly as anticipating many later arguments about privacy. He singles out five points made by Stephen as particularly appropriate and "pregnant":

175

Privacy relates to:
1. intimacy
2. subtleties of relationships
3. meaning for others
4. allowing a person discretion to explore inner feelings
5. certain kinds of affronts

All five aspects of privacy singled out by Schoeman are in fact functional and contingent and certainly not necessary to all human beings at all times. Schoeman ignores the tacit point, made by Stephen and indicated by the italicized phrases, namely, that privacy is inextricably bound with giving and receiving attention. What is distinctive about privacy, then, is its unalterable and irreversible connection with human attention, especially concentration.

Bloustein argues that a person without privacy will lose dignity: autonomy, uniqueness, a sense of self as an individual. But how would a lack of privacy effect this? Basically, by impeding a person's ability to pay attention to self and to attend to his (or her) way of attending to others and to the world (what Stanley Benn calls being able to adopt a point of view and to understand that others have a point of view through which they regard themselves ([1971] 1984:227). Likewise, the cases made for privacy based on arguments in defense of intimacy are all, though unadmittedly, based on attention, because intimacy is simply the concentration at close quarters of people on one another (see Gerstein [1978] 1984; Reiman [1976] 1984).

Thus the development of domestication "meant," among other things, the construction of a technology that simultaneously enhanced the opportunities for concentration by erecting physical barriers against intrusion and interruption; reduced the chances of distraction; and hindered the free-flow capacity of people to pay attention to one another as an undifferentiated feature of the routine of everyday life. The unexpected positive advantages of a materialization of privacy helped set the scene for an expansion of creativity and for the achievement of high levels of creative skill and performance. The unexpected negative drawbacks of such privacy added complicating factors to human interrelationships and communication. A goodly slice of domesticated behavior—thought, psychology, motive, and intention—is generated and conditioned by these circumstances.

The development of the exclusion dimension of attention as spatial, and

176

more generally existential, privacy under conditions of domestication also accentuates certain aspects of power, making them more of an issue and a complicating factor in everyday social behavior. Functional arguments in defense of a right to privacy rest on the proposal that if a person is not left free of inappropriate and unwanted intrusion they suffer "deprivation"— they fail to achieve human dignity, to come by the rewards of intimacy, to be able to undertake adequately all their social and public roles.

Any such instance in which a person, or a group for that matter, unsuccessfully protects himself against unwanted intrusion means that he loses authority over himself. Conversely, any outsider who intrudes on privacy changes the course of the private person's behavior by undermining his or her authority: in this sense an invasion of privacy is a successful demonstration of power and a mark of hierarchy. It is interesting to note in this connection how relative rank is demonstrated not merely by symbols and badges but by the relative inaccessibility of the higher ranks to the lower and by the susceptibility of lower ranks to intrusion from on high. In tyrannies and dictatorships, whether fictional, as in Orwell's *1984*, or factual, as in Nazi Germany, the higher ranks are preserved in private luxury while ordinary people have no privacy whatsoever: "There was of course a not inconsiderable minority for whom the regime's permeation of all spheres of life was intolerable. The fear they felt of revealing their true feelings took many forms. . . . The German Labour Front Leader, Robert Ley, stated complacently—'The only person still leading a private life in Germany today is someone who sleeps'" (Grunberger 1971:27).

Idealistic leaders of utopian communities have quickly recognized that their power over followers depends not only on their charisma and their ability to display divinity, but also on their own privacy, coupled with their own freedom to intrude on, if not eradicate, the privacy of their followers. Shaker villages sometimes had towers from which elders could observe the activities of members, and George Rapp, founder of the Harmony commune, "used a series of underground tunnels to appear suddenly and mysteriously before members" (Kanter 1972:107). Living in common was meant to create an equality between members, and this meant as near as complete reduction of privacy as possible, even, in some instances, going as far as encouraging fellow commune members to confess their "selfish" or "prideful" actions—that is, their private behavior—and/or encouraging companions to "bear-witness" to one anothers' "wrong-doing"—again, mostly to their private actions, thoughts, and intentions.

Note that in these examples the essence of privacy is the resistance to

177

the attention of others, while the nub of the power of some over others is to be able to attend to subordinates' actions at will, to see without being seen. This notion of power versus subordination as the monopoly of attention as against a total deprivation of attention was given a model architectural form in Jeremy Bentham's ideal prison, the Panopticon. A supervisor is seated in a central tower surrounded by cells that are open to his view but quite cut off from the view of any other. Each cell is backlit; the overseer can see the prisoners but they cannot see him. Although he may not be looking at each prisoner all the time, none will ever know whether he is actually under surveillance, so the power of the overseer is complete and no prisoner has any authority over himself or his projects. Bentham remarks that this asserts the power of mind over mind (1843:39). Or, as Michel Foucault comments, the "Panopticon is the diagram of a mechanism of power reduced to its ideal form; its functioning, abstracted from any obstacle, resistance or friction, must be represented as a pure architectural and optical system: it is in fact a figure of political technology" (1979:207).

The Panopticon is the ideal form of the diffuse struggle for power which goes on as part of the daily routine of domesticated life in which, at times, neighbors are, in an insidious way, one another's prisoners and overseers. These tussles between the desire to preserve authority and the compulsion to gain power through watching and hiding come to the surface and are given cultural recognition in such beliefs and practices as witchcraft and the evil eye as well as in gossip and the ever ready vigilance of neighbors. The power that evolves with privacy touches most immediately on neighbors, and the relation "neighbor" is founded on that power.

Historians invariably observe that privacy is a relatively modern development, that the people of early Europe lived in closed, cramped quarters, sharing their beds with one another to keep warm, sharing the domain of the household not only with servants but with their animals, living an exposed and open life. Christopher Hill writes:

All roads in our period have led to individualism. More rooms in better off peasant houses, use of glass in windows (common for copyholders and ordinary poor people only since the Civil War, Aubrey says); use of coal in grates, replacement of benches by chairs—all this made possible greater comfort and privacy for at least the upper half of the population. Privacy contributed to the introspection and soul searching of radical Puritanism, to the keeping of diaries and spiritual journals. [1961:253]

These historians are referring to privacy within the home, where the house itself is divided to allow individual members to secure some degree of separation from one another, where they can either carry out their tasks with greater concentration or can undertake interpersonal relationships with greater independence. This form of privacy is the one that has been developed to a high degree in our urban industrial society but has its beginnings in the mercantile towns and their houses of seventeenth-century Europe. Does this mean that what I have called domestic or Neolithic society does not, in fact, have privacy when I have claimed that spatial privacy was one of its main inventions?

The privacy that I have claimed came into being through domestication is not the privacy within a house, the privacy we associate with intimacy, but the privacy *between* houses and their respective members. In typically domesticated society, the house itself is often only minimally partitioned to allow for the privacy of occupants. In the poor quarter of Cairo, flats and houses were so lacking in the facilities for personal privacy that a European ethnographer found she could not live among her informants. Yet at the same time, the occupants took considerable pains to screen themselves from their neighbors and to ensure that they enjoyed domestic privacy (Wikan 1980:53). In the villages of the Caribbean the house is the focus of life. Internally it is usually only divided in two, and then not effectively. But each house is at the heart of its yard, which may often be fenced and which divides it from its neighbors, and the care bestowed on it displays the respectability of the house and creates the public image of its occupants (Abrahams 1983:141–44).

Because domesticated privacy is between houses and households rather than within them and between individuals, privacy assumes a high degree of political and moral significance. Domesticated people in general do not equate intimacy and privacy. As is suggested in the quotation from Christopher Hill, the interior development of privacy serves to create the setting and technology for intimacy and the ideas of individualism. Only when intimacy and interior privacy have formed does there develop a model for and a technique of creating the concept of the interior, individual, private self. Until then, and "then" is quite recent, members of domesticated society acquired their sense of self from the house and the household, and this sense was sharpened in definition and filled out by their responsibility to represent the house against neighbors. A person's honor was not "his" or "hers" so much as it was the honor of the house to which he or she

179

belonged; the honor and repute of the house descended through the centuries, not of the individual who, nevertheless, was empowered as a part of the whole to damage that honor and to be damaged by whatever diminution other members of the household brought on the house. Morality, then, hews to the house, and moral and immoral actions are defined by their enhancement or diminishment of the house.

The house in domesticated society is the source of social autonomy; it gives form and material basis to a social unit. The household rather than the family is the active unit of everyday life, and a household is rarely a kinship group, for it usually contains the spouses, who are affines, though in some domestic societies spouses are also kin. Adopted children, servants, followers, and, in some societies, slaves, are equally occupants of houses, members of the household. As such they frequently bear as great a responsibility for the reputation of the house as the more authoritative members, and equally, their sense of self, of who they are and who others recognize them to be, is derived from the house. This statement applies, of course, to daily routine behavior—secular behavior if you like—and is less true of periodic, dramatic behavior—ritual behavior if you like. Then, as I have suggested, kinship is more often than not the principal identity.

We take living with a roof over our heads and within four walls so much for granted, as the fulfillment of a "need" for shelter, that we really have not questioned whether shelter is a natural fact of life and whether it makes a difference to the way we are. Freud includes the construction of dwellings as among the first three acts of civilization (the other two being the manufacture of tools and the making of fire). He considers the dwelling house to be the substitute for the mother's womb, "the first lodging, for which in all likelihood man still longs, and in which he was safe and felt at ease" (1961:37–38). This speculation does not conform to the facts of archaeology and therefore should prompt us to rethink Freud's theoretical position. It is a position that has become firmly entrenched in our present view of human nature.

Freud adopts an out and out Hobbesian stance on the original state of human nature: people are naturally, instinctively, and biologically aggressive, and "this hostility of each against all and of all against each, opposes this programme of civilisation" (1961:69). The program of civilization is a "process in the service of Eros whose purpose it is to combine single human individuals, and after that their families, then races, peoples and nations, into one great unity" (ibid.). I have no quarrel with this somewhat

Kantian program, but it is clear that by assuming an instinctive aggression Freud also supposes that people's hostility toward one another has always been at the same high level of intensity. He further disallows the possibility that the scope, breadth, and form of aggression may have changed in response to the changing nature of the human context, and, even more important, Freud overlooks the possibility that evolving conditions may have led to the ever more complex *organization* of aggression.

In a recent illuminating study of aggression, David Gilmore has noted that in psychoanalytic theory aggression is a drive and that drives are distinct from biological instincts. Whereas the instinct concept "implies both the inherited impulse to do something and the actual motoric activity itself," the drives in humans are "quite variable in their final aims. . . . the element of volition is present" (Gilmore 1987:15). Drives, unlike instincts, can be sublimated, rechanneled, repressed, and metamorphosed. And what I am suggesting is that such drives can be directed toward a larger and more complex variety of final aims with the coming of domestication. Once these final aims have been specified it is possible for them to exist before the onset of any aggression and thereby to call on or recruit the drive. When this happens it is appropriate to describe the aggressive drive as being organized—what is being recognized and organized is the *capacity* for aggression—much as Marx argued that it was not labor that capital organized so much as labor power. The organization of the capacity for aggression must surely be considered a step in the evolution of human conduct and a contribution to the growth of civilization as significant as Freud's proposal that the control, sublimation, or renunciation of aggression was a feature of the program of civilization. If a final aim is territorial appropriation, for example, then organizing aggressive drives into a military pattern is an accomplishment of civilization. It is nearly impossible to infer such organization from Paleolithic archaeology, but evidence of such an organization becomes increasingly insistent in the archaeology of the Neolithic era, the period of the domestication of society. The ethnographic parallel is that organized fighting is rarely reported for contemporary hunter/gatherer peoples but is commonplace among domesticated peoples. We must reckon this organization of aggression, as well as such other modes as gossip, witchcraft, displays, the evil eye, and so on, as being among the evolved characteristics of civilization or domestic society in the same way as we acknowledge pottery, sculpture, or writing to be among the constituents of civilization.

181

It is possible, then, that the drive for aggression has evolved, in the sense that it has undergone organization. If sublimation, repression, or renunciation is brought about by the imposition of rules, taboos, and prohibitions as Freud suggests, what factors of human activity have been instrumental in implementing this organization? Freud himself almost stumbles on both the question and the answer when he writes: "We can quite well imagine a cultural community consisting of double individuals like this, who, libidinally satisfied in themselves, are connected with one another through the bonds of common work and common interests. If this were so, civilization would not have to withdraw any energy from sexuality. But this desirable state of things does not, and never did, exist" (1961:55).

Modern ethnography suggests that some hunter/gatherers who are not domesticated and who presumably possess the same human drives and instincts as everybody else maintain a "community" life on the basis of mutual affect rather than rule-bound duty, on common interests and common work. Their affection for one another may not always be long-lived, but it is sustained at least in part because they live under conditions that allow them to pay adequate attention to one another as part and parcel of their routine day-to-day interaction. Attention is an integral aspect of their common interests and work. When people adopted settlement and domestication as a permanent feature of their lives, they did not impinge directly on their drives of aggression and sexuality, but they did impinge directly on the *conditions of attention*. That is, they impeded their sensory ability to monitor. stimulate, and govern these drives. Living behind walls affects the various aspects of attention, and people so affected must respond. This occurs in part by specializing attention, by developing modes of surveillance, supervision, and inspection, and by evolving stratagems of evasion and display.

The effect of cultural development on the senses, especially vision, rather than their direct effects on the instincts and drives, then, leads to efforts to organize as well as intensify aggression. Aggression (and sexuality, too) is, to a considerable extent guided, controlled, and incited by attention—too much of it, too little of it, the misplacement of it. Because they cannot see all that goes on behind neighbors' walls, people feel compelled to organize surveillance; because one is uncertain of having been seen, or is afraid to be seen, one organizes evasion.

The strategy of Freud's argument seems sound to me. He maintains basically that external developments, both natural and cultural, have affected the human constitution, especially the drives and instincts. He does not argue, as do some sociobiologists and such needs theorists as Malinowski, that human biology determines human culture directly and in a straight line. But Freud seems to consider *only* the instincts and drives as important, and he sees cultural evolution as a uniform, undifferentiated process. I would argue that the relations between culture and biology are far more dialectical and considerably more complex. In particular, permanent housing and settlement comprise a cultural event of considerable complexity, the full nature of which has not been properly brought to light. What is more, the senses, in particular vision, have played a far more active and instrumental role in social and cultural evolution than has hitherto been recognized. Freud himself notes that civilization began with erect posture and that this led to the devaluation of olfaction together with the elevation of vision (1961:46–47). But, like everyone else, he then supposed evolution to have stopped, whereas the influence and role of the senses in social and cultural evolution underwent a crucial change with the advent and adoption of domestication. This is why, perhaps, the ethical injunction to "love thy neighbor as thyself" became so important when it did, during the time of domestication, for this was when being a neighbor was established as a social concept and as a social role. Before domestication it had no significance, no social meaning. Freud sees this injunction as more or less futile since, given human aggression, a neighbor becomes the closest object for that aggression. But to be mindful of one's neighbor is, in every sense, a necessary condition of domesticated life. Neighbors, and their instincts, are linked together by and through their senses, especially through visual attention or the lack of it, and it is through these conditions of attention that the instincts are aroused for good as well as ill. Not only attention, of course, arouses instincts, but the occasions are few in which human instincts are not immediately impinged on and stimulated by the senses.

Like Freud, then, I have argued for a thread in human evolution spun out by virtue of the jostling effect a human cultural achievement has—but not on the instincts, on the senses. This point of view in general runs counter to the argument that culture arises out of genetic predispositions to particular cultural accomplishments: it is a reactionary view rather than an actionary view. By stressing that a particular cultural process—domestication—had among its unanticipated consequences an effect on the senses, however, I have sought to broaden our perception of the interrelationship between the human organism and its environment. This has been too much confined to the instincts, as in the manner of Freud. By the same token, the largely materialist outlook of archaeologists and social theorists has led them to concentrate more on the productive and economic aspects of domestication and to have overlooked the more general cultural, social, and psychological aspects. By intimating that a permanent built environment has not always been a feature of human life and is to this day not a necessary feature in all human societies, the revolutionary significance of architecture has been made more apparent, not just in a technological sense but for human psychology and social behavior.

References

Abou-Zeid, Ahmed. 1966. "Honour and Shame among the Bedouins of Egypt." In *Honour and Shame: The Values of Mediterranean Society,* ed. J. G. Peristiany. Chicago: University of Chicago Press.

Abrahams, Roger D. 1983. *The Man-of-Words in the West Indies: Performance and the Emergence of Creole Culture.* Baltimore: Johns Hopkins University Press.

Ahmed, Akbar S. 1976. *Millenium and Charisma among Pathans.* London: Routledge and Kegan Paul.

Arendt, Hannah. 1959. *The Human Condition.* New York: Doubleday Anchor.

Aristotle. 1952. *Politics.* Chicago: Encyclopaedia Britannica.

Austin, John L. 1962. *How to Do Things with Words.* Oxford: Oxford University Press.

Bachelard, Gaston. 1969. *The Poetics of Space.* Boston: Beacon Press. Originally published 1958.

Bagehot, Walter. 1974. *The English Constitution.* In Vol. 5: *Collected Works,* ed. N. St. John-Stevas. London: The Economist. Originally published 1867.

Baroja Caro, Julio. 1964. *The World of the Witches.* London: Weidenfield and Nicolson.

Barth, Fredrik. 1965. *Political Leadership among Swat Pathans.* L.S.E. Monographs in Social Anthropology, no. 19. London: Athlone Press. Originally published 1959.

Benn, Staney I. 1984. "Privacy, Freedom and the Respect for Individuals." In *Philosophical Dimensions of Privacy. See* Schoeman 1984.

Berdan, Frances F. 1982. *The Aztecs of Central Mexico: An Imperial Society.* New York: Holt, Reinhart, and Winston.

Berlin, Isaiah. 1969. *Four Essays on Liberty.* Oxford: Oxford University Press.

Bird, Nurit. 1983. "Conjugal Units and Single Persons: An Analysis of the Social

System of the Naiken of the Nilgiris (South India)." Ph.D. diss., Cambridge University.

———. 1986. Review of C. Schrire, ed., *Past and Present in Hunter Gatherer Societies. Man* 21, 2.

Birdsell, Joseph. 1968. "Some Predictions for the Pleistocene Based on Equilibrium Systems among Recent Hunter-Gatherers." In *Man the Hunter. See* Lee and DeVore 1968.

Black-Michaud, Jacob. 1975. *Feuding Societies.* Oxford: Basil Blackwell.

Bloch, Maurice. 1971. *Placing the Dead.* London: Seminar Press.

———. 1985. *From Blessing to Violence.* Cambridge: Cambridge University Press.

Bloch, M., and J. Parry, eds. 1982. *Death and the Regeneration of Life.* Cambridge: Cambridge University Press.

Bloustein, Edward. 1984. "Privacy as an Aspect of Human Dignity: An Answer to Dean Prosser." In *Philosophical Dimensions of Privacy. See* Schoeman 1984.

Bonner, John Tylor. 1980. *The Evolution of Culture in Animals.* Princeton: Princeton University Press.

Bourdieu, Pierre. 1966. "The Sentiment of Honour in Kabyle Society." In *Honour and Shame: The Values of Mediterranean Society,* ed. J. G. Peristiany. Chicago: University of Chicago Press.

———. 1977. *Outline of a Theory of Practice.* Cambridge: Cambridge University Press.

Bowlby, John. 1973. *Attachment and Loss,* Vol. 2: *Separation-Anxiety and Anger.* London: Hogarth Press.

Briggs, Jean L. 1970. *Never in Anger: Portrait of an Eskimo Family.* Cambridge, Mass.: Harvard University Press.

———. 1982. "Living Dangerously: The Contradictory Foundations of Value in Canadian Inuit Society." In *Politics and History in Band Societies. See* Leacock and Lee 1982.

Bruner, Jerome S. 1973. *Beyond the Information Given: Studies in the Psychology of Knowing.* Ed. Jeremy M. Anglin. New York: W. W. Norton. Originally published 1957.

Campbell, J. K. 1964. *Honour, Family and Patronage: A Study of Institutions and Moral Values in a Greek Mountain Community.* Oxford: Clarendon Press.

Chance, Michael R. A., and R. E. Larsen. 1976. *The Social Structure of Attention.* London: John Wiley and Son.

Clark, J. G. D. 1977. *World Prehistory.* 3d ed. Cambridge: Cambridge University Press.

———. 1980. *Mesolithic Prelude: The Paleolithic-Neolithic Transformation in Old World Prehistory.* Edinburgh: Edinburgh University Press.

Cohen, Mark Nathan. 1977. *The Food Crisis in Prehistory: Overpopulation and the Origins of Agriculture.* New Haven: Yale University Press.

Coulanges, Fustel de. 1969. *The Ancient City.* New York: Doubleday Anchor.

Cunningham, Clark. 1973. "Order in the Atoni House." In *Right and Left: Essays on Dual Symbolic Classification,* ed. Rodney Needham. Chicago and London: University of Chicago Press.

Dixson, A. F. 1981. *The Natural History of the Gorilla.* London: Weidenfeld and Nicolson.

Douglas, Mary. 1970. "Introduction: Thirty Years after Witchcraft, Oracles and Magic." In *Witchcraft Confessions and Accusations,* ed. M. Douglas. London: Tavistock Press.

———. 1972. "Symbolic Orders in the Use of Domestic Space." In *Man, Settlement and Urbanism,* ed. P. J. Ucko et al. London: Duckworth.

———. 1973. *Natural Symbols: Explorations in Cosmology.* London: Barrie and Jenkins.

Draper, Patricia. 1973. "Crowding among Hunter Gatherers: The !Kung Bushmen." *Science* 182:301–3.

———. 1978. "The Learning Environment for Aggression and Anti-Social Behavior among the !Kung." In *Learning Non-Aggression: The Experience of Non-Literate Societies,* ed. M. F. Ashley Montagu. Oxford: Clarendon Press.

Du Boulay, Juliet. 1979. *Portrait of a Greek Mouintain Village.* Oxford: Clarendon Press.

Eder, James F. 1984. "The Impact of Subsistence Change on Mobility and Settlement Pattern in a Tropical Forest Foraging Economy: Some Implications for Archeology." *American Anthropologist* 86, 4:837–53.

Edwards, I. E. S. 1947. *The Pyramids of Egypt.* Harmondsworth: Pelican.

Elias, Norbert. 1983. *The Court Society.* Oxford: Basil Blackwell. Originally published 1969.

Evans-Pritchard, E. E. 1937. *Witchcraft, Oracles and Magic among the Azande.* Oxford: Clarendon Press.

———. 1940. *The Nuer: A Description of the Modes of Livelihood and Political Institutions of a Nilotic People.* Oxford: Clarendon Press.

———. 1971. *The Azande: History and Political Institutions.* Oxford: Clarendon Press.

Favret-Saada, Jeanne. 1980. *Deadly Words: Witchcraft in the Bocage.* Cambridge: Cambridge University Press.

Feeley-Harnik, Gillian. 1980. "The Sakalava House (Madagascar)." *Anthropos* 75:559–85.

Firth, Raymond. 1959. *Economics of the New Zealand Maori.* Wellington, New Zealand: R. E. Owen. Originally published 1929.

Fobes, James L., and J. E. King. 1982. "Vision: The Dominant Primate Modality." In *Primate Behaviour,* ed. James L. Fobes and James E. King. New York: Academic Press.

Ford, Richard I. 1985. "The Presence of Plant Food Production in Prehistoric North America." In *Prehistoric Food Production in North America,* ed. Richard I. Ford. Museum of Anthropology Papers, no. 75. Ann Arbor: University of Michigan Press.

Forge, Anthony. 1970a. "Learning to See in New Guinea." In *Socialization: The Approach from Social Anthropology,* ed. Philip Mayer. London: Tavistock Publications.

———. 1970b. "Prestige, Influence and Sorcery: A New Guinea Example." In *Witchcraft Confessions and Accusations. See* Douglas 1970.

————. 1972. "Normative Factors in the Settlement Size of Neolithic Cultivators (New Guinea)." In *Man, Settlement and Urbanism*, ed. P. J. Ucko et al. London: Duckworth.

Fortune, Reo. 1963. *Sorcerers of Dobu: The Social Anthropology of the Dobu Islanders of the Western Pacific.* New York: E. P. Dutton. Originally published 1932.

Foster, George. 1961. "Interpersonal Relations in Peasant Society." *Human Organization* 19, 4:174–84.

————. 1965. "Peasant Society and the Image of Limited Good." *American Anthropologist* 67, 2:293–315.

Foucault, Michel. 1979. *Discipline and Punish.* New York: Vintage Books.

————. 1980. *Power/Knowledge: Selected Interviews and Other Writings, 1972–1977.* Brighton: Harvester Press.

Freeman, Derek. 1983. *Margaret Mead and Samoa.* Cambridge, Mass.: Harvard University Press.

Freud, Sigmund. 1961. *Civilization and Its Discontents.* New York: W. W. Norton. Originally published 1930.

Fried, Morton H. 1967. *The Evolution of Political Society: An Essay in Political Anthropology.* New York: Random House.

Frisby, John P. 1979. *Seeing: Illusion, Brain and Mind.* Oxford: Oxford University Press.

Gallup, Gordon G. 1977. "Self-Recognition in Primates: A Comparative Approach to the Bi-Directional Properties of Consciousness." *American Psychologist* 32:329–38.

Gallup, G. G., L. B. Wallnau, and S. D. Suarez. 1980. "Failure to Find Self-Recognition in Mother-Infant and Infant-Infant Monkey Pairs." *Folia Primatologica* 33:210–19.

Gardner, Peter M. 1966. "Symmetric Respect and Memorate Knowledge: The Structure and Ecology of Individual Culture." *Southwestern Journal of Anthropology* 22:389–415.

Geertz, Clifford. 1960. *The Religion of Java.* Glencoe, Ill.: Free Press.

————. 1980. *Negara: The Theatre State in Nineteenth-Century Bali.* Princeton: Princeton University Press.

Gerstein, Robert S. 1984. "Privacy and Intimacy." In *Philosophical Dimensions of Privacy. See* Schoeman 1984.

Gibson, J. J. 1979. *The Ecological Approach to Visual Perception.* Boston: Houghton Mifflin.

Giddens, Anthony. 1984. *The Constitution of Society: Outline of the Theory of Structuration.* Cambridge: Polity Press.

Gilmore, David. 1987. *Aggression and Community: Paradoxes of Andalusian Culture.* New Haven: Yale University Press.

Gittens, S. P. 1980. "Territorial Behaviour in the Agile Gibbon." *International Journal of Primatology* 1, 4:381–400.

Gluckman, Max. 1955. *Custom and Conflict in Africa.* Glencoe, Ill.: Free Press.

Godelier, Maurice. 1977. *Perspectives in Marxist Anthropology.* Cambridge: Cambridge University Press.

188

Goffman, Erving. 1959. *The Presentation of Self in Everyday Life.* New York: Doubleday Anchor.

———. 1961. *Asylums: Essays on the Social Situation of Mental Patients and Other Inmates.* New York: Doubleday Anchor.

———. 1967. *Interaction Ritual: Essays on Face to Face Behavior.* New York: Doubleday Anchor.

Goldman, Irving. 1963. *The Cubeo: Indians of the Northwest Amazon.* Illinois Studies in Anthropology, no. 2. Urbana: University of Illinois Press.

Goodall, Jane van Lawick. 1974. *In the Shadow of Man.* London: Fontana/Collins.

Goodall, Jane, et al. 1979. "Intercommunity Interactions in the Chimpanzee Population of Gombe National Park." In *The Great Apes,* ed. D. Hamburg and E. McCown. Menlo Park, Calif.: Benjamin/Cummins.

Goody, Esther. 1970. "Legitimate and Illegitimate Aggression in a West African State." In *Witchcraft Confessions and Accusations. See* Douglas 1970.

Goody, Jack. 1977. *The Domestication of the Savage Mind.* Cambridge: Cambridge University Press.

Gould, Richard. 1980. *Living Archaeology.* Cambridge: Cambridge University Press.

Gregor, Thomas. 1977. *Mehinaku: The Drama of Daily Life in a Brazilian Indian Village.* Chicago: University of Chicago Press.

Gregory, Richard. 1979. *Eye and Brain.* London: Weidenfeld and Nicolson.

Griaule, Marcel, and G. Dieterlen. 1954. "The Dogon of the French Sudan." In *African Worlds,* ed. Daryll Forde. London: Oxford University Press for the International African Institute.

Grunberger, Richard. 1971. *The Twelve-Year Reich: A Social History of Nazi Germany, 1933–1945.* New York: Holt, Rinehart, and Winston.

Guemple, D. L. 1965. "Saunik: Name Sharing as a Factor Governing Eskimo Kinship Terms." *Ethnology* 4:323–35.

Gumpert, Marc. 1981. "Paradigms Lost: An Analysis of Anthropological Models and Their Effect on Aboriginal Land Rights." *Oceania* 52, 2:103–23.

Hall, Edward T. 1966. *The Hidden Dimension.* New York: Doubleday Anchor.

Hamilton, Annette. 1982. "Descended from Father, Belonging to Country: Rights to Land in the Australian Western Desert." In *Politics and History in Band Societies. See* Leacock and Lee 1982.

Hanson, F. Allan and Louise. 1983. *Counterpoint in Maori Culture.* London: Routledge and Kegan Paul.

Harris, Marvin. 1977. *Cannibals and Kings: The Origins of Cultures.* New York: Random House.

———. 1985. *Culture, People, Nature: An Introduction to General Anthropology.* 4th ed. New York: Harper and Row.

Hart, C. W. M., and A. Pilling. 1960. *The Tiwi of North Australia.* New York: Holt, Rinehart, and Winston.

Havelock, Christine M. 1978. "Art as Communication in Ancient Greece." In *Communication Arts in the Ancient World,* ed. Eric A. Havelock and Jackson P. Hershbell. New York: Communication Arts Books/Hastings House.

Hayek, F. A. 1960. *The Constitution of Liberty.* London: Routledge and Kegan Paul.

189

————. 1976. *Law, Legislation and Liberty,* Vol. 2: *The Mirage of Social Justice.* London: Routledge and Kegan Paul.

Higham, C. F. W. In press. *The Archaeology of South East Asia.* Cambridge: Cambridge University Press.

Hill, Christopher. 1961. *The Century of Revolution.* London: Nelson.

Himmelfarb, Gertrude. 1968. *Victorian Minds.* London: Weidenfeld and Nicolson.

Hirschman, Albert O. 1970. *Exit, Voice and Loyalty: Responses to Declines in Firms, Organizations and States.* Cambridge, Mass.: Harvard University Press.

Hodder, Ian. 1984. "Burials, Houses, Women and Men in the European Neolithic." In *Ideology, Power and Prehistory,* ed. D. Miller and C. Tilley. Cambridge: Cambridge University Press.

Holmberg, Alan. 1969. *Nomads of the Long Bow.* New York: Garden City Press. Originally published 1950.

Holy, Ladislav. 1983. "Symbolic and Non-Symbolic Aspects of Berti Space." *Man,* n.s., 18:269–88.

Holy, Ladislav, and M. Stuchlik. 1983. *Actions, Representations and Norms: Foundations of Anthropological Inquiry.* Cambridge: Cambridge University Press.

Hugh-Jones, Christine. 1979. *From the Milk River: Spatial and Temporal Processes in Northwest Amazonia.* Cambridge: Cambridge University Press.

Hugh-Jones, Stephen. 1979. *The Palm and the Pleiades: Initiation and Cosmology in Northwest Amazonia.* Cambridge: Cambridge University Press.

Humphrey, Nicholas. 1984. *Consciousness Regained: Chapters in the Development of Mind.* Oxford: Oxford University Press.

Huntingdon, Richard, and Peter Metcalf. 1979. *Celebrations of Death: The Anthropology of Mortuary Ritual.* Cambridge: Cambridge University Press.

Ingold, Tim. 1983. "Territoriality and Tenure: the Appropriation of Space in Hunting and Gathering Societies." Paper presented at the Third International Conference on Hunter-Gatherers, Bad Homburg, West Germany.

Jay, Robert R. 1969. *Javanese Villages: Social Relations in Rural Modjokuto.* Cambridge, Mass.: MIT Press.

Kahn, Joel S. 1981. "Marxist Anthropology and Segmentary Societies: A Review of the Literature." In *The Anthropology of Pre-Capitalist Societies,* ed. Joel S. Kahn and Josep R. Llobera. London: Macmillan.

Kanter, Rosabeth Moss. 1972. *Commitment and Community: Communes and Utopias in Sociological Perspective.* Cambridge, Mass.: Harvard University Press.

Kapuscinski, Ryszard. 1984. *The Emperor: Downfall of an Autocrat.* New York: Vintage Books.

Katz, Richard. 1982. *Boiling Energy: Community Healing among the Kalahari Kung.* Cambridge, Mass.: Harvard University Press.

Keenan, Jeremy. 1981. "The Concept of Mode of Production in Hunter-Gatherer Societies." In *The Anthropology of Pre-Capitalist Societies. See* Kahn 1981.

Kemp, Barry J. 1983. "Old Kingdom, Middle Kingdom and Second Intermediate Period: 2686–1553 B.C." In *Ancient Egypt: A Social History,* ed. B. G. Trigger et al. Cambridge: Cambridge University Press.

Kenny, Michael. 1966. *A Spanish Tapestry: Town and Country in Castile.* New York: Harper and Row.

Keyes, Charles F. 1977. *The Golden Peninsula: Culture and Adaptation in Mainland Southeast Asia.* New York: MacMillan.

Klima, Bohuslav. 1954. "Paleolithic Huts at Dolní Věstonice, Czechoslovakia." *Antiquity* 28:4–14.

Kluckhohn, Clyde. 1967. *Navaho Witchcraft.* Boston: Beacon Press. Originally published 1944.

Leach, Edmund. 1976. *Culture and Communication: The Logic by Which Symbols Are Connected.* Cambridge: Cambridge University Press.

Leach, H. M. 1984. *One Thousand Years of Gardening in New Zealand.* Wellington: A. H. and A. W. Reed.

Leacock, E., and R. B. Lee, eds. 1982. *Politics and History in Band Societies.* Cambridge: Cambridge University Press.

Lee, Richard B. 1979. *The !Kung San: Men, Women and Work in a Foraging Society.* Cambridge: Cambridge University Press.

———. 1984. *The Dobe !Kung.* New York: Holt, Rinehart, and Winston.

Lee, R. B., and I. DeVore, eds. 1968. *Man the Hunter.* Chicago: Aldine Atherton.

Lévi-Strauss, Claude. 1963. *Structural Anthropology.* Vol. 1. New York: Basic Books.

———. 1966. *The Savage Mind.* Chicago: University of Chicago Press.

———. 1984. *Paroles données.* Paris: Plon.

Lukes, Steven, ed. 1986. *Power: Readings in Social and Political Theory.* Oxford: Basil Blackwell.

Lumley, H. de. 1969. "A Paleolithic Camp Site at Nice." *Scientific American* 220, 5:42–50.

Macfarlane, Alan. 1970. "Witchcraft in Tudor and Stuart Essex." In *Witchcraft Confessions and Accusations. See* Douglas 1970.

McKenna, James J. 1982. "The Evolution of Primate Societies, Reproduction and Parenting." In *Primate Behavior. See* Fobes and King.

McKinnon, John. 1978. *The Ape within Us.* London: Collins.

McLurg, William Alexander. 1983. *The Architecture of Paradise: Survivals of Eden and Jerusalem.* Berkeley and London: University of California Press.

Maddock, Kenneth. 1972. *The Australian Aborigines: A Portrait of Their Society.* London: Allen Lane.

Malinowski, Bronislaw. 1928. *The Sexual Life of Savages.* London: Routledge and Kegan Paul.

———. 1961. *Argonauts of the Western Pacific: An Account of Native Enterprise and Adventure in the Archipelagos of Melanesian New Guinea.* New York: E. P. Dutton. Originally published 1922.

Maloney, Clarence, ed. 1976. *The Evil Eye.* New York: Columbia University Press.

Manuel, Frank, and Fritzie Manuel. 1979. *Utopian Thought in the Western World.* Cambridge, Mass.: Harvard University Press.

Maple, T. 1980. *Orang-Utan Behavior.* New York: Van Nostrand Reinhold.

Marshall, Lorna. 1976. *The !Kung of Nyae Nyae.* Cambridge, Mass.: Harvard University Press.

Marwick, Max. 1967. "The Sociology of Sorcery in a Central African Tribe." In *Magic, Witchcraft and Curing,* ed. John Middleton. New York: Natural History Press.

Marx, Karl. 1967. *Capital.* Vol. 1. New York: International Publishers.

Marx, Karl, and F. Engels. 1970. *The German Ideology,* ed. C. J. Arthur. London: Lawrence and Wishart.

Mauss, Marcel. 1967. *The Gift: Forms and Functions of Exchange in Archaic Societies,* trans. Ian Cunnison. New York: W. W. Norton. Originally published 1925.

Meek, Ronald L. 1976. *Social Science and the Ignoble Savage.* Cambridge: Cambridge University Press.

Metge, Joan. 1976. *The Maoris of New Zealand: Rautahi.* Rev. ed. London: Routledge and Kegan Paul.

Morris, Brian. 1976. "Whither the Savage Mind? Notes on the Notional Taxonomies of a Hunting and Gathering People." *Man,* n.s., 11:542–57.

———. 1982. *Forest Traders: A Socio-Economic Study of the Hill Pandaram.* London: Athlone Press.

Morris, Desmond. 1962. *The Biology of Art.* New York: Knopf.

Munn, Nancy D. 1973. *Walbiri Iconography: Graphic Representation and Cultural Symbolism in a Central Australian Society.* Ithaca: Cornell University Press.

Needham, Rodney. 1971. *Introduction Rethinking Kinship and Marriage,* ed. R. Needham. London: Tavistock.

———. 1978. *Primordial Characters.* Charlottesville: University of Virginia Press.

———. 1979. *Symbolic Classification.* Santa Monica, Calif.: Goodyear.

Ng, Sik Hung. 1980. *The Social Psychology of Power.* London: Academic Press.

Oliver, Douglas L. 1967. *A Solomon Island Society: Kinship and Leadership among the Siuai of Bougainville.* Boston: Beacon Press. Originally published 1955.

Ortiz, Alfonso. 1969. *The Tewa World: Space, Time, Being and Becoming in a Pueblo Society.* Chicago: University of Chicago Press.

Pastoral Production and Society. 1979. Proceedings of the International Meeting on Nomadic Pastoralism, Paris 1976. Published by Cambridge University Press.

Peters, Emrys. 1978. "The Status of Women in Four Middle Eastern Communities." In *Women in the Muslim World,* ed. Lois Beck and Nikki Keddie. Cambridge, Mass.: Harvard University Press.

Peterson, Nicolas, ed. 1976. *Tribes and Boundaries in Australia.* Canberra: Australian Institute of Aboriginal Studies.

Pitt-Rivers, J. A. 1961. *The People of the Sierra.* Chicago: University of Chicago Press.

Plato. 1952. *The Republic.* Chicago: Encyclopedia Britannica.

Polanyi, Karl. 1957. *The Great Transformation: The Political and Economic Origins of Our Time.* Boston: Beacon Press. Originally published 1944.

Popper, Karl. 1972. *Objective Knowledge.* Oxford: Oxford University Press.

Raphael, D. D. 1980. *Justice and Liberty.* London: Athlone Press.

Rappaport, Roy A. 1968. *Pigs for the Ancestors: Ritual in the Ecology of a New Guinea People.* New Haven: Yale University Press.

———. 1979. *Ecology, Meaning and Religion.* Richmond, Calif.: North Atlantic Books.

Redman, Charles L. 1978. *The Rise of Civilization: From Early Farmers to Urban Society in the Ancient Near East.* San Francisco: W. H. Freeman.

Reiman, Jeffrey H. 1984. "Privacy, Intimacy and Personhood." In *Philosophical Dimensions of Privacy. See* Schoeman 1984.

Reining, Conrad. 1966. *The Zande Scheme*. Evanston: Northwestern University Press.

Renfrew, Colin. 1984. *Approaches to Social Archaeology*. Edinburgh: Edinburgh University Press.

Reynolds, Vernon F. 1966. "Open Groups in Hominid Evolution." *Man*, n.s., 1, 4:441–52.

Riches, David. 1982. *Northern Nomadic Hunter-Gatherers: A Humanistic Approach*. London: Academic Press.

Rodman, P. 1979. "Individual Activity Patterns and the Solitary Nature of Orangutans." In *The Great Apes*, ed. D. Hamburg and E. McCown. Menlo Park, Calif.: Benjamin/Cummins.

Rosen, Stephen I. 1982. "An Introductory Survey of the Primates." In *Primate Behavior*. See Fobes and King 1982.

Rubel, Paula, and A. Rosman. 1978. *Your Own Pigs You May Not Eat: A Comparative Study of New Guinea Societies*. Canberra: Australian National University Press.

Rykwert, Joseph. 1976. *The Idea of a Town: The Anthropology of Urban Form in Rome, Italy and the Ancient World*. Princeton: Princeton University Press.

Sahlins, Marshall. 1974. *Stone Age Economics*. London: Tavistock Publications.

———. 1976. *Culture and Practical Reason*. Chicago: University of Chicago Press.

Salomon, Frank. 1986. *Native Lords of Quito in the Age of the Incas: The Political Economy of North Andean Chiefdoms*. Cambridge: Cambridge University Press.

Schaller, George B. 1967. *The Year of the Gorilla*. Harmondsworth: Penguin.

Scheffler, Harold W. 1978. *Australian Kinship Classification*. Cambridge: Cambridge University Press.

Schoeman, Ferdinand D., ed. 1984. *Philosophical Dimensions of Privacy: An Anthology*. Cambridge: Cambridge University Press.

Schneider, David. 1984. *A Critique of the Study of Kinship*. Ann Arbor: University of Michigan Press.

Schurman, C. L. 1981. "Courtship and Mating Behavior of Wild Orang-utans in Sumatra." In *Primate Behavior and Sociobiology*, ed. A. B. Chiarrelli and R. S. Corruccini. Berlin and New York: Springer-Verlag.

Service, Elman R. 1966. *The Hunters*. Englewood-Cliffs, N.J.: Prentice-Hall.

Shackley, Myra. 1980. *Neanderthal Man*. London: Duckworth.

Shore, Bradd. 1982. *Sala'Ilua: A Samoan Mystery*. New York: Columbia University Press.

Shostak, Marjorie. 1983. *Nisa! The Life and Words of a !Kung Woman*. Harmondsworth: Penguin.

Silberbauer, Georg B. 1981. *Hunter and Habitat in the Central Kalahari Desert*. Cambridge: Cambridge University Press.

Sillitoe, Paul. 1979. *Give and Take: Exchange in Wola Society*. Canberra: Australian National University Press.

Silverwood-Cope, Peter. 1972. "A Contribution to the Ethnography of the Colombian Macu." Ph.D. diss., Cambridge University.

Simmel, Georg. 1950. *The Sociology of Georg Simmel*. Ed. Kurt Wolff. Glencoe, Ill.: Free Press.

Singer, Andre and B. V. Street, eds. 1972. *Zande Themes: Essays Presented to Sir Edward Evans-Pritchard*. Oxford: Blackwell.

Smith, Adam. 1976. *The Theory of Moral Sentiments*. Glasgow ed. Oxford: Oxford University Press. Originally published 1759.

Smith, Bruce James. 1985. *Politics and Remembrance: Republican Themes in Machiavelli, Burke and Tocqueville*. Princeton: Princeton University Press.

Solecki, Ralph. 1971. *Shanidar: The First Flower People*. New York: Alfred Knopf.

Srinivas, M. N. 1976. *Rampura: A Village Remembered*. Delhi: Oxford University Press.

Stevenson, Charles L. 1944. *Ethics and Language*. New Haven: Yale University Press.

Strathern, Andrew. 1971. *The Rope of Moka: Big Men and Ceremonial Exchange in Mount Hagen, New Guinea*. Cambridge: Cambridge University Press.

————. 1979. *Ongka: A Self Account by a New Guinea Big Man*. London: Duckworth.

————. 1984. *A Line of Power*. London: Tavistock Publications.

Strathern, Andrew, and M. Strathern. 1971. *Self-Decoration in Mount Hagen*. London: Duckworth.

Street, B. V. 1975. *The Savage in Literature*. London: Routledge and Kegan Paul.

Strong, Roy. 1984. *Art and Power*. Woodbridge: Boydell.

Teleki, Geza. 1973. *The Predatory Behavior of Wild Chimpanzees*. Lewisburg, Pa.: Bucknell University Press.

Thomas, Keith. 1984. *Man and the Natural World: Changing Attitudes in England, 1500–1800*. Harmondsworth: Penguin.

Thomson, Judith J. 1984. "The Right to Privacy." In *Philosophical Dimensions of Privacy. See* Schoeman 1984.

Tuan, I. Fu. 1974. *Topophilia: A Study of Environmental Perception, Attitudes and Values*. Englewood-Cliffs, N.J.: Prentice-Hall.

Turnbull, Colin M. 1962. *The Forest People: A Study of the Pygmies of the Congo*. New York: Doubleday Anchor.

————. 1966. *Wayward Servants: The Two Worlds of the African Pygmies*. London: Eyre and Spottiswoode.

————. 1973. *The Mountain People*. London: Jonathan Cape.

Turner, David H. 1980. *Australian Aboriginal Social Organization*. Atlantic Highlands, N.J.: Humanities Press; Canberra: Australian Institute of Aboriginal Studies.

Volkman, Toby Alice. 1985. *Feasts of Honor: Ritual and Change in the Toraja Highlands*. Illinois Studies in Anthropology, no. 16. Urbana: University of Illinois Press.

de Waal, Frans. 1982. *Chimpanzee Politics: Power and Sex among the Apes*. New York: Harper and Row.

Weber, Max. 1947. *The Theory of Social and Economic Organization*, ed. T. Parsons. New York: Free Press.

————. 1948. *From Max Weber: Essays in Sociology*, trans. and ed. H. H. Gerth and C. Wright Mills. London: Kegan Paul, Trench, Trubner.

————. 1958. *The Protestant Ethic and the Spirit of Capitalism*. New York: Charles Scribner's Sons. Originally published 1904–5.

Westin, Alan. 1967. *Privacy and Freedom*. New York: Atheneum Press.

Wheatley, Paul. 1971. *The Pivot of the Four Quarters: A Preliminary Inquiry into the*

Origins and Character of the Ancient Chinese City. Chicago: Aldine Publishing Company.

Wiener, Annette. 1976. *Women of Value: Men of Renown.* Austin: University of Texas Press.

Wiessner, Polly. 1982. "Risk, Reciprocity and Social Influences on !Kung San Economics." In *Politics and History in Band Societies. See* Leacock and Lee 1982.

Wikan, Unni. 1980. *Life among the Poor in Cairo.* London: Tavistock Publications.

———. 1982. *Behind the Veil in Arabia: Women in Oman.* Baltimore: Johns Hopkins University Press.

———. 1984. "Shame and Honour: A Contestable Pair." *Man,* n.s., 19:635–53.

Williams, Raymond. 1975. *The Country and the City.* London: Paladin.

Wilson, Bryan R., ed. 1971. *Rationality.* New York: Harper and Row.

Wilson, Edward O. 1980. *Sociobiology.* Abridged ed. Cambridge, Mass.: Belknap Press. Originally published 1975.

Wilson, Monica. 1951. *Good Company: A Study of Nyakyusa Age-Villages.* London: Oxford University Press for the International African Institute.

Wilson, Peter J. 1983. *Man, The Promising Primate: The Conditions of Human Evolution.* 2d ed. New Haven and London: Yale University Press.

Wilson, Peter J., et al. 1974. "More Thoughts on the Ik and Anthropology." *Current Anthropology* 16, 3:343–51.

Winch, Peter. 1958. *The Idea of a Social Science.* London: Routledge and Kegan Paul.

Wittfogel, Karl A. 1957. *Oriental Despotism: A Comparative Study of Total Power.* New Haven: Yale University Press.

Wolters, O. W. 1982. *History, Culture and Religion in Southeast Asian Perspectives.* Singapore: Institute of Southeast Asian Studies.

Woodburn, James. 1968a. "An Introduction to Hadza Ecology." In *Man the Hunter. See* Lee and DeVore 1968.

———. 1968b. "Stability and Flexibility in Hadza Residential Groupings." In *Man the Hunter. See* Lee and DeVore 1968.

———. 1979. Universal Politics: The Political Organization of the Hadza of North Tanzania. In *Politics and Leadership: A Comparative Perspective,* ed. W. A. Shack and P. S. Cohen. Oxford: Clarendon Press.

———. 1980. "Hunters and Gatherers Today and Reconstruction of the Past." In *Soviet and Western Anthropology,* ed. Ernest Gellner. London: Duckworth.

———. 1982a. "Egalitarian Societies." *Man,* n.s., 17:431–51.

———. 1982b. "Social Dimensions of Death in Four African Hunting and Gathering Societies." In *Death and the Regeneration of Life,* ed. Maurice Bloch and Jonathan Parry. Cambridge: Cambridge University Press.

Yates, Frances. 1969. *The Art of Memory.* Harmondsworth: Peregrine. Originally published 1966.

Yellen, John. 1977. *Archeological Approaches to the Present: Models for Reconstructing the Past.* New York: Academic Press.

Young, Robert. 1985. *Darwin's Metaphor: Nature's Place in Victorian Culture.* Cambridge: Cambridge University Press.

Index

*   *   *

Nam nil aegrius est quam res secernere apertas
ab dubiis, animus quas ab se protinus addit.

—Lucretius, *De rerum natura*, 4.467–68